ARTIFICIAL INTELLIGENCE AND EXPERT SYSTEMS

ELLIS HORWOOD BOOKS IN COMPUTING SCIENCE

General Editors: Professor JOHN CAMPBELL, University College London, and BRIAN L. MEEK, King's College London (KQC), University of London

Ellis Horwood Series in Artificial Intelligence

Series Editor: Professor JOHN CAMPBELL, Department of Computer Science, University College London

Boguraev, B.K.	**Natural Language Interfaces to Computational Systems***
Bramer, M.A. (editor)	**Computer Game Playing: Theory and Practice**
Campbell, J.A. (editor)	**Implementations of PROLOG**
Campbell, J.A., Forsyth, R., Narayanan, A. & Teague, M.	**Dictionary of Artificial Intelligence***
Campbell, J. A. & Cox, P.	**Implementations of PROLOG, Vol. 2***
Carter, D.	**Interpreting Anaphors in Natural Language Texts**
Davies, R. (editor)	**Intelligent Information Systems: Progress and Prospects**
Elcock, E.W. & Michie, D. (editors)	**Machine Intelligence 8: Machine Representations of Knowledge**
Evans, J.B.	**Structures of Discrete Simulation***
Forsyth, R. & Rada, R.	**Machine Learning: Applications in Expert Systems and Information Retrieval**
Gabbay, D.M.	**Programming in Pure Logic***
Gergely T. & Futó, I.	**Artificial Intelligence in Simulation***
Glicksman, J.	**Image Understanding and Machine Vision***
Gottinger, H.W.	**Artificial Intelligence: The Commercialisation of Intelligent Systems***
Harland, D. H.	**An Architecture for Object-oriented Knowledge-based Systems***
Hawley, R. (editor)	**Artificial Intelligence Programming Environments***
Hayes, J.E., Michie, D. & Mikulich, L.I. (editors)	**Machine Intelligence 9: Machine Expertise and the Human Interface**
Hayes, J.E., Michie, D. & Pao, Y.-H. (editors)	**Machine Intelligence 10: Intelligent Systems: Practice and Perspective**
Hayes, J.E. & Michie, D. (editors)	**Intelligent Systems: The Unprecedented Opportunity**
Hunter, J.R.W., Gotts, N.M. & Sinnhuber, R.K.E.W.	**Artificial Intelligence in Medicine***
Łukaszewicz, W.	**Nonmonotonic Reasoning***
Lopez de Mantaras, R.	**Approximate Reasoning and Knowledge Acquisition***
Mellish, C.	**Computer Interpretation of Natural Language Descriptions**
Michie, D.	**On Machine Intelligence, Second Edition**
Mortimer, H.	**The Logic of Induction***
Mozetic, I.	**Machine Learning of Qualitative Models***
Partridge, D.	**Artificial Intelligence: Applications in the Future of Software Engineering**
Ramsay, A. & Barrett, R.	**AI in Practice: Examples in POP-11**
Savory, S.E.	**Artificial Intelligence and Expert Systems**
Spacek, L.	**Advanced Programming in PROLOG***
Sparck Jones, K. & Wilks, Y. (editors)	**Automatic Natural Language Parsing**
Steels, L. & Campbell, J.A. (editors)	**Progress in Artificial Intelligence**
Torrance, S. (editor)	**The Mind and the Machine**
Turner, R.	**Logics for Artificial Intelligence**
Wallace, M.	**Communicating with Databases in Natural Language**
Wertz, H.	**Automatic Correction and Improvement of Programs**
Yazdani, M. (editor)	**New Horizons in Educational Computing**
Yazdani, M. & Narayanan, A. (editors)	**Artificial Intelligence: Human Effects**

* *In preparation*

ARTIFICIAL INTELLIGENCE AND EXPERT SYSTEMS

Editor:
STUART E. SAVORY, B.Sc., Ph.D.
Head of Artificial Intelligence Research
Nixdorf Computer AG, Paderborn, West Germany

Translator and Translation Editor:
M. W. ROGERS
Commission des Communautés Européennes, Brussels, Belgium

ELLIS HORWOOD LIMITED
Publishers · Chichester

Halsted Press: a division of
JOHN WILEY & SONS
New York · Chichester · Brisbane · Toronto

This English edition first published in 1988 by
ELLIS HORWOOD LIMITED
Market Cross House, Cooper Street,
Chichester, West Sussex, PO19 1EB, England
The publisher's colophon is reproduced from James Gillison's drawing of the ancient Market Cross, Chichester.

Distributors:
Australia and New Zealand:
JACARANDA WILEY LIMITED
GPO Box 859, Brisbane, Queensland 4001, Australia
Canada:
JOHN WILEY & SONS CANADA LIMITED
22 Worcester Road, Rexdale, Ontario, Canada
Europe and Africa:
JOHN WILEY & SONS LIMITED
Baffins Lane, Chichester, West Sussex, England
North and South America and the rest of the world:
Halsted Press: a division of
JOHN WILEY & SONS
605 Third Avenue, New York, NY 10158, USA

This English edition is translated from the original German edition *Künstliche Intelligenz und Expertensysteme* edited by S. E. Savory and published in 1985 by R. Oldenbourg Verlag GmbH, Munich, © the copyright holders.

British Library Cataloguing in Publication Data
Artificial intelligence and expert systems. —
(Ellis Horwood series in artificial intelligence).
1. Expert systems (Computer science)
I. Savory, Stuart
II. Künstliche Intelligenz und Expertensysteme. *English*
006.3'3 QA76.76.E95

Library of Congress Card No. 87–29766

ISBN 0–7458–0147–1 (Ellis Horwood Limited)
ISBN 0–470–21038–9 (Halsted Press)

Phototypeset in Times by Ellis Horwood Limited
Printed in Great Britain by Unwin Bros., Woking

Contents

Preface to the English edition

This book originally appeared in German, published by Oldenbourg Verlag, Munich, in 1985. The material dated from 1984. During 1986 it was revised and appeared as a second revised edition in 1986. Mike Rogers of the EEC produced this English translation in 1987, adding Appendices A and C. I then amended his translation to include some more up-to-date research work, and also updated the bibliography where possible. So the book you hold in your hand is current today. Biographical details of the (senior) authors of each paper have also been added as Appendix B.

Paderborn, FRG
7th November 1987

Stu Savory

Introduction

0.1 OBJECTIVES

The objective of this book is to give the reader an overall insight into a specific area of industrial research in Artificial Intelligence (AI): that of Expert Systems.

Artificial Intelligence is a key technology for the software of the future. AI concerns itself with the areas of application that involve human reasoning, in that it attempts to imitate reasoning and draw inferences. AI, it should be stated, is not a special methodology, but a framework of interwoven processes that are used together to achieve these goals.

The application areas that are included in the common definition of AI include, amongst others:

— knowledge based systems or expert systems
— intelligent/learning systems
— natural language translation/understanding
— automatic programming with correctness proven
— understanding/generation of speech
— image and scene analysis in real time.

The major part of the above list reflects priorities that are apparent in industrial research and development, especially as seen by one leading company, Nixdorf AG of the Federal Republic of Germany. Nixdorf have been committed to research and development of expert systems since 1982, with an ever increasing team.

The core of this book is made up from contributions of results from this team, or from complementary co-ordinated work in universities. The work is presented in such a way as to represent a complete, albeit brief, overview of the developments up to 1984/85. Subsequent looks by Dr Savory will decribe further progress made in 1985/86 and onwards.

The reader will be able to gain an insight into what can realistically be expected from a current state of the art in knowledge based systems in the sense of what it can and, more importantly perhaps, what it cannot do.

0.2 CHAPTER 1

This is a scene setting overview of the mature state of the art in AI in general, as well as a brief résumé of the historic stages in the main research areas over three decades. The seminal publications are referred to.

The objective of the chapter is to give the reader a feel for the type of application that may be supported by AI tools and methods. In order to make the subsequent sections more palatable, the reader needs to appreciate just what expert systems are and where they fit into the scheme of AI.

0.3 WHAT IS AN EXPERT SYSTEM?

Expert systems are a specific group of methods and tools as a subtopic in the wider area of artificial intelligence. What is AI, though? Almost every author has his own opinion and endless debate on this topic is commonplace.

Some of the more notable definitions are:

[R. Davis and D. B. Lenat] in *Knowledge Based Systems in Artificial Intelligence* (1982):

> AI is the symbolic, non algorithmic reasoning process. Intelligence can be explained as a symbol manipulating activity, and that this can be realised on a physical symbol machine such as a digital computer.

This view is shared by Newell and Simon in a classic Turing Award lecture in 1976 [Newell and Simon].

[N. J. Nilsson] in *Principles of Artificial Intelligence* (1982) states that:

> Human activities such as writing books, computer programs, commonsense reasoning, natural language understanding or driving a car are said to be demanding a level of "intelligence". Over the years, computer programs have been built that can perform tasks such as these. We might say that such systems possess some degree of artificial intelligence.

[E. Rich] in *Artificial Intelligence* states that:

> AI is the study of how to make computers do things at which, at the moment, people are better. This ephemeral definition only betrays the current state of the art, not the objectives.

However, probably the widest accepted definition is that of Minsky [in Semantic Information Processing, 1982]:

> AI is the science of making machines do things that would require intelligence if done by humans.

This is an attractive definition, since it avoids saying anything about "intelligence" of course.

0.4 WHAT IS AN EXPERT?

An expert is commonly accepted to be someone who has specialist knowledge in a domain, in the form of facts and rules coupled with, most importantly, personal experience. Experience is composed of heuristics (i.e. rules of thumb), associative experience, decision making quality based on personal past experiences, and experimental experience. This expertise allows the expert to select a strategy to solve a seemingly complex problem that should offer the highest chance of success. Yet experience is often very vague and difficult to express. An expert, when confronted with a problem that uses his past experience, can only increase the probability of success; he can seldom assure it totally. It is the imprecision of the experience which has prevented a representation to be easily developed that could be used effectively to represent the different degrees of "vagueness".

Expert systems are computer programs where it has been possible to capture both the factual and the experiental knowledge, and where a problem solving engine is also implemented. Some use heuristics, "fuzzy knowledge", and are able, based on their database, to draw conclusions themselves. At any one time they can supply details of hypotheses under consideration, why certain strategies were preferred to others and which inferences have already taken place, and how the program flow arrived there.

0.5 TWAICE

All expert systems have certain common components. Therefore they can be considered in groups with certain technical similarities. They can also be considered as universal tools (i.e. shell systems) applied to different technical problems (knowledge domains).

Nixdorf Computer AG have developed the Expert System Shell called TWAICE, for the development and construction of individual expert systems. The main use is in the area of advisory or diagnostic expert systems. This book uses TWAICE as an example of an expert system shell. TWAICE runs on the Nixdorf TARGON Series under Unix, and the Nixdorf 8890 under VM/CMS. It is written in PROLOG, a declarative language based on predicate logic.

TWAICE's components are:

— data acquisition
— knowledge acquisition
— access to relational database systems
— multiple inference mechanisms
— quasi-natural language interface
— explanation modules.

Based on these, various knowledge bases can be developed and used as expert systems in certain application domains.

0.6 CHAPTER 2

This chapter looks at the commercial industrial expert systems angle. The first two sections concern themselves with market potential, and where expert systems could be applied successfully. Emphasis is placed on those areas requiring routine knowledge, which is a large component of expertise and still requires "intelligence". Some applications are sketched out, including a simple example.

Based on market expectations, and how the expert system technology could impact it, Section 2.3 looks at the requirements of an expert system before they could expect to be commercially useful. Such limitations to acceptability as:

- user interface
- tools for knowledge acquisition
- knowledge engineering shortcomings
- user viewpoints
- advisory role concepts

are discussed.

Finally, the problems of technology transfer out of the universities (where much of the historic work has been done) into the market place (where skills are a pre-requisite to use) via industry is noted. The central theme is how related real world practical problem solving is exposed to the university pure research-led work.

0.7 CHAPTER 3

The functional capabilities of TWAICE are discussed here, with the rationale for the basic design decisions such as:

- the knowledge representation used
- the inference mechanism implemented
- the factual data representation used

explored, and related to the well-established EMYCIN paradigm.

The possibilities and limitations are also explored from a practical point of view.

0.8 CHAPTER 4

This aims to acquaint the reader with PROLOG, the predicate logic-based language used to implement TWAICE. Based on a simple example, some aspects of PROLOG are demonstrated and their implications in AI work are discussed. The problems of PROLOG in large scale commercial software packages are discussed.

0.9 CHAPTER 5

This chapter deals with "Knowledge Engineering"—the method of representing expert knowledge, other knowledge in general inside the expert system itself. The capture and representation problems are primarily discussed.

0.10 CHAPTER 6—LEARNING

This section of the book describes the various perspectives under which the development of semi-automatic learning knowledge acquisition took place for TWAICE and similar systems. The viewpoint taken is that knowledge acquisition is currently a bottleneck, and searches are made for semi-automatic methods to ease this. Are learning systems a useful contribution to expert system technology, and if so, to what degree can they provide more effective means of knowledge acquisition?

0.11 CHAPTER 7 AND ONWARDS

While Chapters 1 to 6 are heavily related to work undertaken by Nixdorf AG in the framework of its AI R & D programme, the remaining chapters are contributed by academia in complementary research.

The appendices are designed to give practical information to the reader who wishes to delve deeper into the various problem domains touched upon. A substantial appendix describes work currently underway in major collaborative programmes in this area.

0.12 GUIDING NOTE

The primary objective has been to describe realistically what has been achieved, what may be achieved in the near future, and what is unlikely to be available soon. Thus "media-hype" and the raising of false expectations are avoided. In a science so prone to false starts, unrealised hopes and deceptions, a pragmatic approach taken by the research team with sound rationales has enabled a commercial product to be built, and we attempt to tell its story here.

1

Some Views on the State of the Art in Artificial Intelligence

Stuart E. Savory
Nixdorf Computer AG, Paderborn, FRG

1.0 INTRODUCTION

"Artificial Intelligence" or "AI" is a phrase liable to (perhaps deliberate or anthropomorphic) misinterpretation, as has been pointed out by Professor Wolfgang Bibel [Bibel 1980] and others. You are all no doubt aware of stories ranging from the early GOLEM myth via Mary Shelley's "Frankenstein" and Karel Čapek's "R.U.R." to Asimov's Laws of Robotics in modern science fiction.

Therefore I should first like to give a definition for AI.

Winston [1979] has stated that the aims of AI are to make computers "smarter" and to research the phenomenon of natural intelligence. This chapter concentrates on the first aim, that of making computers smarter. To this end AI is defined here as being a collection of computer supported techniques emulating some of the natural capabilities of human beings. This collection includes primarily:

— problem solving
— understanding natural language
— vision and robotics
— expert systems and knowledge acquisition
— knowledge representation methodologies.

These aspects are the ones discussed in this chapter.

An excellent overview of AI research and its epistemological base has been given in Daiser's doctoral dissertation [Daiser 1984] which complements this chapter.

1.1 A SHORT HISTORY

As Julius Caesar might have said, "the whole is divided into three parts"; and one could think of the history of AI research as being divided into three decades.

1.1.1 The First Decade: 1955 to 1965

In the first decade researchers investigated their belief that a single general-purpose problem solver having sufficiently powerful inference capabilities could solve all of AI's problems. The General Problem Solver (GPS) was developed by Newell, Shaw and Simon, beginning in 1957 and continuing until 1969.

The important contribution to this work was the idea of "means–end analysis" which searched the state space in what was then a new manner. GPS turned out to be the wrong paradigm, and the next decade concentrated on "less inference" and "more knowledge"—because the power lies in the knowledge. The early work was summarised in collections of papers edited by Feigenbaum and Feldman [1963] and by Minsky in 1968.

On the mathematical side Slagle's MIT doctoral dissertation implemented a "Symbolic Automatic Integrator" in LISP, which performed at college freshman level and was a progenitor of MACSYMA [cf. Slagle, J. R. 1963].

First-decade natural language systems generally assumed that the syntax of a sentence was sufficient to derive all meaning from it.

Lindsay's SAD-SAM [1963] used a context free grammar and a 1700-word dictionary of basic English to process sentences about kith and kin relationships.

The first simple information retrieval parser (BASEBALL) was written at Lincoln Laboratories, also in 1963. Weizenbaum's famous program of the same year, ELIZA (simulating a psychiatrist's dialogue) [Weizenbaum 1966], told us perhaps more about American psychiatry than it did about artificial intelligence, but it did illustrate pattern matching techniques rather well.

In retrospect, all three contributions were unsophisticated and were consequently thrown off track by ambiguities.

Research on speech recognition in the 1960's concentrated on the recognition of isolated words spoken by a known speaker.

1.1.2 The Second Decade: 1965 to 1975

During the second decade, the research work was subdivided into three major fields.

The first field was computer vision, where the seminal book was perhaps Winston's "The Psychology of Computer Vision" [1975]; the second field was understanding natural language as exemplified by Winograd's 1972 book; the third field was on the deeper and more fundamental issues of representation and understanding, where Bobrow's and Collins [1975] masterfully summarised the state of the art in the 1970's. The best known vision research of this period is that of Horn and colleagues at MIT, who researched "shape from shading" in the miniature world of children's toy blocks. This "blocks world" was also used in Winograd's 1972 program SHRDLU which could answer questions about the position of the blocks on the table top and about some of SHRDLU's internal states. Winograd used simple "fill-in-the-blank" text generation techniques (somewhat modified by heuristic pronoun generators) for the natural language output.

Speech input research was funded in the 1970's by DARPA where, by the end of the decade the following had limited success rates of up to 94% at the word level, and 17% to 68% at the sentence level:

— HARPY
  whose pronunciation representation was an integration network
— HEARSAY II
  which used pronunciation graphs and the blackboard model
— HWIM
  using segmented lattices
— DRAGON
  CMU research subsequently utilised by IBM.

Symbolic mathematics peaked in this decade with MIT's MACSYMA package in 1974.

1.1.3 The Third Decade: 1975 to to-day

Whereas the second decade of AI was characterised by mainly "ivory tower" research with little practical use, the third and latest decade has re-addressed the emphasis on real world applications.

Forerunners were Shortliffe's [1976] MYCIN for the diagnosis of infectious bacterial diseases such as meningitis; Hendrix's LADDER system for providing natural language access to databases; and Mitchell's thesis leading to the DENDRAL program for handling mass spectrometry analysis of chemical compounds which enable computer scientists (Buchanan and Mitchell [1978]) to contribute to chemistry research literature. Following these specific systems, Davis' TEIRESIAS [1982b] was a system generalised beyond the bounds of medical diagnosis applications.

Using these results and other progress, computer companies began to develop in-house AI applications such as DEC's R1, which was initially developed by CMU [McDermott 1984], and Nixdorf's CONAD. Both were used to help configure complete computer systems from incomplete order information. Other applications have been in computer hardware diagnosis (Genesereth's DART program for IBM, and Savory's FAULT-FINDER at Nixdorf); in oil well analysis such as the DIPMETER advisor at Schlumberger; and in fault finding in diesel locomotive (CATS by P. Bonnissone).

In the last two years of this third decade a new type of commercial software has begun to appear. These are AI based tools and range from an English language front end for database access (for example INTELLECT or THEMIS) to full expert system builder kits like KEE, ART, LOOPS, S.1 or TWAICE.

Special AI hardware is also available from a number of vendors such as LMI, Symbolics, Xerox, Texas Instruments and so on.

AI is experiencing a boom such as never before. The public and politicians (and the military) are beginning to believe that machines can really be made to "think". If AI fails to live up to these high expectations this time, there will be an "AI winter" from which it may take a very long time to recover.

With this in mind, this book describes what can actually be done today and thus dispels exaggerated claims as "media-hype".

1.2 SOLVING PROBLEMS

The three basic methods of problem solving are

— search-based
— algorithmic-based
— knowledge-based.

The algorithmic method is associated with a curious phenomenon, that is, as soon as an algorithmic method for solving a problem is known, people cease to regard the problem as being one in the area of artificial intelligence! The corollary is that the algorithmic solution no longer separates its domain knowledge from its inference mechanisms, so that the self-explanation capability disappears.

All the basic methods of (artificial) intelligence appear to involve searching through a space of possible solutions whilst optimising a (pre-defined) evaluation function.

This can lead to the well known "combinatorial explosion" of the number of states in the search space versus their depth. Chess has some 10 to the power 120 possible positions. Knowledge (often in the form of heuristics) is used to guide and constrain the search space. The methods used can range from simplex hill climb via alpha–beta techniques to knowledge "chunking".

As an example, the chess game of a king and three pawns versus a king and three pawns requires an explicit table of 500 000 moves and a run time of orders of magnitude longer than the lifetime of the universe. The main success of the CMU "chunker" program is that (by using chess domain knowledge) it reduces this run time to a minute.

However, current artificial intelligence systems, despite much progress, are still woefully limited in their knowledge compared to what general "commonsense" intelligence requires.

We have programs like MACSYMA and DENDRAL which have specialised knowledge of postgraduate standard in symbolic algebra and isomer chemistry respectively, but we have no progress in commonsense reasoning of even a small child. I will quote what each of these systems can do by means of an example.

MACSYMA contains knowledge about symbolic algebra such as integration and differentiation and, by using an algebraic simplifier technique together with pattern matching, is able to solve the algebraic equation problems input by the user.

DENDRAL searches through all possible isomers of a number of hypothesised chemical formulae while trying to find one which satisfies the mass spectrographic data of an unknown sample, and thus discover its chemical formula. Its knowledge base includes the laws of chemistry such as valence theory, tables of atomic weights, NMR resonance frequencies and physical laws like mass balance conservation.

The major approach of problem solving now in use is that of knowledge controlled search, which is also in use for natural language processing and expert systems, as will be subsequently described.

1.3 NATURAL LANGUAGE UNDERSTANDING

The current state of the art ranges from robust parsing systems, such as SRI's TEAM system, via Fujitsu's research efforts to provide automatic Japanese to English (and vice versa) translation, to commercial products such as Intellect or THEMIS. For reasons of familiarity, the HAM-ANS system is taken as representative of the state of the art.

The HAM-ANS system was developed at Hamburg University by von Hahn, Wahlster and colleagues; one domain of discourse is that of hotel reservations where its inference component can even over-answer yes/no questions with appropriate explanations. The following short dialogue extract demonstrates some of these features:

Caller:
Von Hahn, University of Hamburg, here.
Do you have a room for next Tuesday for me?

HAM-ANS:
Yes, we have 4 single rooms for the night of 2nd October free.

Caller:
Is it quiet enough?

HAM-ANS:
Yes, because it faces the courtyard.

The system is able to cope with anaphora, ellipses and dereferencing pronouns on input. It over-answers the question using its inference component to provide reasonable explanations. For further details, Wahlster's dissertation is recommended [Wahlster 1981]. Unfortunately, HAM-ANS can tie up a single PDP-10 and take 15 to 60 seconds to reply.

A second example is SRI's TEAM system as demonstrated at the COLING 1984 Conference on a Symbolics 3600. Its strong points are:

— graphics support for knowledge acquisition eases adaptation to new conceptual databases
— high speed parsing with a large American/English grammar of 1–3 seconds per sentence on a Symbolics 3600 basic machine.
— exemplary test, trace and debugging capabilities.

Its weak points are:

— there is no inference mechanism, merely database access
— there is no generation of natural language output
— the implementation of SODA is weak
— the LISP interface to SODA for the parsing results is only extendable with great difficulty.

Yasukawa's research on lexical functional grammars is also worth reading.

It must be noted that, despite popular press reports, none of the systems above have speech input or output. All use keyboards and CRT displays, and none are real-time systems as such.

The trend in natural language research is away from toy worlds such as in SHRDLU to real-world applications in limited domains, such as:

BACON — room planner and congress travel

BLAH — US income tax planner

HAM-RPM — hotel booking and street scene analysis

INTELLECT — access to dBASEII and VISICALC

KIPUS — unemployment situation

LUNAR — Apollo lunar rock sample analyser

NAND — Natural Language access to an expert system shell

PLIDIS — control over emission of dirty water

POL — loading of ships

ESP — the Erlangen Speech Project on Railway Timetables

Straight Talk — database access

SYSAN — documentation of a program library.

1.4 SPEECH PROCESSING

Speech processing can be subdivided into speech input and speech output, whereby the input recognition problem is the harder of the two. Several chip based sets are available (e.g. VOTRAX) which can convert either phonemes or individual words of text to a rather mechanistic form of speech. Generally these use phoneme tables or a linear prediction synthesiser and are at present (although not in principle) limited to an American dialect subset of English. Nixdorf Computer AG is participating in a co-operative research programme which is building an LPC chip to speak unrestricted German text. DEC already has a system called the DEC-talker which utters American speech from English text. However, it has no contextual or syntactic knowledge and thus, for example, in the question "have you read the book that I just read?" pronounces both instances of the word "read" identically as it pronounces "reed".

Similarly it has problems with the syllable "ough", as in bough, dough, enough, ought, through, hiccough, thorough.

As stated above, the existing natural language understanding programs like TEAM and HAM-ANS merely accept input from keyboards, not spoken input. Spoken input is currently handled by several different approaches. Recognition of word-at-a-time speech by a device trained by each of its individual users is already commercially available. Recognition of continuous speech still remain elusive, although progress is being made. Perhaps the best known effort was the ARPA-SUR 5-year project of the 1970's, whose goal was to develop a system that could understand normally spoken sentences constrained to a 1000 word vocabulary, which was acceptable to the military. It was to have an error rate of under 10% and to be virtually "real-time". The main results were the HARPY system and the HEARSAY-II system from CMU which used a layered blackboard model to transmit intermediate results and hypothesise between semi-disjunct knowledge bases. The success rate ranged from 63% to 94%; user feedback indicated that error rates of less than 1% were needed in practice, and that it was not a real-time system.

In Japan, NEC have an advanced system which we have witnessed performing speaker independent recognition of continuous spoken short sentences. Coupled with automatic translation systems, it enabled an English speaker to communicate with a Spanish speaker at a simple level.

In the USA I have seen a recent demonstration of a point-and-say system for military commanders, but the restrictions on information about the system prevent further details being published.

1.5 VISION AND ROBOTICS

SRI's "Shakey" robot, with the aid of some dubious publicity, was the first to fire the public's imagination. It also caused a certain backlash echoing the Golem myths, Karel Čapek's "R.U.R", and Asimov's stories, as basic human fears. The real world, however, uses mainly non-mobile industrial robots, although the military are attempting to build autonomously fighting land vehicles.

Existing industrial robots are mainly manipulator arms which are pre-programmed to perform a repetitive action, often without the benefit of any sensory input. It is the purpose of the vision system component to make such robots more flexible by performing a scene analysis.

Gerald Barber of MIT has listed some of the capabilities that vision systems should provide for robots:

— location, e.g. of objects on a conveyer belt
— orientation, e.g. of randomly ordered objects in a bin
— identification, e.g. of different components in a bin
— inspection, e.g. to discard faulty items via comparison
— error correction, e.g. for manipulator positioning.

All of these are present to some degree or other in state of the art vision systems, depending on the target application generally.

An example of the use of a vision system to control a robot manipulator has been demonstrated by a large manufacturer of household vacuum cleaners. At the beginning of their demonstration the various parts of the vacuum cleaner are scattered on the floor around a mobile robot arm with a vision system. The robot has been given a pre-determined assembly sequence and a "lexicon" of parts of the major components, and determines their location and orientation. The manipulator arm then grasps the pieces in the pre-determined sequence, assembling one part onto the other. The vision system identifies the required fastener (typically one of various different-sized screws) enabling the robot to fasten the pieces together. This process proceeds until the vacuum cleaner is completely assembled, whereupon inspection of the floor checks that no pieces remain unused.

Marr [1978] discusses the problems of representing visual information.

It is possible to draw an analogy between this type of vision system recognising a limited number of known objects in a restricted environment and the word-at-a-time speech recognition system outlined previously. Applications typically involving aerial photography interpretation in real time are much more complex but are hidden behind the military security screen, the corresponding analogy being with recognition of continuous speech of a random speaker having a huge vocabulary. Probably the foremost vision research has been done at SRI by Barrow and Tenenbaum [1983], although Japanese researchers have shown significant results at their Fifth Generation Computer Systems conferences.

In Japan and the USA it has now been realised that it is much too expensive to design workplaces around the capabilities of limited robots, and researchers are now concentrating on building truly intelligent, flexible and autonomous robots which can work in a "human" environment. Therefore the following AI techniques are being increasingly applied:

— spatial reasoning about geometry to solve problems such as grasping, trajectory, and assembly problems
— temporal reasoning over time to solve co-ordination and efficiency problems
— sensory reasoning about the capabilities of sensors and task requirements to solve sensor application problems and to assimilate different sensory modalities
— task planning systems combining spatial, temporal and sensory reasoning to plan tasks efficiently and mediate their co-ordinated execution.

1.6 EXPERT SYSTEMS

What are expert systems?

Someone is considered an expert if he has a large knowledge domain in the form of facts and rules, and in addition has individual experience generally not found in the literature of the domain. Experience consists of heuristics, analogies, judgements on the basis of individual decision criteria, etc. Such experience and knowledge enables the human expert to choose promising problem solving strategies or, if these turn out to be unsuccessful, to go back to the point from where the strategy failed and try another alternative.

Expert systems are computer based programs which store experts' factual and inferential knowledge. They use heuristics and vague knowledge and are able to draw conclusions from given case data. In addition, they can inform the user at any point of the solution what hypothesis they are currently pursuing, why they have chosen a particular strategy, what conclusion have been drawn so far, and why these conclusions were drawn.

Expert Systems are thus intrinsically knowledge based system. Early knowledge based systems, such as Stanford's MYCIN for the diagnosis of infectious diseases or Nixdorf's CHICO for generating commercial application program suites, did not separate their knowledge clearly from their inference mechanisms. Furthermore, they had either no explanation component or only a rudimentary one, as in MYCIN. The necessity of having a good explanation capability was stated as early as 2000 years ago by Virgil, "Felix qui potuit rerum cognoscere causas", which means "he is a fortunate man who has managed find out the causes of things".

The first efforts are now more than a decade old. R1 remains the most often quoted successful commercial expert system, in use by DEC on a daily basis.

The following is an example of an explanation capability taken from Savory's FAULTFINDER as documented at the GWAI84 Workshop:

FAULTFINDER
Is disc 1 write-enabled? << YES
Are the errors all on the same cylinder? << WHY?

FAULTFINDER
I am investigating the state of the fault "a servo track on disc 1 is suspect"

This is a possible cause of "disc 1 is suspect"

This in turn is a possible cause of the "peripherals chassis contents are suspect"

This in turn is a possible cause of "the 8832 has a defect"

Now I must ask you again:
Are the errors all on the same surface? << YES

FAULTFINDER
The fault is:
a head on disc 1 is suspect.
It requires a repair to fix it.
The appropriate exchange–replace unit is disc 1
Its position is at the lower left of the front side of the peripheral's chassis.

FAULTFINDER REPAIR PLAN:
— please switch off disc 1 on/off
— switch is at the centre left of the front side of the peripheral chassis
— etc. etc.

Other expert systems that are often quoted in the literature are:

— SRI's PROSPECTOR
  helps a geologist search for mineral or deposits
  [Hart and Einaudi 1978]
— Schlumberger's DIPMETER ADVISOR
  aids in borehole analysis in search for oil deposits
  [Smith 1984]
— DEC's R1
  is a computer configuration advisor for the DEC series
  [McDermott 1984]
— Stanford's DART
  localises and supports repair of faults in computer systems

More detailed overviews are available in Nau [1983] and in Michie [1982].

All this applications related work has led to the development of so-called expert system shells, a concept first developed by von Melle in EMYCIN. Such shells contain no domain dependent knowledge but support all the other facilities such as several inference mechanisms, database access methods, explanation facilities, etc. There are about a dozen such shells on the market currently.

Such a shell becomes a complete expert system only when the appropriate domain knowledge is added by the process of knowledge engineering. An example of a dialogue with an elementary prototype shell is given in Savory [1983]. Smith [1984] has given a fairly good review of the development of a commercial expert system. Davis [1982a] has also given an amusing review of "where we were, where we were going".

Restrictions on the rapid advancement of the state of the art include:

— knowledge of narrow domains of expertise only
— fragile behaviour at boundaries of applications
— limited knowledge representation facilities
— limited I/O
— limited explanation capabilities
— underdeveloped knowledge acquisition facilities.

The last of these issues is the current bottleneck in the wider application of expert systems technology. A number of workers are now actively engaged in this area (Michalski, Michie, ESPRIT projects 12, 82, 112, 304 and 1098). It is the weak point of Rank Xerox's LOOPS, Nixdorf's TWAICE and Teknowledge's S.1, to name but three.

1.7 REPRESENTATION OF KNOWLEDGE

The core which is central to all of the previously discussed AI application areas is the problem of knowledge representation. The main methods of knowledge representation in use today are:

- AI programming languages
- actor systems
- inference nets
- frames
- semantic nets
- production rule systems
- logical calculi:
  - predicate logic
  - modal logic
  - temporal logic
  - fuzzy logic
  - non-monotonic logic.

There are a number of knowledge representation languages now available. The most popular first generation language was and still is LISP. Second generation languages include PLANNER and CONNIVER from MIT, Fuzzy from Rutgers and Smalltalk from Xerox.

The third generation AI languages can be subdivided into four main subgroups:

- antecedence systems such as
  - AMORD from MIT
- frame oriented systems such as
  - KRL from Xerox
  - FRL from MIT
  - KL-ONE from BBN
  - OBJTALK from Stuttgart University
- actor languages such as
  - CSSA from Bonn University
  - M-Actors from Kyoto University
- production and logic oriented languages such as
  - OPS from CMU
  - PROLOG from Marseilles University.

The chosen language for the Japanese Fifth Generation Computer Systems initiative is PROLOG, and it is also frequently adopted in European programmes such as ESPRIT and the UK's Alvey.

The following small example shows how the same knowledge may be represented as:

- natural language

— frames
— a semantic net
— PROLOG.

For a detailed overview of recent research issues in knowledge representation, see Brachman and Levesque [1983].

Natural Language
"The Nixdorf 8832 is a fault tolerant computer system. The software includes PROLOG and PASCAL; the PROLOG alone is interpretive. The hardware has multiple processors . . . ".

Frames

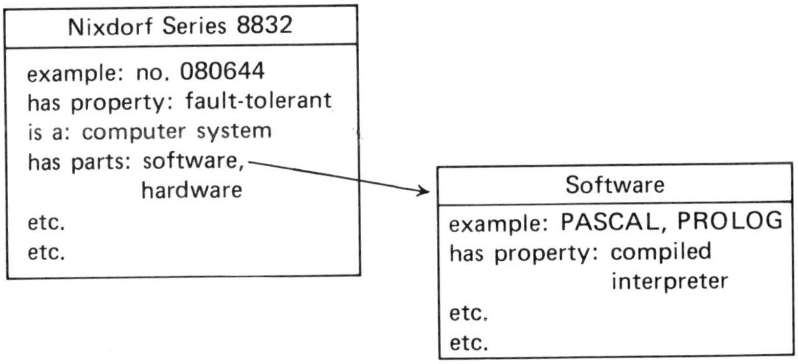

Semantic Net

Prolog

facts: is_a(nixdorf_8832, computer_system).
part_of (nixdorf_8832,sw).
part_of (sw,prolog).
has_property (prolog,interpretive).

(inheritance rule): has_property (X,Y):– part_of (X,P),
has_property (P,Y).

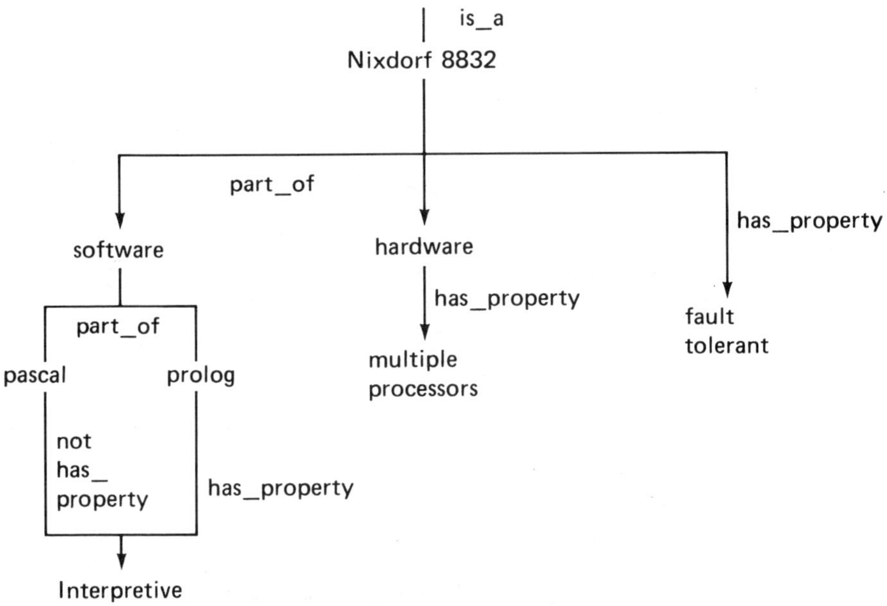

1.8 THE FUTURE OF ARTIFICIAL INTELLIGENCE

This chapter attempts to give a brief overview of systems that were state of the art in recent times and have become the "mature" flag carriers of examples of successful AI based systems. It is much more difficult to predict the future developments, but it would be useful to contrast two extremes, based on pessimism and on optimism.

1.8.1 Pessimism

In America, serious plans are under consideration to replace prison guards by mobile robots—thus released prisoners will most likely become neo-Luddites. The military plans involve developing autonomous fighting vehicles which may "learn" to become paranoid. Remember the words on the GOLEM's forehead: EMETH (i.e. truth) is easily changed into METH (i.e. death).

Social resistance to AI products may thus hinder not only the more "nightmare"-type applications but also the more routine ones such as financial advisor systems. Voltaire's 1777 claim, "tout est pour le mieux dans le meilleur des mondes possibles", a generalisation of the Orwellian "1984" government propaganda, would then turn out to have a hollow ring indeed.

1.8.2 Optimism

The driving force of intellectual competition, in particular the concerted and totally peaceful Japanese research work on Fifth Generation Computer Systems, will lead to a new kind of machine to serve mankind. Expert advisors to see, hear, talk and think while communicating worldwide via electronic networks may not just appear in either Delaney's or Pohl's science fiction world, but could be with us sooner than one may imagine.

2

Expert Systems for Commercial Use

Hannelore Roesner
Nixdorf Computer AG, Paderborn, FRG

2.1 THE PROBLEM

Since the dawn of the computational age, it has been the objective of "computer" programmers to lighten the seemingly endless, mind numbing, routine procedures that man surrounds himself with in order to justify his own self-perpetuating existence. Generally, it can be said that wherever an algorithm exists to describe a procedure or process, a computer program could be used just as effectively to reach the same results through the automatic application of a predetermined rule set.

Yet there are certain areas where, despite the existence of rules and procedures which are a pre-requisite to any organised process, any attempts to implement the descriptive algorithm describing the process in an automatically executable form, have so far met with little or no success. These classes of areas, or "domains", are characterised by requiring a high degree of "intelligence", usually due to the potentially large search space where the solution may reside, or due to the uncertain nature or "fuzziness" of the knowledge involved. Intelligence and intelligent behaviour usually is meant to include the following capabilities:

— the ability to infer
  that is, to reach logical, consistent reproducible conclusions from the facts by applying a rule set
— the use and evaluation of fuzzy knowledge
  that is, the use of facts which have some uncertainty associated with them implicitly or explicitly
— the use of heuristics and default values based on experience
  that is, the application of rules of thumb, and knowing what is reasonable, based on experience
— the inclusion of new/altered facts and rules in the solution process on a dynamic basis
  that is, maintaining a knowledge base and always using the latest and best facts to infer a higher quality solution

— the interpretation of time dependent and multi-valued data that is, temporal reasoning and handling ambiguity.

The domains in which problem solving requires generally a higher degree of intelligent behaviour than could be provided by traditional sequential programming of third generation programming languages such as Pascal and Ada include, for example:

— error diagnosis and repair strategies for instruments
— diagnosis of diseases and illnesses and associated strategies for treatment and monitoring recovery
— the configuration of systems of a high inherent complexity from modular, functional subsystems
— planning and design with global boundary constraints
— process and control situations requiring value based judgements, as in large power plants
— forecasting, using semi- or totally non quantitative measures
— intelligent tuition, computer aided instruction; CAI.

These domains are characterised by the need for highly specialised knowledge of the subject matter (i.e. the context), as well as experience in the solutions of problems that typically arise in the domain. A person who combines these two skills to varying degrees may be classed as a domain expert. In relative human values, the more problem solving history an expert has accumulated, the higher he is regarded on the scale of "expertise".

Experts in a domain are generally few and far between. As a rule, they have to cover large geographical areas (due to their scarcity, of course) so that in theory their expertise is available where it is most needed. Nevertheless, it is far more common for that expertise to be not readily available at the time it is required or, perhaps more frustrating, to be available too late. Some classical situations are:

— the knowledge of an investment analyst in a bank is frequently only available to a small sub-office of that bank via an expensive and circuitous route
— the expertise of a system developer is generally located in the Research and Development facility of a company, and only very exceptionally is available to a market outlet of that company or that product line
— specialist bacteriological knowledge of a tropical disease consultant is not available to the general practitioner who is faced with unusual symptoms in a tourist returning from some exotic location
— the skills to plug a blowout in an oil well are generally not only

unavailable locally, but found in only a handful of people worldwide (e.g. Red Adair).

Yet a large number of problems that are faced by the expert are purely routine in nature. By the time they are with him, however, the procedure is much the same. He generally has few tools to lighten this load, and this could result in a number of problems arising over time:

— overload by routine prevents attack on new problems and the extension of expertise by rapid acquisition of new (leading-edge) knowledge
— important but non-urgent work is forced to take a back seat so that new problems can be handled as they arise
— seemingly routine problems are not submitted to the expert and are handled, or rather mis-handled, often on a local basis. The case of the Chernobyl nuclear power station is perhaps a good example; routine procedures followed once the accident had occurred would have minimised the effects.

By the provision of appropriate tools, the cost, quality and time scale of many expert consultations could be altered dramatically. A typical example is that of the overall Nixdorf Computer AG product line. The installed and serviced base of machines generate about 1 000 000 service/enquiry calls throughout the year. If by the appropriate provision of tools, the time taken for each service call could be reduced by only 6 minutes (that is, by much less than 10% of an average repair time), this would result in a company saving of about US$ 5 000 000 at 1986 prices. However, if software that does not simply follow a pre-determined (i.e. humanly determined) well-defined algorithm is to be accepted by experts, the software must afterwards be able to rationalise its procedural flow. It must retain a trace of its thinking flow and decisions made at every stage so that this can be checked and possibly overridden, but mainly so that the user can build up trust in the software's abilities.

2.2 ARTIFICIAL INTELLIGENCE AND EXPERT SYSTEMS

2.2.1 The Broad Domain of Artificial Intelligence

In the domain of Artificial Intelligence, as a subsidiary domain of general Informatics/Computer Science, research of some description has been going on since the 1950†s into various aspects of processing knowledge as opposed to pure numeric data. The 1950' and 1960's were characterised by research into methods and specific tools, often of only academic interest. A popular example was that of heuristics and game playing machines, as games are in a finite closed world (i.e. within a set of all encompassing rules to cover every eventuality) but can have large search spaces (e.g. in chess). Other research was directed at proving mathematical theorems, or (re-)discovering mathematical concepts using inductive principles.

It was not until the third decade of this new science that the relevance of work in artificial intelligence for practical applications came to be evident. The major factor in this revelation were the developments of a small number of systems using conventional software languages and hardware systems that nevertheless worked. Amongst these are often cited:

— MYCIN for the medical area
— EMYCIN, PUFF, ONOCIN, HEADMED for specific medical areas such as respiratory diseases (PUFF)
— PROSPECTOR, DIPMETER ADVISOR for geological mineral work
— DRILLING ADVISOR, DART for error diagnosis in machinery
— R1/XCON for computer configuration advice.

Using these methods and tools, coupled to significantly higher powered computational engines than have hitherto been available (perhaps one should add that this greater power will come at an affordable price), it is now possible, for the first time in the short history of computers, to simulate the behaviour of experts in terms of knowledge and procedures for the more routine (i.e. repetitive) tasks that everyone encounters in their occupation. As a result, the narrow domain of "Expert Systems" has become an important field within the whole area of artificial intelligence—and the first area that has seen commercial use.

Expert Systems are by now quite well documented. It is important at the outset to gather a fair overview of the state of the art, as many systems described may still be in the experimental stage. The following are recommended for further reading (full references are in the Bibliography): Bibel and Siekmann [1982], Hayes-Roth [1983, 1984], Nilsson [1982] and Winston [1975].

Also, to end this book, an overview of some systems in another application domain is provided as a lateral look at the problems discussed, and as a reminder that domain dependencies are still paramount in the requirements and implementation of today's state of the art systems. The "Handbook of Artificial Intelligence" by Barr and Feigenbaum (1981) is still regarded as the ultimate reference text by many.

In association with the literature there is a healthy offering of seminars, application groups and more or less technically oriented conferences:

— IJCAI
International Joint Conference on Artificial Intelligence, the next to be held in Milan in 1987 (bi-annually)
— AAAI ("Triple A" I)
American Association of Artificial Intelligence, held annually
— ECAI
European Conference on Artificial Intelligence, held bi-annually, in 1986 in the UK, and in 1988 in Munich, FRG.

Every year has many conferences on associated themes, the most common being:

Databases
Application of expert systems
Ada and artificial intelligence
Machine learning
Knowledge representation
Computer architectures
PROLOG and languages
5th Generation computer systems
Artificial intelligence and computer-integrated manufacturing.

Most major conferences now have exhibitions running in parallel. Manufacturers of hardware, and software vendors, find exhibitions to be useful opportunities to broadcast product information to the relevant people, who are usually widely scattered geographically. However, the atmosphere of such exhibitions rarely allows for real analysis of a product, so its evaluation prior to a possible acquisition is still done by visits, or trial periods, or both.

2.2.2 The Market for Artificial Intelligence and Expert Systems

Though covered elsewhere, it is revealing to look at the market diagnosis for just one country, the USA , where the market is most advanced:

US Market Estimates
Artificial Intelligence
1983–1993

(turnover in Millions of US $ at 1984 prices)

Application Domain	1983	1985	1987	1991	1993
Factories	4	57	210	575	1305
Offices	28	110	365	1025	3850
Home	1	13	120	520	2435
Research & Development	33	39	70	200	435
Education	1	2	15	80	510
Totals	67	221	780	2400	8535

These figures were speculated at the beginning of 1984, and imply a growth rate of Artificial Intelligence and AI-type products of between 30% and 120% per annum over the decade 1983–1993. Compared to an overall level of growth of 13% p.a. sustained by the computer industry in the current decade (1976–1986), these figures are impressive, to say the least. By 1986, though, worldwide expenditure on data processing had exceeded US $100 000 million, so the market penetration of Artificial Intelligence products is still very low. An interesting comparison is provided by the programming language Ada, developed for the US Department of Defense by a European design team under Honeywell Bull in Paris in 1975. This language will be an ISO standard in 1987, and, despite the force of the military market behind it and public funding for product development, the worldwide Ada market is likely to be just about US $1000 million in the year 1986 [Rogers 1985].

The current boom in popular articles about the subject is equally symptomatic of the enthusiasm with which the current expert systems are being greeted by technical and general media alike. Many journals are devoting full issues to the topic, and many attempts to popularise the work are currently under way. Some typical articles and papers are listed in the Bibliography. They appear almost daily, and with the state of the art evolving rapidly, the cited articles are by now more of a historical record of how the subject was perceived at those times.

2.2.3 The First Applications of Expert Systems

The first applications of Expert Systems occurred in the USA as a result of close co-operation between industry and academia. The majority of these systems were developed within the framework of the famous "Heuristic Programming Project" (HPP) at Stanford University under the direction of Feigenbaum, described in detail elsewhere [Barr & Feigenbaum 1981]. Definitive overviews at the time were incomplete [Bramer 1982, Feigenbaum and McCorduck 1983, 1984] because of the scattered location of research, but games were specifically excluded, and yet the list was impressively long.

However, it is the more speculative yet relatively rare application in industry that has brought artificial intelligence into the world headlines. Use of these techniques for mineral prospecting (system "Prospector") and for computer system configurations (Digital Equipment Corporation's use of R1) are classic examples of relatively simple systems, in industrial everyday use for some time already.

Yet one has to ask why the penetration has been so shallow, bar a few isolated cases? After looking at a typical example, the requirements of an expert system will be analysed in more detail in order to try to answer that very question.

2.2.4 A Typical Example of an Expert System at Work with Non-technical Users or The European Vacation Hay Fever Expert System

This is a small subset of an allergies knowledge of about 130 rules used only to demonstrate the possible application areas for an expert system shell like TWAICE. The principal features are:

— user-friendly dialogue
— use of probabilities
— simple output features
— use of "fuzzy" terms.

The knowledge engineering was by Ludwig and Koehler, while Savory added the English user interface, and the adaptation of the shell to support dialogue in English and German—an important marketing point. Please note that the example is not intended for serious medical use in the context it is presented here.

There are four modes of consultation possible with the system:

1. To locate a particular pollen allergy
2. Predicting which pollen will be ambient in an environment
3. Advising suitable vacation locations, given certain allergies
4. Simple allergy analysis.

The following sections contain example dialogues with the Hay Fever Expert System, which are very straightforward user consultations and do not demonstrate the explanation capabilities within TWAICE. These can answer WHY it asks a specific question, HOW it deduced some particular result, WHAT a specific term may mean, and provide advisory support to aid answering of difficult questions. The more sophisticated knowledge engineering tools contained in TWAICE are also not evident in the examples—but the example is intended to show the advantages of a straightforward, simple yet powerful user interface. In the dialogue that follows, the user prompt character is "?>" . The questions asked by the system are numbered for convenience "(1)". A mixture of Menu and Natural Language input is demonstrated. Explanatory text for this publication is contained within "<< >>" strings.

EUROPEAN VACATION HAY FEVER ADVISORY SYSTEM.
NIXDORF Computer AG, 1985 copyrighted.
Hello

(1) Please choose the type of advice desired:

1: allergy and vacation area
2: prediction of allergies
3: vacation area
4: allergy

?> 1

<<example of a menu driven question—always useful at the start of a session in case the user is not familiar with the system>>

(2) What is the surname of the patient ?> Schmitt

(3) Is the patient male or female (reply M or F)
?> S

<<an incorrect response is given; the system aids the user to guide him to the correct choice>>

The only possible answer to the last question was M or F. Your reply S is not valid. Please try again:

(3) Is the patient male or female (reply M or F)
?> m

(4) Date of Birth ?> 8 June 1944

<<Note that no rigid response format was notified to the user. The system accepts a variety of inputs and, knowing the properties of the essential components of "date", tries to parse the input and abstract a valid, sensible date of birth from the information. If it does not succeed, it can prompt by example for an alternative format from the user>>

(5) In which environment did the patient spend most of their time recently?

1: Meadows
2: Suburbs
3: Heathland

?>M

<<note that only the minimum response is needed to identify the choice uniquely>>

(6) In which month do the symptoms occur worst

?>mya
= May

<<note that the system has spotted the spelling mistake, corrects it and issues it to the user interface so that the user is assured that his error has been corrected to the response he intended. Validation of this kind increases the acceptability of the system to the user>>

(7) For which month is vacation planned?> Ju

The input "JU" could refer to JUne or JUly. Please try again:

(7) For which month is vacation planned?> July

<<The system now analyses the particular pollen allergies that the patient may possess, and weights them with confidence factors in the range of 0 (being absolutely excluded) to 1000 (absolutely certain). Then a recommendation is made regarding which areas of Europe are suitable for a vacation with the minimum hay fever exposure for the current patient. More sophisticated medical expert systems do not require any medical tests to be performed on the patient directly, thus making it an especially useful technique for haemophiliacs and avoiding any types of allergy shocks. The knowledge in the system itself is abstracted from public domain knowledge issued by Fisons Allergy R & D Ltd, UK.>>

ALLERGY AND VACATION AREA ANALYSIS:
Mr. Schmitt, born on 8 June 1944

Your symptoms in the month of May, for location Meadows imply an allergic reaction to some of these pollen:

Plane Tree	150	probable
Dock	250	probable
Grasses	250	probable
Oak	300	probable
Birch	50	less probable

<<note the sum of weights is 1000>>

For your chosen vacation month, JULY, the corresponding areas of Europe are as follows:

West	325	less recommended
South	326	less recommended
North	362	less recommended
Central	505	not recommended
East	505	not recommended

<<note that the most recommended area always appears first. The other areas are listed to give the user an idea of the strength of the conclusions relative to each other—in this case the recommendations of West and South are virtually identical>>

(8) Please choose the type of advice desired:

1: allergy and vacation area
2 : prediction of allergies
3: vacation area
4: allergy

?> 2

<<the second type of advice in the specimen database predicts the type of pollen which will be airborne in a particular environment during a specific month, but only in Germany, where the knowledge base was constructed. The advice would thus only be valid in that geographical region>>

(9) In which environment did the patient spend most of their time recently?

1: Meadows
2: Suburbs
3: Heathland

?>2
Suburbs

<<compare the answer to question (5). Here the user uses the numeric reference to the menu, and the system accepts this as unique and intended>>

(10) For which month is advice sought ?>6
June

<<the same comment as above>>

PREDICTION
Mr. Schmitt, born on 8 June 1944, during JUNE you must bear in mind in the suburbs the following predicted densities of airborne pollen:

Grasses	500	Strong
Dock	250	Weak
Nettles	250	Weak

<<note again the total of all prediction probabilities>>

(11) Please choose the type of advice desired:

1: allergy and vacation area
2: prediction of allergies
3: vacation area
4: allergy

?>vac

<<the third selection provides recommendations concerning suitable vacation areas within Europe, bearing in mind certain allergies to be avoided. The response to the question above is understood unambiguously by the system, though one would not use this facility if the choice were 1 or 4, as the

minimum string to avoid ambiguity would be much longer than a single letter>>

(12) This vacation advice is only valid for Europe in the months MAY to SEPTEMBER.

<<note—the user is clear about applicability of reasoning>>

The following pollen have been included:

Ash	Alder	Beech	Birch
Chenopodium	Dock	Grasses	Hazel
Mugwort	Nettles	Oak	Olive
Plane Tree	Plantain	Ragweed	

Select by name, and give a confidence factor

?> ?

<<the user inputs ?, universally interpreted as a help signal>>

To answer this question, give a list of pollen sources with a confidence factor (cf) for each. End with a <CR>. For example: ash cf500 oak cf100 <CR>. The question will be repeated now:

(12) This vacation advice is only valid for Europe in the months MAY to SEPTEMBER.
The following pollen have been included:

Ash	Alder	Beech	Birch
Chenopodium	Dock	Grasses	Hazel
Mugwort	Nettles	Oak	Olive
Plane Tree	Plantain	Ragweed	

SElect by name, and give a confidence factor

?>hazel cf600 mug cf400
alder cf999

<<note—the menu was given automatically in alphabetical order, but the user's replies can be in any order and the cf's need not add up to 1000>>

VACATION AREAS IN EUROPE
Mr. Schmitt, born on 8 June 1944, for your proposed vacation month AUGUST, the corresponding areas are:

South	240	recommended
East	320	less recommended

North	320	less recommended
West	320	less recommended
Central	399	less recommended

<<the fourth type of advice is a subset of the first, being an advisor on allergy analysis, without any vacation analysis. This width of choice, however, enables use in a medical environment or a travel agency that wishes to provide a high level of service—the knowledge bases required are compatible!>>

END OF HAY FEVER ADVISORY SYSTEM. Thank you.

2.3 REQUIREMENTS FOR EXPERT SYSTEMS IN INDUSTRIAL USE

2.3.0 Introduction

As mentioned earlier, a number of Expert Systems for applications have already been developed. Yet few of the academic/scientific community have conspired successfully to develop Expert Systems which undertake serious, planned, systematic information cost/benefit analysis of the essential requirements Expert Systems in commercial use need to meet. It seems that applications have been attacked without a great deal of consideration about an explicit analysis of the domain in which the Expert Systems will operate. The following sections will try to give some insight into why, whenever an Expert System is developed, the environment in which it is intended to operate should be continuously borne in mind during planning, development and use—in fact the environment is a part of the system , as the system has information about the environment in which it operates.

2.3.1 Requirements of the Application Domain

The first requirement of the application domain is not related to the content of the Expert System, but to the concept only. However, it is often forgotten that *Expert Systems should only be developed for those application domains where a proven need exists.*

The quality of an expert system is limited by the quality and extent of its knowledge base. The development of the knowledge base is an expensive undertaking, in terms of cost and resources, and requires scarce knowledge extracted from an expert relating to the actual nature of his job tasks, and thus the nature of his expertise. Heavy and significant investment can therefore only be justified where a real need exists, and where other methods fail to solve the problem to hand.

As the development of an Expert System is dependent on the co-operation of the expert who possesses the essential technical knowledge about the application domain, it is essential that such experts are sufficiently motivated to help create a serious, complete system that encompasses significant (i.e. non-trivial) knowledge. There may be psychological motivation to produce a shallow "toy" system. It is doubly important as, in a serious system, the representation of serious knowledge in a large knowledge base gives rise to problems that are rarely apparent in a small or trivial knowledge base. These problems (often concerning conflicting knowledge) can only be resolved by the motivated co-operative domain expert.

Such motivation can be found in the first instance in the areas specified previously, where experts are rare and/or are drowned by a large amount of "routine" that requires only some (generally quite small) expertise. Another area is one of decision support systems in areas that require the evaluation of numerous data of a heterogenous nature, often under time pressure. Some typical application areas are:

— error diagnosis in technical equipment (in assembly and in maintenance/test phases)
— assembly of components and/or sub-assemblies to larger, more complex units (robotics, bin picking, etc.)
— interpretation of data in large, complex industrial processes such as power stations, chemical plants, telephone exchanges, etc.

Should one view the Expert Systems developed in the academic sphere, the suspicion may arise that, in the choice of domain for the application of the Expert Systems being developed, none of these considerations played a role. Only chance directed the early applications (and the source of the finance to support the work). The medical domain featured prominently because of its clear dependence on levels of expertise, but this in turn produced early acceptance problems due to differing views on what was the state of the art in a medical domain at any one time!

Prototypes could have been developed just as easily for in-house applications, had developer and expert had the joint motivation to build highly functional systems that extended the throughput of the expert. This would have allowed the acquisition of know-how for developing of systems that would have had subsequent use in non-academic domains. The penetration of Expert Systems today, had this route been taken, may have been much deeper.

2.3.2 The User Interface

Again, the requirements of the user interface are really quite independent of the system application. The age-old requirement for a comfortable, easy to use, friendly user interface is still far from being realised in many systems—even in more traditional data processing applications programmed in 3rd or 4th generation programming languages.

Irrespective of how good and all-knowing the knowledge base is, how smart the inference mechanism is, if the user interface exhibits only limited intelligence, or is awkward to use, human nature being what it is will soon stop using the system on a routine basis. Therefore the system stops evolving and does not learn, and will be quickly consigned to the corporate graveyard, along with the investment and the knowledge gained to date!

It is a characteristic defect of much academic research that the value of progress is placed on the way the knowledge is implemented in the machine (i.e. the systematic representation and the inference component), often to the detriment of the external appearance of the system, which of course impacts its attraction for a potential, albeit reluctant, user. Admittedly, developing a good user interface would appear to have little or nothing to do with the basic research that is still prevalent (and undeniably necessary) in this area. Yet it is often overlooked by those who seek out experts that when a dialogue takes place, this is at the level of the user interface. The expert is not treated as a naked inference engine by the interviewer; but one observes the social conventions of a face-to-face meeting. The experts in turn attempt to interpret their specialised domain knowledge to the person who has consulted them, though much of the inferential reasoning to answer a question will have occurred in the expert's own knowledge representation, using his meta-knowledge, levels of reasoning and inferential styles. The output of this internal "thinking" is translated via his user interface (using the expert's cognitive model of the listener) to a form that he thinks the listener will understand—how often we hear experts explaining concepts to non-experts by using analogy. Analogy is the adaptation of facts and reasoning to a different model of the world that contains the same essential reasoning framework.

Fortunately, with the advent of low cost, high power work stations a great deal of work on user interfaces is now beginning, even in the universities, and some will have relevance to use with Expert Systems. More generally, it is now recognised that the user interface is a great barrier to the introduction and willing use of modern information technology in many potential situations.

What are the relevant requirements of a user interface? What are the tools needed, and is the requirement to include real-time response (or even "reasonable" time response) and behaviour? The collection of experience through automatic learning is usually an important point. If the user interface can reconfigure to reflect the current user viewpoint (by changing the level of detail, or by adaptation to the user capability or expertise with the system), then there are obvious potential benefits.

2.3.3 A Comprehensive Advisory Capability

The third substantial requirement of Expert Systems in commercial/industrial use is the development of a comprehensive advisory concept. The development of a knowledge base is expensive and very time consuming. Therefore it is necessary to consider, well in advance of major design decisions being made about the structure of the Expert Systems as a whole, the following issues:

— what are the problems of the domain?
— can Expert Systems technology address them?
— who are the end users?
— what are their (reasonable) requirements?

— what are the requirements for the Expert Systems to integrate into the organisational structure?
— what user training is necessary?
— what type and number of staff are needed?
— what is the time plan for implementation?
— are there any (better) alternatives?

An advisory concept, implying close collaboration with humans, will only succeed if the above topics are duly considered.

2.3.4 Knowledge Engineering and the Education of Knowledge Engineers

The fourth substantial requirement of Expert Systems for commercial use still bears little relation to the level of expertise or intelligence exhibited by the final system. This particular requirement relates to knowledge acquisition and maintenance. Sight should not be lost of the fact that expert knowledge is often of a nature that should be evident at the user interface, but whose precise internal representation is often the intellectual property right of the organisation employing the expert, and as such it should not be easily accessible or capable of being edited by the user. This often requires that organisations implementing expert systems need to retrain some professional staff as knowledge engineers to maintain the knowledge base and thus protect their investment (i.e. their expertise).

If the user documentation, training or system tools are poor, badly maintained or even "user hostile", then again no matter how expansive and all knowing the knowledge base is, the use to which it will be put will be limited to the capability of the local knowledge engineer, and it will never achieve the status of a widely used system. This automatically restricts its exposure to a special class of problems only, and thus the learning to manage a wide set of problems never takes place.

Also, instead of acquiring more and more additional knowledge to "improve" the expert systems a question at least as interesting is how far one can go with an expert system. The search for new paradigms and less elegant but quicker solutions is a constant trade-off between shallow (heuristic) and deep knowledge analysis, requiring an experienced knowledge engineer to exploit and balance properly.

2.3.5 Embedding an Expert System into the Existing Organisational Structures

The fifth requirement of expert systems to be considered from the earliest moment in an organisation is that the system to be built will not be used later in a vacuum! It will be used inside an existing organisational framework, into which it will have to integrate well in order to perform well. This again gives rise to further requirements that have little, if any, connection with the inherent knowledge of the system. Some of these issues involve considerations of:

— development/delivery hardware (host/target issues)

— existing computational facilities in the organisation
— tools for development
— tools for use
— tools for maintenance
— what demands are not met by the system
— maintenance and customising of interfaces
— security of knowledge
— structural (managerial) integration
— education/training/re-training implications
— cost/benefit analysis
— evolution in the long term life of the organisation.

It is usually recommended that these issues are handled by a mixed team drawn from different levels in an organisation, as well as the technical development team.

2.3.6 Requirement for the Expert System to Exhibit "Intelligence"

The requirement for a computer based system to exhibit intelligence in commercial or industrial applications is only essential where existing methods fail to arrive at a solution, or arrive at a relatively trivial solution in a resource intensive way (e.g. taking up experts' time in routine tasks), where the problem is sufficiently important that a cost-effective route to the solution has to be sought by other means, using a new technique such as Expert Systems.

There is only one unavoidable component for systems that should draw conclusions based on knowledge and solve a specific problem: the INFERENCE MECHANISM. This is the heart of every Expert System. Depending on the problem domain, specific logical inference techniques are invoked (primarily forward and/or backward chaining).

In order to validate the inferring process and thus to enable the user to trust the system in the decisions it makes, the system must be able to trace its reasoning to the user. Therefore a subsidiary requirement is fast becoming a "must" for all expert systems: the EXPLANATION SYSTEM. This allows the historic, current and potential future inferrals to be presented to the user via the user interface, and possibly even influenced or modified by the user on-line.

Depending on the precise nature of the problem domain, certain other capabilities should be available in expert systems for commercial/industrial use:

— fuzzy logic for imprecise knowledge
— knowledge consistency checkers, where very large knowledge bases are built up by more than one expert
— knowledge editors to maintain consistency of the knowledge base
— data acquisition and validation from sensors (e.g. in process control applications)
— belief revision, so that during a goal-oriented search strategy a belief and

all its downstream consequences can be revised and a new rule or rule set selected
— knowledge partitioning, for ease of maintenance and more efficient searching
— constraint reasoning, as with global constraints it is possible to limit the state space of the search to improve performance times significantly
— reasoning about time, where data vary over time, such as clinical data on daytime/night-time metabolism variations
— reasoning with time, including time as an element of the reasoning process itself
— analysis of natural languages, for the user interface
— synthesis of natural languages, for the user interface and for the generation of explanation text, analysis and conflict resolution
— a learning capability, especially where knowledge in the knowledge base is frequently modified on the basis of new facts
— computer aided instruction capability, where the system itself can act as a tool to train users in the decision making processes and advisory function of the expert whose knowledge is in the knowledge base, but who cannot fulfil all the educational functions required of him, because he is usually not at the site of the expert systems.

Intelligent systems are necessary today, as a number of routine tasks requiring some intelligence have to be completed, and the human resource to do this is too scarce, expensive or unreliable.

However, an expert system can at best be seen as the kernel of a more substantial reasoning environment that embeds this layer of "intelligence" into the user's computational support environment. The open question from the industrial users point of view, as systems begin to be used more seriously, is which of the requirements explored above require further basic research, and what progress each of the breakthroughs expected in the areas could contribute to the market potential of the technology as a whole, and the expert systems product of the day.

2.4 ON TECHNOLOGY TRANSFER BETWEEN ACADEMIC RESEARCH AND INDUSTIAL DEVELOPMENT

2.4.0 Introduction

We differentiate between research and technological development. Fundamental, basic research is an absolute essential for the eventual emergence of new technologies. It is expensive and has a long lead time until pay-back—if there is any at all! It is therefore unlikely that this type of research will be carried out in the industrial framework, where returns on investment horizons are generally short. Three years is already an aeon in the minds of many company accountants, required to produce quarterly or six-monthly company reports with optimal profit figures on the bottom line. Initiatives like ESPRIT [Rogers 1986] allow industry to take a slightly longer term approach to these fundamental problems by encouraging a medium term view of 3 to 5 years before a concept moves to the product phase (the so-called pre-competitive phase). Fundamental research should therefore be supported by public or quasi-public funding, where the requirement of the support is only to contribute to the long term intellectual well-being of the society funding the research [Feigenbaum 1979]. However, the unique position of academic research has long ago established its own legitimacy. The inherently different nature and limitations/constraints of academic research and industrial development limit the usefulness of basic research for industrial development, and thus limit the potential technology transfer from academia to industry.

Programmes for Information Technology Research and Development, such as the Commission of the European Communities' ESPRIT (European Strategic Programme of Research and Development in Information Technology), RACE (Research and Development in Advanced Communications for Europe), the German BMFT (Bundesministerium fuer Forschung und Technik) IT-Foerderungsprogramm and the United Kingdom's ALVEY programme all aim to capitalise on this largely latent potential by encouraging joint projects between academic and industrial organisations.

2.4.1 Constraints of Industrial Development

2.4.1.0 Introduction

There are characteristics of industrial development that are determined by the framework in which it takes place, and the exceptions are few. Small start-up companies with high risk venture capital often engage in less constrained R & D. The industrial giants, who represent 80% of the R & D resources in IT per year in Europe, generally succumb to a variety of the problems itemised below.

2.4.1.1 Integration of the Developing Product into the Market

The market needs a product line that solves the problem, at least better than the previous one, or a market has to be developed afresh. The development, in any case, is thus emerging into an environment into which it has to be integrated, or which it helps to shape. There are viewpoints that this angle, that of the user being the ultimate judge of everything and thus driving R & D towards his and only his needs, is good for the long term potential of a supplier, and isolated cases bear this out [Luft 1986]. However, somewhere, someone needs to do the R & D for the next product.

In the context of developing expert systems, it is essential to consider the software environment (and eventual hardware target machine) in which the system is due to operate. The potential market and its collective requirements precede individual attentions. In the US, expert systems made their first widespread market penetrations when they could be operated on common hardware systems, such as DEC's VAX series, or on PC's. European development concentrated on very specific one-off projects. Recently, a major system written for an aircraft pilot decision support system was developed on a specific LISP machine, which of course could never be installed in the aircraft. Finally had to be rewritten in Ada and then delivered!

2.4.1.2 *Concentration on Generic Problems*

The considerations outlined previously determine that, with only very few exceptions, the emphasis must be on solving generic problems or classes of problems at all times, rather than the single problem of a single organisation or individual. A domain of applications exhibit common characteristics that can be exploited by the use of common or generic tools, or tool kits that can handle variability within the domain. It is a cost-benefit conclusion that it is always preferable, at this stage, to design solutions for groups of problems, rather than one optimal solution for a very specific problem (which is rarely transparent to the developer of such a solution anyway). This may seem rather an obvious solution, but in the past, European industry at least has specialised in high expertise, sacrificing width of experience in solution design. Exceptions are very few. Satellite-specific software systems and huge industrial plant configurations are two such special cases where even now software development is becoming more generic. NASA have declared that the Space Station of the 1990's will use Ada, a language where cost-benefit arises out of re-use of much of the developed software components, although the initial development is more expensive than traditional 3rd generation languages.

If the objective of a potential expert system user is to genuinely relieve the organisation's experts of routine work as quickly and completely as possible, then the knowledge acquisition component and a user friendly interface are more crucial than individual problem directions which may be tailored into the user interface.

2.4.1.3 *Team Products*

Team products have a higher inherent value than the product of an individual in an organisation. The addressing of an entire domain of problems usually forces collaboration as the explicit expertise required stretches beyond one individual, and often beyond departmental boundaries. Also, invariably, the inconsistencies that arise will have to be discussed in the team framework, as several different functions are usually influenced by conflicting knowledge bases. Some organisations realise the overlaps of activity for the first time when such an analysis is completed prior to the introduction of an expert system into the organisational framework.

2.4.1.4 *Cost-Benefit Approach*

All products developed in an individual environment inevitably come under scrutiny of a cost-benefit analysis. There are a number of factors to take into account in this case:

- — priorities must be determined in the main by the requirements of the market
- — after a point, further development that may make the system nicer to use may be prohibitively expensive and sometimes impossible once installed at a customer site

— any changes must be introduced in full consultation with the users, and with any planned educational support that may be required
— consideration should be given to the fact that after some time in use, the value of the expert system resides in the knowledge in the system, explicitly or implicitly in the inferences it can make from the plethora of case histories it has gathered in its life. This is the sum total of the investment made in the system and the experts — the organisation must have a way of protecting it.

2.4.1.5 Flexibility of Constraints

Once the objective has been set for the development of such an expert systems product, bearing in mind the immature state of the art and the early stages of the market, the constraints on development should be regarded as flexible and reviewed frequently in the light of new developments and new markets.

2.4.2 Limitations of Academic Research

2.4.2.0 Introduction

Academic research, especially in European universities, is based on individual performance which tend to limit its usefulness to companies engaged in the pursuit of technological advance. It is this loose coupling of research that has given much impetus to the diversity under which Europe's industrial structures now labour. Universities, ivory towers at best of times, exert a strong regional influence, and sometimes also exert a secular influence over whole governments in their endeavours to determine the direction to which industry must look in order to remain popular. Conversely, government may influence the direction of research, which is arguably not their role. War time may generate exceptions, as in the case of the research associated with radar, the atom bomb or the Enigma machine. The highly controversial Lighthill report in the 1970's on the state of research in artificial intelligence in the UK effectively reduced funding for research in that area to a trickle for half a decade. Arguably, funding ought not to be directed, except in the loosest sense, so that basic research can progress unhindered by short to medium term market forces or, even worse, political influences.

2.4.2.1 Integrated Research Traditions and Research Structures

Success in academic research is not manifest in market penetration, or market share, or profitability, or return on investment. It is the recognition by a peer group that determines the measure of standing and thus success. This requires that work is reported and recognised within an existing framework (one's peer group) and within the current literature. Anyone seeking to break out of this has a very difficult time indeed in the formative years of a new technology [Bernold and Albers 1985]. Therefore new areas of research, or those that concern interdisciplinary aspects of existing fields of research, are inherently made more difficult to fund, execute and have accepted. Artificial intelligence suffers from all these complications, and, as such, has had a difficult time emerging from the "lunatic fringe/mad professor" image to the edge of respectability and industrial applications.

2.4.2.2 Concentrating on Intellectually "Nice" Topics

The environment for research requires that the problems that remain currently unsolved are at the forefront of those topics to be attacked with the next funding grant, and to be endlessly pursued to the next conclusion (the insolvent in pursuit of the insoluble?). Few serious researchers concern themselves with the problem of collecting all the solutions of the day and interpreting them in some greater framework. This often leads to neglecting the testing of solutions "in the large", and interest quickly focusses back on the next detailed problem. A classical example is the current large number of knowledge representation formalisms that are available throughout the mainstream artificial intelligence languages and their endless dialects. These are still rapidly expanding, in the quest for solving narrower and narrower problems more and more elegantly, at the expense of generality. The functionality of existing tools hardly comes into play—the more esoteric a new representation is, the greater the intellectual status attained by the developer in the eyes of his peer group.

2.4.2.3 Emphasis on Individual Career Progression

This problem is not as acute in some countries as in others. It is at its worst where the academic staff are employed as civil servants, and least harmful where free contract agreements, often no more than a loose statement of intent, define an individual's domain of research. Fortunately, even academia has now discovered that some problems can only be solved by teamwork, although the potential career progression for the individual is still highly related to the rate of single-name publications, a crude but often used measure of the skill of a researcher. This emphasis, together with the best tradition of accrediting, requires individual research, looking at narrow or isolated problems. Little wonder that the domain of results is finally littered with a mass of heterogeneous models of often startlingly similar essence.

2.4.2.4 Art for Art's Sake?

The responsibility of creating real and lasting long term benefit for society is that of the individual, but he is not educated in how to exercise it. There is no place for such sophisticated role modelling in education—when did any scientist last attend courses on morality or responsibility? The system places a great deal of trust on the individual to gather these concepts by emulating his peers—the only source of comparable experience. This encourages the maintenance of the status quo, unfortunately.

The "art for art's sake" attitude often predominates in the absence of a strong responsible leadership in an area of research. This drifting is often very convenient, as it removes the requirement to examines one's long term goals or the desirability of the work in hand. This further reinforces insularity, giving rise to orthogonal sets of solutions that scatter to other areas, instead of a group of cohesive questions being answered in an orderly fashion that should produce widely usable results at the end of the day for a whole group of researchers and downstream for industry.

2.4.2.5 Inflexibility of Funding Mechanisms and Organisational Framework of the Academic Institutions

The mechanism of support and the framework of the institutions in which research is carried out usually require precise detailed documentation of methods, processes to be used, costs and resources analysed, all well in advance of funding and actual work commencing. This does not induce more comprehensive, flexible or inter-disciplinary research, where problems only become apparent once work has started. Equally, if a promising new line of research appears, the inflexibility usually prevents this being explored directly. About the only item that does not need explicit justification in most academic institutions is the salary, and thus much incentive for high risk, flexible research is surrendered to administration. One could speculate that many large companies exhibit the selfsame characteristics, not to mention administrations; so perhaps it is unfair to single out academia, except that is vital that in this environment there is less constraint than elsewhere. One good example is the length of time taken to create a new course in artificial intelligence in a university [Biorci, 1986] in Europe.

2.4.3 Shortcomings in Research

The result of all these constraints and attitudes in research seems to be that, in the case of artificial intelligence at least, only isolated results have emerged where the work fitted in with traditional research scenarios, and these have often been the result of a singular or very small team of workers. Their importance is recognised only by their frequent citation. They are characterised by small scale, in general. Some examples of well-investigated areas in artificial intelligence are:

— the world of "John and Mary"
— knowledge representation of biblical geneology
— animal kingdom taxonomy
— blocks on tables
— search spaces for the 8 and 15 puzzle
— solutions for the above
— learning from pattern recognition.

Deficits in research can be identified with the following:

— knowledge representation for complex and comprehensive knowledge domains
— techniques for knowledge engineering for complex problems
— variable expert viewpoints
— possibility of stepwise knowledge engineering where different experts tackle different aspects of the overall problem

— techniques for user friendly interfaces
— classification of knowledge domains and the typical problems associated with them
— capability of varying paradigms under real field test conditions
— user acceptance considerations
— insertion of technology into organisational patterns.

Of course, this should come as no great surprise. The academic centres do not have expertise on applications in general, nor do they have the channels of contacts that would need to be in place if this expertise needed to be acquired; or to interface with it so that their research expertise can be brought to bear on the users' aspects of the problem. The typical researcher is just not able (or willing?) to develop any practical knowhow, as against, say, the practising physician, industrial chemist or astronomer. The knowledge that is acquired in the course of his work is so highly specific that it will sustain him in the next endeavour if it is in the same tunnel of technology, or on an even narrower path! The knowledge is isolated, only partially communicated and rarely if ever supported by a vast width of applications. In that sense, apart from acquiring experience in the techniques of "doing research" the expertise acquired is not "expert knowledge" in the sense of being useful for expert system rules of thumb, for example.

From another point of view, one could argue to the contrary — that the academic has deep knowledge, and in that sense is an expert, but in a very narrow domain. He is an expert in the conduct of methodical research, the abstraction of knowledge from text (literature search type abstraction), and in the communication of unique research findings (to others not in his narrow domain). There is certain expertise of a more conventional nature available at most universities, often in more "engineering oriented" departments, and this could be a useful source for expert systems input, and would certainly begin to remedy some of the points above.

Typical problems (i.e. routine ones in the expert systems sense) requiring expert knowledge in an academic environment include:

— advice on local DP system use
— presentation of reports and scientific papers
— advisory service for software libraries
— debugging programs service
— documentation services such as library, literature surveys, etc.
— resource scheduling
— experimental design in laboratory subjects
— student counselling services.

It is strange that these are precisely the areas that researchers often complain take up so much valuable time as to be irritants, and reduce the overall ability to research. Yet it has not generally occurred to the developers of expert systems that an in-house application may be an ideal starting point (or if it has, it is not well advertised, another problem with successful expert systems applications).

The use of expert systems technology to further aid the development of next-generation expert systems seems so obvious.

2.4.4 The Possibilities for Technology Transfer

Considerations of the different fundamental processes of academic research and industrial development indicate that there are deep disparities that give rise to structural reasons why technology transfer from academia to industry is constrained. Whether academic research fulfils its social role in the long term and wider sense is no concern of industry, directly at least, nor should it be. University is a source of highly skilled labour at a low price for industry. It is clear, however, that in the realm of artificial intelligence research today, academia can now only make a limited contribution in the building of practical expert systems. It may be an over-simplified paraphrase of a complex reality, but it could be argued that research stops where user requirements begin!

A valid approach is that it is the role of academia to deliver the principles only for a solution to a problem, and that industry takes on the development of the final prototypes. This overlooks the fact that the realisation of products gives rise to a number of theoretically and intellectually demanding problems at a late stage that are not visible at the "principles" stage. These problems, due to their fundamental nature, are best researched in academic environments. In the context of expert systems, such problems include:

— structure of examples
— development of analogies
— learning by example
— structure of expert knowledge
— elicitation of knowledge
— explanations and their structure
— discourse analysis
— non-verbal communications, gesture, etc.
— user viewpoint in the interface.

Technology transfer should not be seen as a one-way street, from academia to industry, but as a feedback loop with some gain in it. Applications related expertise in a domain is fed back to academia for it to tackle the problems listed above, and thus generally to encapsulated the nature and use of the expertise into their own research model. The question of whether this can occur in today's structures is still unresolved, but the possibility of a positive step in this direction is increasing almost daily.

Academia still needs to be convinced that applications oriented problems are worthy of its serious consideration when planning advances in the state of the art in fundamental research.

2.5 CONCLUSIONS

The current situation for expert systems and their commercial applications may be summarised thus:

— Experts are rare, difficult to access and frequently overloaded by routine. It is important that today's expert systems products try to address the area of routine expert knowledge where a known market waits eagerly.
— When attempting a requirement analysis, it becomes obvious that expert systems, much more than traditional sequential algorithmic software, need to take account of the whole environment where they will eventually operate.
— The technological "knowhow" for the realisation of such systems, despite the wealth of basic research, is limited beyond a certain point in the case of artificial intelligence, expert systems and knowledge based systems.
— Academic research traditionally concentrates on the individual, on individual problems with examples usually stripped of extraneous details to illustrate a point at best. Demanding problems embedded into a realistically useful user interface barely come into the picture. Therefore, when industry decides to develop an expert system, there is little incentive to search out practical methods and tools from the academic arena.
— What is certain is that with the increasing demands placed on systems, much more research is required in this area. It is to be hoped that academia will recognise that the applications context of an eventually used system can give rise to problems that do not appear in the computer laboratory, and these are in part worthy of leading edge research.

The fact that such leading edge research may require the Artificial Intelligence researcher to cross barriers into other disciplines such as cognitive psychology, epistemics, etc., must be overcome; and maybe will reap rich rewards of cross fertilisation. For the first time in such an area it may be possible to generate usable systems where, in value terms, the sum of the whole may indeed exceed the sum of the (ex-) parts.

3

Functionality and Operational Features of the Expert System Shell "TWAICE"

Bernhard Mescheder
Nixdorf Computer AG, Paderborn, FRG

3.0 INTRODUCTION

Nixdorf's Artificial Intelligence Research and Development team has produced a generic expert system building tool called "TWAICE", which has been marketed since the spring of 1985. TWAICE is implemented in PROLOG, the first order logic language popular with the implementors of so-called Fifth Generation systems. A subset of PROLOG is used to enable this kernel to be portable [Noelke and Savory 1984]. As a consequence of this, TWAICE runs on hardware systems from Nixdorf, DEC, Amdahl, Fujitsu, Sun and IBM.

TWAICE currently has German and English interfaces, though it is a notable point that due to the localisation of natural language interfaces, the addition of other languages is a well structured and easily accomplished task. TWAICE has a number of knowledge acquisition tools that help overcome the knowledge acquisition bottleneck for commercial applications (see Chapter 2). Further tools being built include consistency checkers, as well as induction tools. To assist the knowledge engineer in finding gaps in his knowledge base, negative reports are generated and explained. Thus the knowledge engineer and the user are able to get not only explanations of the system's results but also explanations of why the system was unable to conclude otherwise. Other projects include accessing relational databases; separating strategic knowledge of how to use knowledge at the domain level from the domain knowledge itself; generating natural language text output from formal knowledge representations; and the development of a hardware realisation of a parallel computer architecture that would suit TWAICE execution. The implemented functions in TWAICE are particularly aimed at two types of applications:

— Diagnosis, for example in electronic equipment
— Advisory, for example in financial advice situations.

Chapter 3 is structured in the following way:

Section 0	Introduction
Section 1	Basic design decisions taken in TWAICE
Section 2	Systems architecture and main components
Section 3	The knowledge base
Section 4	The knowledge representation
Section 5	Inferring
Section 6	Possibilities and limitations for the application of TWAICE.

3.1 DESIGN OBJECTIVES

3.1.1 Historic Development of the Shell Concept

The very early work in the area of artificial intelligence was carried out in the late 1950's and early 1960's and concentrated very much on the development of very powerful general purpose problem solving methods such as GPS of Newell and Simon. General problem solving techniques that arose out of this work included

— means-end analysis
— problem reduction
— heuristic search.

These techniques emerged as important contributions to the general development of broader techniques. Unfortunately it became apparent that the general ability to solve a problem required much more than each of these techniques could encapsulate. Their capabilities were quickly left behind once a class of specialised problem solvers had been developed—but these each had limited applicability (for comparison, see Barr and Feigenbaum [1981], pp. 113–118). In the 1970's, however, a new trend emerged for problem solving systems. A group of systems characterised by large knowledge bases about specific subjects became the focal point of development. These included:

AM	Lenat [1976]
CRYSALIS	Engelmore and Nii
DENDRAL	Feigenbaum, Buchanan and Lederberg, Michie and Buchanan
MOLGEN	Martin, Friedland, King & Stefik
MYCIN	Shortliffe [1976]
SU/X	Nii and Feigenbaum.
TEIRESIAS	Davis [1976].

Outline descriptions and full references are given in [Barr and Feigenbaum 1981].

In these first expert systems the problem solving strategies were relatively simple, though systems such as MACSYMA and DENDRAL were highly specific in their applicability in an invariably narrow domain. Although the general capabilities of these systems were impressive in a domain, a basic weakness also emerged. The knowledge contents of many of these systems were encapsulated and implemented in LISP functions. The development of these systems, consequently, was difficult and very costly—especially the extension and modification of knowledge which ideally should have been achieved automatically but instead involved major restructuring of extensive portions of native code, and could therefore only be accomplished by someone intimately familiar with the program itself. As the knowledge resided in the structure of the code and functions, editing often resulted in side effects and inconsistencies. Furthermore, there were no tools to support any of this detailed work [Buchanan and Shortliffe 1984, p. 149] as the concept of computer manufacturers at that time was that the provision of a compiler was already a major concession to the needs of software developers!

A precondition to the successful exploitation of expert systems in the market place is their usability. This implies an acceptable cost/benefit ratio not just at the construction phase (because that is highly unlikely anyway) of such a complete system, but also at the maintenance phase of a knowledge base. This phase lasts much longer, of course, and is not really just maintenance, it is a learning phase also. An expert system that learns as it is used becomes more valuable as time passes, therefore the cost/benefit analysis should take this longer term view into account. Systems that require possible code changes after (or during) use will never meet this criterion. It was important for a method to be developed that would delineate between:

— the domain knowledge, specialist knowledge
— the program to evaluate it and infer from it.

Much greater flexibility was attainable in the construction of expert systems. Most notably, this separation aided the extension and modification of knowledge bases for domain specific systems such as those listed above. A further degree of flexibility could be attained by making the program for evaluating the knowledge independent of the application domain, and hence the term "Expert System Shell" (cf. van Melle [1980]) was coined. In this situation, it is possible to use a domain independent shell for different applications. This development was also the basis for economically viable developments and maintenance of expert systems, thus opening the way for the commercial exploitation in a number of application areas.

In parallel to the shell concept developing, the main emphasis moved from implementation of routines that evaluated rigidly structured knowledge to a much broader based discipline of knowledge engineering. Knowledge engineering is the process of creating an image of the expert's knowledge about a domain in a form of knowledge representation that can be utilised more or less directly by an expert system [Bernold, 1985, pp. 133–140].

3.1.2 Design Objectives of TWAICE

In order that the knowledge engineering function receives effective support, two possible viewpoints must be taken into account when an expert system is designed:

— the user's viewpoint that expects the system to deliver a solution to his problem
— the knowledge engineer's and/or expert user's viewpoint for the ease of creation and maintenance of the knowledge base.

In the rest of this chapter, the designation "user" refers to the user in the first category—the person who consults the system and expects to receive competent advice on the current domain to help his problem solving requirement. (He also picks up the bill for the development of the expert system, therefore it is his priorities which prevail.) The knowledge engineer/ expert user is not excluded, of course, from his own consultations with the knowledge base—in fact this is essential during development, testing and maintenance. These aspects were uppermost in the minds of the developers of TWAICE. Overall, seven specific design objectives were developed:

1. Domain Independence
   The developed expert system should be an expert systems shell so designed that it can be used for a variety of different application domains.
2. Capability
   The Knowledge Representations employed in TWAICE, as well the inference mechanism, should be powerful enough to solve real, complex problems. The system should be capable of working with knowledge that has imprecision associated with it.
3. Incremental Development of the Knowledge Base
   TWAICE should enable incremental building of a knowledge base of expertise and experience. This must be especially applicable to the knowledge that is domain specific. This must be extendable and adaptable. This is equally true of those parts of the user interface that contain domain specific elements, such as highly detailed menus, or the representation of specific results through, say, customised icons. These aspects should remain separated from building the logical kernel of the knowledge base which should only contain independent components.
4. Easily Modifiable
   A highly related goal to that above in paragraph 3 is for an easily modifiable and extendable expert system. Only when this is achieved will the performance and capability of a system be of sufficient quality to envisage its extensive use over a prolonged period.
5. Tools for Testing Knowledge Bases
   The knowledge engineer must be supported by the appropriate tools in TWAICE, or in any other expert system shell for that matter. The most important of these tools is for the location and resolution of erroneous and/or conflicting knowledge, and it is heavily used during the initial construction phase.

6. Explanation Capability
   TWAICE must be capable of explaining its reasoning and conclusions. This should enable the user to gain an insight into the nature of the reasoning of the system, i.e. how a conclusion was arrived at, and allows the knowledge engineer to assess the quality of that reasoning. It also allows the user to gradually build up his confidence in the system.
7. Usability
   The user interface should be so designed and constructed that even a naïve user can conduct a consultation with the expert system, without major training on the user's part (ideally without any training, or with the minimum of online training). Components of the knowledge base should be protected from being over written by the user, and be modifiable only by the knowledge engineer or domain expert(s).

Based on the current status of the TWAICE development, considerable success has been achieved in meeting all of these objectives to an extent that a marketable system has resulted.

3.1.3 Fundamental Design Decisions Taken for TWAICE

There were four absolutely fundamental design decisions that had to be taken in the design phase of TWAICE, that would shape its future:

— the knowledge representation
— the inference engine
— the representation of basic facts
— the implementation language.

3.1.3.1 The Knowledge Representation for TWAICE

The single most important representation for expert knowledge in TWAICE is that of rules. This decision was taken based on good experience accumulated from the prototype expert system "ICE" [Savory 1983] that was presented by Nixdorf as early as 1983 at the annual Hannover Fair.

Rules are widely used and consequently are a "natural" way to represent dependencies in a domain. Examples may be found in all walks of life:

— Laws of the State: IF (any person) (terminates a pregnancy) THEN (they) (will have offended) (section 218) (of the German Penal Code)
— Advice: IF (you are non-resident in UK) AND (have over 20 000 pounds sterling) THEN (invest) (in Widget Plc) AND (earn 12.5%)
— User Manuals: IF (power light is ON) AND (master disk is loaded) THEN (hit the RETURN key)
— Health : IF (you smoke) THEN (your health) MAY (suffer).

Therefore rules are also meaningful to non-programmers/experts and thus a natural means of expression for the vast majority of the potential user market for any particular expert system. Furthermore, production rules can also express a large amount of expert knowledge quite succinctly. The rules are usually independent, or well grouped, and can thus be handled, edited and manipulated over time with experience largely independent of each other, or with easily identifiable side effects. The dialogue between the knowledge engineer and the expert, during the so-called knowledge acquisition phase, can concentrate on small components such as "elements" or "atoms" of knowledge. Explanations can later utilise the same rules as the system uses them for regeneration of the reasoning chains. In direct contrast to the knowledge representations used in PROSPECTOR [Barr and Feigenbaum 1981, Vol. 2, p. 155] and in the Nixdorf expert system FAULT-FINDER which are based on nets, these rules possess a high degree of inherent modularity. In the process of inferring, rules are not called by other rules, or by the inference engine directly, but by their contents. Therefore the addition or deletion of a rule can be effected without any effect on other rules generally. The systems capability remains the same, but the overall quality of the decision making may be improved or reduced by modifying the number of rules in use at inferral time. Consequently, the use of rules is a convenient method for incremental building of a knowledge base over time with the minimum of expert intervention.

The strength of an "if–then" relationship may be expressed by a modification that reflects different degrees of belief, based on natural language interpretation of qualifiers such as:

Belief Strength		Everyday Speech
if then always	⇒	certainty
if then almost always	⇒	most probably
if then usually	⇒	probably
if then possibly	⇒	possibly
if then improbably	⇒	unlikely

The United Kingdom H.M. Government Health warning on all cigarette packets is a good example of the strength of belief, and belief revision in the light of other pressures. The anti-smoking lobby from the medical world wanted the rule "Smoking will Damage your Health" to appear on all packets, but by the use of statistics and "belief weakening", (and possibly from revenue fears) the government modified the word WILL to MAY. This downgrades the rule from an IF-THEN-ALWAYS to IF-THEN-POSSIBLY, and will affect the fundamental reasoning process of an expert system that has this rule in it, when using it in an inference chain.

The qualifiers may also be given some numeric probability as they are in TWAICE and as exemplified in the Hay Fever advice example in Chapter 2. The numeric probabilities are propagated along chains of rules and can be accumulated in cases of multiple evidence for the same fact. Thus the need to interpret natural language is removed, also making the process more independent of application domain or location. The qualifier can be adapted and refined in the light of case histories, or rules based on better expertise when it is available. Either way, uncertainty can be represented and modified in the light of experience directly or indirectly.

3.1.3.2 The Inference Mechanism

The principal method employed in ICE and, for the same reasons as explained in 3.1.3.1, in TWAICE is backward chaining. Goal oriented problem solving and its mode of operation are well known to both experts and users. Over and above that, a backward chaining inference process allows a much more focussed dialogue with the user, and a simple question/answer dialogue on the user interface. As the backward chaining proceeds, argument chains are built up that later provide the greater framework for information requests from the system [Davis and Lenat 1982, pp. 260–265].

3.1.3.3 Representation of Atomic Facts and Taxonomic Knowledge

In TWAICE, unlike the prototype system ICE which only used propositional logic, rules were intended for use in more than just the singular context of IF (a condition) THEN (some consequential action or condition). For example, a rule that describes the selection of a particular type of keyboard based on the requirements of a customer should, of course, be applicable to all keyboards in a computer system range. This requirement implies that TWAICE needs to represent attributes not only as a carrier of absolute or relative values, but also for explicit references to objects and object instances. Therefore, apart from the knowledge represented in rules about the interdependencies of object–attribute–value triples, TWAICE requires knowledge about the objects in a domain, their attributes, and their possible values. This knowledge is taxonomy oriented, or "domain vocabulary" knowledge. The usefulness of this knowledge is apparent in designing simple syntactic tests for rule knowledge and user responses.

This structural/syntactic knowledge and the inferred facts are represented in TWAICE by a frame structure. Generic object frames contain certain types of slots for describing:

- the object hierarchy (FATHER-Slot)
- the method of instantiation (INSTANTIATION-Slot),
- the legal number of object instances (NUMBER-Slot)
- the associated goals (GOAL-Slot)
- the initial data (INITIALS-Slot), etc.

By the prescribing of goal attributes, the knowledge engineer identifies those attributes that the inference component must investigate after the instantiation of an object instance.

By the prescription of initial data attributes, the knowledge engineer identifies those attributes that the inference component must acquire from the user directly after the instantiation of an object instance, independent of the application of rules (see Fig. 3.1).

Differentiating different objects and object instances requires that in the evaluation of the rule propositions, the relevant instantiations related to the listed objects in the current premise have to be determined. This is the so-called instantiation context.

For example, a rule that includes in its proposition the objects workstation and keyboard can, in a configuration like Fig. 3.2, be evaluated in instantiation contexts:

(workstation—1,keyboard—1)
(workstation—1,keyboard—2)
(workstation—2,keyboard—3)

but not in contexts:

(workstation—1,keyboard—3)
(workstation—2,keyboard—1)
(workstation—2,keyboard—2)

In order for the expert system to be able to determine the instantiation context, it is necessary to include, apart from pure taxonomy knowledge, some further knowledge about hierarchical relationships between the objects in the knowledge base. So, for example, in the context of a computer system configurator, the object "keyboard" is always hierarchically below the object "workstation". These hierarchies are described as components of the taxonomy knowledge in so-called FATHER-slots in the object frames (see Fig. 3.5).

FATHER slots describe a static tree representation (see Fig. 3.3a). In the course of a consultation, this object tree is populated and expanded by the instantiations of new object-instances. This results in dynamic tree structures, for example as in Fig. 3.3b. The hierarchical relations in a dynamic object tree are represented through FATHER-INSTANCE in the instantiated object frames.

3.1.3.4 Implementation Language

For the development of TWAICE, the language PROLOG was chosen (PROgramming in LOGic). The detailed advantages of this choice are explained in Chapter 4. There is little doubt that for the criteria listed here, PROLOG is a language that is extremely suitable for simplifying many of the problems in expert systems and other problems in the domain of artificial intelligence. The manipulation of symbols, for example, is supported by unification. Goal oriented search and selection strategies for rules are supported by backtracking. The selection of PROLOG, as opposed to LISP, was also influenced by such issues as availability, implementations and support by vendors offering implementations. Campbell [1984] discusses some technical issues in this area.

```
OBJECT           printer                 : object declaration
FATHER           workstation             : name of father object
                                           in object tree
INSTANTIATION    trace_NUMBER            : method of instantiation
NUMBER           0–2                     : legal number of objects
INITIALS         speed                   : initial attributes
GOALS            order_code              : goal attributes
END

A Generic Object Frame

ATTRIBUTE        printer.paper_transport : attribute declaration
MULTIVALUED      no                      : multi valued attribute
ANSWER           ask,unk,no_cf           : question and answers
RESULT           yes                     : result attribute
VALUES_LIST      roller;                 :
                 single_sheet;           : legal values
                 tractor                 :
END

A Generic Attribute Frame
```

Fig. 3.1 — Generic frames in a configurator advisor example.

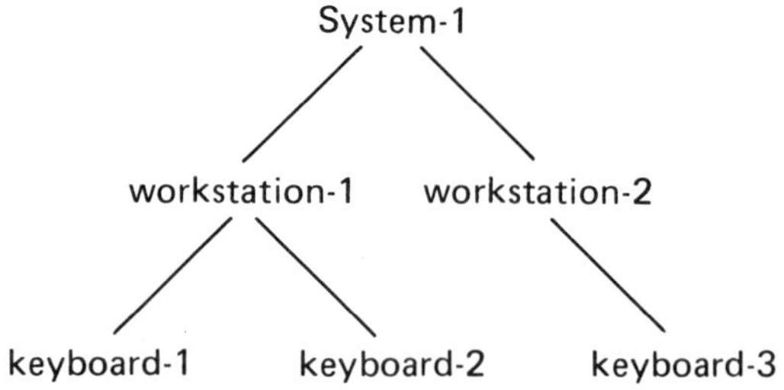

Fig. 3.2 — Instantiation context in a configuration of a computer system.

3.1.4 Classification of Paradigms

The design decisions

— production rules for prime method for knowledge representation
— backward chaining as principal inference mechanism

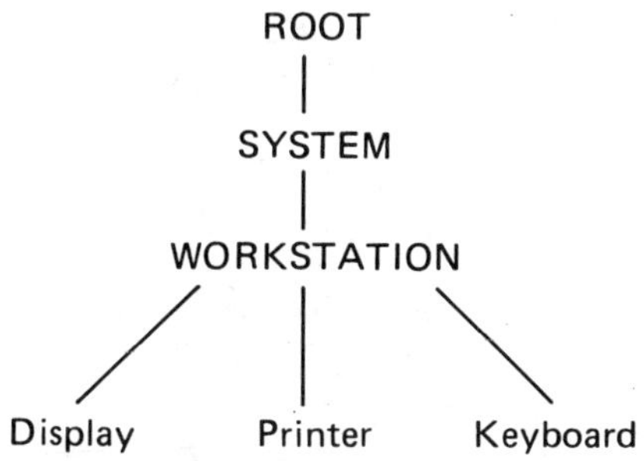

Fig. 3.3a — Example of a static object tree for a computer configuration expert system.

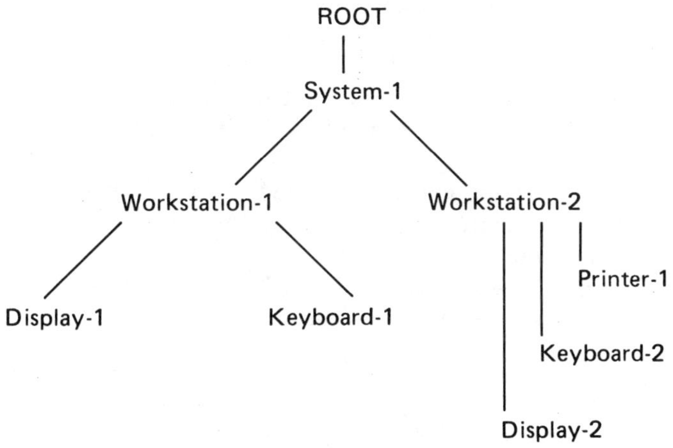

Fig. 3.3b — Example of a dynamic object tree for a computer configuration expert system.

— representation of facts as object–attribute–value triples
— representation of hierarchical relationships as trees

are characteristic of a whole family of expert systems that have been developed subsequent to the paradigms employed in MYCIN. Therefore TWAICE is close to MYCIN in the conceptual ideas that have been implemented in detail. An important consequence of the success of MYCIN was the development of EMYCIN (for Empty MYCIN), which was the MYCIN concept stripped of any domain knowledge. From the mid 1970's onwards, a number of expert systems were developed from the starting point of the EMYCIN shell in different domains, not always with initial full success [Clancey and Letsinger 1984] when the domain is fundamentally different to the origins of the MYCIN system as in the case of PARNISSE, an expert on exchange rates; but with enough consistent progress demonstrated to ensure that following the design decisions above would represent the least risk strategy.

A number of distinct expert systems have been developed based on EMYCIN that have proved to be quite successful, for example [van Melle 1980] :

— SACON: an advisory system for engineers in the use of software system libraries for structural analysis in engineering disciplines
— CLOT: a system for the diagnosis of illnesses of the thrombosis class
— PUFF: a diagnosis system for lung disease, and for occupational lung disease diagnosis
— HEADMED: a system for diagnosis of psychological illnesses.

The original work done in EMYCIN was extended in TWAICE in several ways. One extension focusses on the improvement of knowledge representation capabilities by allowing quantifiers in rules, term evaluation, table look-ups and procedure calls. Rules can also control the instantiation of objects and reason about defaults. Another focus is in the use of generic frames to represent taxonomic knowledge and to control the inference strategy.

By offering a number of knowledge acquisition tools for acquiring rules and taxonomy and for building the end-user interface TWAICE provides an easy to use interface for the knowledge engineer. Case history files help in testing the knowledge base. Extensive trace and explanation facilities help in debugging the knowledge base.

3.1.5 Current Work in TWAICE.

Current work in TWAICE concentrates on the following topics:

— separating strategic knowledge (meta-knowledge) of how to apply domain knowledge from the domain knowledge itself
— building consistency checkers to help the knowledge engineer in testing the knowledge base
— building completeness checkers to help the knowledge engineer in testing the knowledge base
— generating reports of why TWAICE failed to apply knowledge sources in order to help the knowledge engineer debug the knowledge base and the user to understand why the system did not arrive at a specific conclusion
— generating natural language text output from formal representations
— improving the dialogue interface by using graphics
— integrating TWAICE with a relational database management system to access large quantities of data
— allowing TWAICE to reason about hypothetical situations.

3.2 SYSTEMS ARCHITECTURE OF TWAICE

The design of the architecture is represented in Fig. 3.4. It demonstrates the conceptual realisation of the shell concept, as well as taking multiple user viewpoints into account.

The main components are:

— the external knowledge base
— the expert system shell TWAICE.

The external knowledge base can be further decomposed into modules for:

— rule knowledge
— tabulated knowledge
— procedural knowledge
— taxonomy knowledge
— knowledge on subject specific natural language
— formulations, e.g. specialist terminology
— knowledge about user aids (help systems).

The components of the external knowledge base can be edited by knowledge engineers both outside and inside the TWAICE environment in their external representation. The components of the knowledge base will be described in greater detail in section 3.3.

In the rest of this section, the components of the expert system shell TWAICE and the implemented functions will be described.

3.2.1 Dialogue Control.

The dialogue control function in TWAICE has two tasks, essentially:

— it gives access for the knowledge engineer or domain expert or user to the system functions
— it handles the requirements of the other system components for dialogue with the (human) dialogue partner.

By the separation of two levels of user interface, protected by different passwords, the dialogue control interface ensures that only certain functions are accessed by the user, and others by the expert and/or the knowledge engineer.

All TWAICE system functions can be selected by an integrated menu and command interface. While the novice knowledge engineer can use a well-structured hierarchy of menus, the more experienced engineer will use easy commands. A number of help facilities assist the knowledge engineer in learning the commands. The dialogue interface is adaptable in that the menus can be switched off so that they only work with direct commands.

In order for the processing of various requests from different components of the system to proceed reliably, special request formulations have to

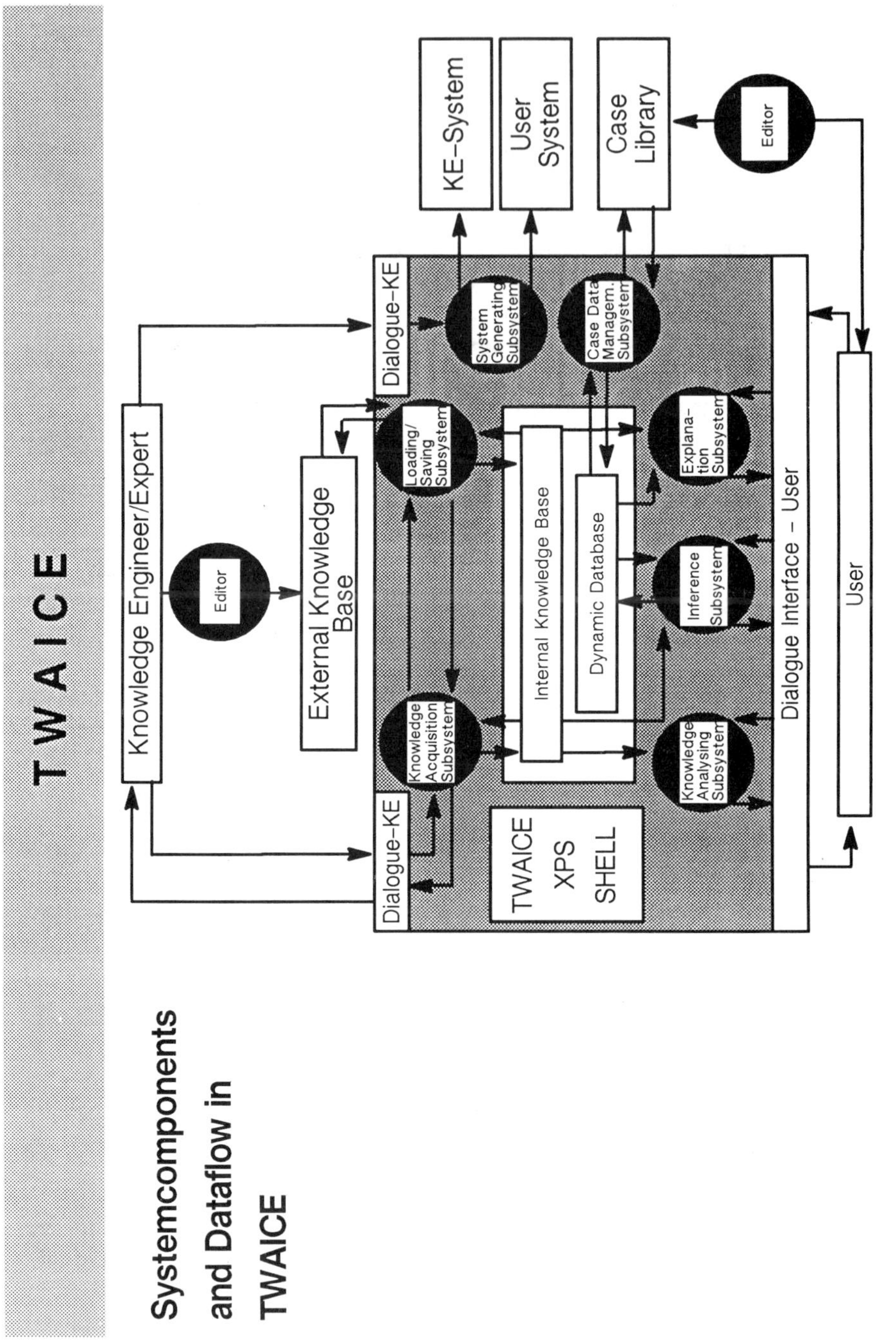

Fig. 3.4 — System components and information flows in the TWAICE shell system.

be generated, and the syntactic correctness of the answer has to be checked. Upon any responses from the user the taxonomic consistency of new information has to be checked, and any spelling mistakes located and corrected as far as is unambiguously possible.

The command "?" can, at any time, be issued by the user to check the currently possible responses.

The dialogue controller also copies the entire user dialogue into a file for possible later analysis of the whole session—useful for recreating special situations or generating a historical record of the consultation.

3.2.2 Loader / Lister

The components of the external database are loaded into the internal knowledge base of TWAICE by the loader. During the loading process, the external representations of the rules are compiled into the internal structure required by TWAICE. Also, in parallel, the loader checks the syntactic correctness of the rules and their taxonomic consistency. Should the loader check meet errors it cannot correct, then the knowledge acquisition component is automatically called up, and a short dialogue follows with the current user in order to attempt to remove the erroneous condition and restore the knowledge base to a consistent and correct form. The knowledge engineer can introduce new terms into the taxonomy at this stage, or a specific rule can be flagged as erroneous and it will be excluded from the current consultation. After the whole loading process has been completed, all the erroneous rules may be examined and edited for reloading. At the end of the loading process, the internal TWAICE knowledge base contains a syntactically correct image of the external knowledge base, and in a form for direct use by the TWAICE system.

The syntactic check serves to prevent the value of the expert system being reduced by very obvious irregularities in the rules. The knowledge engineer/expert should be able to concentrate on the logical inconsistencies in the knowledge base.

Global semantic checks for conflicts, redundancy, subsumption and loops are not currently (1984) in the checking procedures. Also, unlike ONCOCIN [Buchanan and Shortliffe 1984, pp. 159–170] which has then, combinatorial checks, are not included in TWAICE, but can be realised within the framework of the existing design, and will be included in an extension of the knowledge checking components (1986). Currently a consistency checker is being developed that allows checking of the knowledge base for conflicting rules, subsumptions and redundancies; it will be released in 1987.

TWAICE is, however, in a position to recognise loops during a consultation. Rules that lead to these loops are not further utilised, and the trace of the consultation is annotated with the essentials of the decision to exclude these rules.

The knowledge acquisition components operate only on the internal knowledge base. The external knowledge base can be updated with the aid of the Lister. This also performs housekeeping over the modifications in the internal knowledge base, so that the knowledge engineer is reminded, at the end of a session, which parts of the knowledge base have been modified and require securing to the external knowledge base via the Lister.

3.2.3 Inference Component

The inference component is activated when the internal knowledge base is operationally loaded, and the consultation begins. The main function of the component is the execution of the consultation and the controlling of the inference process. A part of this task is the selection and modification of goals and sub-goals, the selection of knowledge sources and checking their applicability, as well as the formulation of queries to the dialogue controller. On request, the inference module informs the knowledge engineer/expert user about the flow of the inference process via a trace. Acquired results are placed into TRACED_RESULT slots of the attribute frames, as well as a protocol over the source of the result and the context in which it was acquired. These items are interpreted by the explanation module at a later stage. Responses from users are specially flagged, so that at the end of a consultation they may be stored in a case history library. The precise nature of operation of this component may be found in section 3.5.

3.2.4 Explanation Component

The function of the explanation component is the reason for questions arising out of the inference component (WHY explanations) and the justification of the deduced facts (HOW explanations). The explanation module needs access to the protocols generated by the inference system through the reasoning process built up under backward chaining. Every explanation consists of a definition of the subject matter under explanation, and an explanation itself.

A WHY explanation subject matter is an extract from the argumentation chain. Basic components of such an explanation include:

— the current goal
— the current rule under investigation
— the currently satisfied premises.

Recurrent invoking of the WHY explanations window the reasoning chain differently, and cause explanations to be generated that relate to hierarchically higher order goals.

A HOW explanation subject matter is an entry in the TRACED_RESULT slot of an attribute frame (i.e. a fact). The basic components of a HOW explanation include:

— the knowledge source employed
— the context of acquisition, which may consist of
    — supporting facts, which in turn can be
    — investigated by further HOW investigations.

The concept employed in TWAICE for explanations is closely allied to that used in the expert system TEIRESIAS [Davis and Lenat 1982, pp. 259–286, Davis 1976]. The assumption is that an insight into the flow of execution in the inference component is a sufficient basis for an understandable explanation. Explanations therefore only regurgitate the history of the reasoning and associated events, and are not oriented towards a user model [Savory, 1984]. Further work on developing this is foreseen however.

Another problem with explanations in TWAICE today is that a state of the art knowledge base contains both domain knowledge and strategic knowledge of how the domain knowledge should be applied. Therefore, by separation of the strategic knowledge, explanations are improved as they concentrate on the logical dependencies within the domain.

3.2.5 Knowledge Analyser

The function of this component is to make available a variety of retrieval mechanisms to access the knowledge in the knowledge repository. This includes the location and marking of rules based on content criteria, as well as the marking of associated taxonomic elements. The selection criteria may be given in differing levels of detail. The actual retrieval is activated over a simple command interface.

Examples of retrieval functions activated by the knowledge analyser are:

— THEN Order-Number of Keyboard
  show all rules deducing the attribute "keyboard. Order No."
— IF Keyboard.Order No.=TA–061
  show all rules that use the premise "Keyboard. Order No.=TA–061"
— TO 50
  show all rules that conclude about premises of rule 50.

The knowledge analyser may be called up via a menu, or by a command from the consultation dialogue itself. In order to relieve the short term memory of the user, once the knowledge analysis has been completed, the dialogue of the consultation is continued by restating the currently unanswered questions.

3.2.6 The Knowledge Acquisition Component

Errors in rule knowledge can occur in the following forms:

— erroneous results due to erroneous rule conclusions
— incorrect application of rules due to weak rule premises
— incorrect exclusion of rules
— missing results due to incomplete knowledge/rule set.

If the knowledge engineer discovers any of these while testing the knowledge base, he can correct them directly with the help of the knowledge acquisition component, so that the internal knowledge base is as correct as possible at all times. Corrections are updated in the external knowledge base with the aid of the Lister. Amongst the functions available to the knowledge engineer are:

- for rules:
  - listing
  - deletion
  - modification
  - insertion
- for object and attribute frames:
  - listing
  - deletion
  - insertion
  - modification
  - for questions, result formulations, user support texts and object announcements:
    - listing
      - deletion
      - insertion
      - modification.

The component operates only on the internal knowledge base. With the aid of the Loader/Lister the modified parts of this may be spooled and secured to the external knowledge base. Housekeeping during the session (of the changes made) will aid the knowledge engineer in deciding which modified portions to secure, and which have been secured already.

3.2.7 Case History Administration

The purpose of the case history administrator is to assist the knowledge engineer in building a library of case histories for the testing of the knowledge base. Case histories are defined as all values elicited from the user during a consultation as well as all values of attributes marked as results. These data can be secured at the end of a consultation into a case history library. The knowledge engineer can commence a consultation by prescribing the case history to be used. The dialogue module will then attempt to complete all queries to the user in the first instance from the library data, only asking the user for any missing data. The library of cases can be edited internally and externally to TWAICE. The generation of case histories is an interesting aspect of the problems in this task.

The case history system along these lines places the user in the position of being able to use the expert system incrementally. An incomplete configuration consultation could be executed by temporary use of the "unk" ("unknown") value. The system generates a provisional configuration plan. When the "unk" values are later defined or revoked the case history can be modified, and a final plan generated. Such a system is also able to gain knowledge by "listening" to a user who wishes to enter data at the start of a session voluntarily. Acquiring an extensive case history eventually allows more efficient solutions to be implemented. The case history administration also includes functions for comparing answers and results of a consultation with different case histories. This function is especially useful for the user and the knowledge engineer who wish to find out the consequences of their answers with respect to the values of the result attributes. Case histories can also serve as an information buffer to other programs that need to use the results acquired by the consultation of an expert system.

3.2.8 System Generator Component

The function of this component is to secure the entire current state of the system (that is, TWAICE shell plus internal knowledge base) as a PROLOG-object database. In other words the component generates a subject specific expert system, in that it integrates the expert system shell and the internal knowledge base. The generated system may be allocated different user levels (the ordinary user, the expert, or the knowledge engineer user) in order to prevent unauthorised changes in the knowledge base.

3.3 CONSTITUENTS OF THE KNOWLEDGE BASE

The knowledge base consist of the following modules:

Name	Module for	Requirement
.etx	taxonomy knowledge	obligatory
.erl	rule knowledge	obligatory
.tab	tabulated knowledge	optional
.sup	user support tests	optional
.prc	procedural knowledge	optional
.que	question formulation	optional
.prt	results formulation	optional
.ann	formulation of object instantiations	optional

Each module is prefixed by a name that indicates the domain of application, e.g. the configuration of a computer system may have just CON.etx, CON.erl, CON.tab and CON.prt as constituent modules.

In order to support the incremental development of the knowledge base, only the modules .etx and .erl are required, as these form the kernel of the knowledge base. For the initial phases of the knowledge engineering tasks, the modules .que, .prt, .ann and .supp can be dispensed with altogether. In this case TWAICE defaults to standard formulations for questions and answers and denies the existence of user support texts. This may actually help an engineer concentrate on the kernel of the knowledge base in the early phases, but is not recommended in the long term! The inclusion of the modules .tab and .prc is dependent on the application in hand. If the application contains subject specific algorithmic data, then the module .prc is essential.

3.3.1 Taxonomy Knowledge

The taxonomic knowledge in TWAICE encompasses conceptual, hierarchical and consultative knowledge.

The conceptual knowledge includes an enumeration of permissible objects, attributes and values in each application domain, as well as a description of their well-ordered allocation.

The hierarchical knowledge includes the hierarchical description of relations between the permitted objects. The need for these two types of knowledge was rationalised in section 3.1.3.3.

The necessity for consultative knowledge was already recognised as far back as MYCIN [Buchanan and Shortliffe 1984, p. 60]. Backward chaining as a central inference mechanism leads to goal oriented and logically based argumentation chains, but does not take into account the needs of the user for a focussed "natural" consultation dialogue. Pure backward chaining leads to a disjointed consultation flow. The following elements of taxonomic knowledge allow the knowledge engineer to focus the dialogue of the consultation:

GOAL-ATTRIBUTES:
Every object can be allocated a list of goal attributes, the achieving of which will be given (left to right) priority after the instantiation of the related object—"object related goal focussing"

INITIALS-ATTRIBUTES:
Every object can be allocated a list of standard attributes, the values of which will be elicited, independent of the rules used, after an instantiation of the related object. This relates closely to real world problem solving strategies—"object related question focussing"

INSTANTIATION:
Every object can be allocated a specific type of instantiation method, whereby each instance of an object is created. TWAICE distinguishes three types of instantiation:

— trace_NUMBER:
  Number of instantiations is determined in advance
— trace_EXISTMORE:
  After investigation of an object instance the necessity of further instantiations is examined. The first instantiation is made automatically
— trace_EXIST:
  This is similar to trace_EXISTMORE. However, the first instantiation is not made automatically, but only if required.

3.3.2 Rule Knowledge

3.3.2.0 Introduction

The most important knowledge source in TWAICE is the RULE. In order to implement goal oriented and event driven inference mechanisms, TWAICE supports both forward and backward rules. The use of rules also allows the description of logical dependencies and consultative knowledge to be expressed easily.

3.3.2.1 Forward and Backward Rules

When the knowledge engineer does not specify any method for use, the rules from the inference component are combined by backward chaining in the inference process (backward rules).

The knowledge engineer can, however, define a rule as a forward rule. Forward rules have trigger attributes attached to them to control the firing of the rule. The forward rules are always examined when one of the attached trigger attributes has been traced. This allows event driven inferences to be defined by forward chaining. These types are useful to improve the efficiency of the whole process, as they avoid unnecessary questioning, and trigger associated processes. As in the analysis of the premises of forward rules new intermediate goals may be inserted, it is possible to utilise these rules also as demons. Demons will trigger an excursion into the main inference process under certain triggering conditions.

3.3.2.2 Rules Syntax

3.3.2.2.0 Introduction

The external form of rules used in TWAICE is identical for all rule types. Each rule consists of two portions:

— the premise (the IF component)
— the conclusion (the THEN component).

The premise component allows con- and disjunction of elementary premises to any depth or level and the negation of elementary premises. A disjunction on a single value can also be expressed via a premise. The conclusion component allows the conjunction of elementary conclusions. Uncertain knowledge is accommodated by the explicit weakening of the IF–THEN relationship by adding a confidence factor ranging from 1 to 1000 (from very UNLIKELY to absolutely CERTAIN).

3.3.2.2.1 Elementary premises

The elementary premises implemented in TWAICE permit the description of relationships between attributes and values (relational elementary premises), as well as the description of consultative situations (consultative premises). Amongst the relational elementary premises are:

Equality:

e.g. workstation.memory = 512k
workstation.memory = customer.memory_requirement

Inequality:
e.g. workstation.memory <>512k

Greater than, greater than or equal to:
e.g. workstation.printer_NUMBER > 0
e.g. workstation.printer_NUMBER >= customer.required_printers

Less than, less than or equal to:
e.g. workstation.keyboard_NUMBER < 3
e.g. workstation.keyboard_NUMBER <=
customer.keyboard_requirement

Quantifiers:
e.g. ALL workstation OF system:
(.memory = 512k AND .keyboard_number<3)
e.g. NOT EXIST workstation OF system:
(.memory = 512k AND .keyboard_number<3)

3.3.2.2.2 Consultative Elementary Premises

Consultative situations are described through consultative elementary premises, such as:

Known:
e.g. keyboard.lock EVALKNOWN
keyboard.lock KNOWN
Unknown:
e.g. keyboard.lock EVALNOTKNOWN
keyboard.lock NOTKNOWN

Unknown by the user:
e.g. keyboard.lock UNANSWERED

Differentiating between known/evalknown and notknown/evalnotknown enables rules to be used to model a typical problem solving situation where the pursuit of the goal is heavily influenced by the current situation as pictured by the dynamic database.

KNOWN evaluates to TRUE only when the value of the respective attribute is currently known, and exceeds a certain level of confidence (which is thresholded). As long as it is not known, or the degree of confidence limit is not reached, the KNOWN premise is regarded as not satisfied.

EVALKNOWN attempts to establish the attribute, and only evaluates to FALSE when this is not achieved, or fails to reach a certain level of confidence.

KNOWN could therefore be interpreted as meaning "known in the current state", and EVALKNOWN as "determinable"; correspondingly the term NOTKNOWN interprets to "not known in the current state", and EVALNOTKNOWN as "not determinable".

3.3.2.2.3 Use of Rule Premises

If the first premise to be used in a rule is of the consultative type, then the evaluation of subsequent premises is dependent on the known state of the system. An example is a forward rule that is dependent on two intermediate results, then to be activated only when the intermediate results are established (i.e. known). For example:

```
FORWARD RULE 10
        TRIGGER workstation.order_code
                workstation.e_box
        IF workstation.order_code KNOWN
             AND workstation.e_box KNOWN
        THEN PRINT(workstation,order_code,e_box)
END
```

Had one used the consultative premise EVALKNOWN in rule 10, as soon as one of the premise attributes became known, the evaluation of the others would have been started as a side effect. This is not the desired course in this instance. Consultative elementary premises also allow the assignment of standard values in rules, called conditional default reasoning, for example:

```
RULE 20
IF     display.type NOTKNOWN
       THEN display.type = NX123
END
```

(in rule 20, the attribute display.type is assigned the default value of NX123 when the value cannot be established through rules, that is, there is no dialogue with the user preceding it to establish the current actual value)

```
RULE 30
IF     display.type = UNANSWERED
       THEN display.type = NX124
END
```

(in rule 30, the attribute display.type is assigned the value NX124 only when the user responds to the corresponding question with the reply "unk" for unknown).

This ensures that is is possible to tailor the consultation to the optimal state of knowledge by the user.

3.3.2.2.4 Elementary Conclusions

In the conclusions several methods for establishing values are implemented, as well as accessing of other knowledge sources such as tables, term evaluations and procedures. TWAICE differentiates between assigning values on the one hand, and actions on the other.

Examples of value assigning elementary conclusions:

Simple value assignment:
e.g. display.type = NX122

Value transfer:
e.g. display.type = display.monochrome

Table look up:
e.g. display.order-no =
LOOKUP (display-data,display.type)
here display-data is a name of a table that stores information about display types, and display.type is a parameter for the lookup.

The table lookup is particularly useful, in that it allows the quasi-automatic inclusion of other knowledge sources such as definitions, technical specifications, etc., in databases . The interface for the calling of tables is so designed that there is much scope for further development for the access of relational database structures.

An example of a Procedural call is:

```
SYSTEM.number_V24-lines =
PROC (V24count, system.number_host-lines,
                system.number_remote-channels)
```

where V24count is a procedure that computes the number of V24 lines available, depending on the number of host lines and remote channels.

The use of procedural calls allows access to subject-specific algorithmic knowledge that is implemented in PROLOG as a knowledge source. We also use this interface to call procedures written in other programming languages, for example, for the error diagnosis of computer test boards, and to ease the integration of expert systems into the working environments of the users with the minimum overheads and disruption.

Counting/enumeration functions example:

```
system.number_of_NX123 =
                COUNT (workstation.type = NX123)
```

where the result is a count of all the workstations of type NX123.

Term Evaluation example:

```
system.number_of_communication_controllers=
((_WS + _HL) / 4)
WITH
_WS = system.number_of_workstations
_HL = system.number_of_host_lines
```

where the result is computed by using the given formula.

3.3.2.2.5 Actions

Actions currently implemented in TWAICE are confined to output actions. They can be qualified by format, title, range definitions that refer to the information in the module .prt. Default output formats are also automatically invoked if .prt is not defined in the current system:

e.g. PRINT (workstation.type)

3.3.3 Table Knowledge

An extract from a table describing computer display types is shown below.

Type	Inventory Order No.	Article type	Size (dm^3)	Power (Watts)
NX123	DPY–4	CRT	1.2	250
NX124	DPY–7	CRT	0.8	150
NX123S	DPY–5	CRT	1.2	200
9″ CRT	DPY–0	CRT-RGB	0.9	175

Tables are assembled in the module .tab, and referenced through an entry in a data dictionary which describes the interface between the knowledge and the inference component in an explicit (thus independence is assured) manner. This allows the relatively easy addition of databases as knowledge sources to TWAICE. An example from the configurator advisor system is given above.

3.3.4 Procedural Knowledge

The procedural knowledge is gathered in the module .prc. A procedure is a PROLOG predicate of the form:

proc (PROCNAME,OBJECT,INST,PARAMLIST,VALUELIST)

If a procedure is called during a rule conclusion, the inference component calls the routine with the name PROCNAME, and transfers

in OBJECT the object name
in INST the instantiation number
in PARAMLIST the parameter list.

The parameter list may be composed of constants or actual value lists associated with the related attribute.

The procedure can evaluate the parameters and return values by unifying them with VALUELIST.

3.3.5 Knowledge about Natural Language Formulations.

Knowledge about natural language formulations can be in the form of question formulations, results formulations and object instantiation definitions. Also, TWAICE offers a language to permit the knowledge engineer to design fill-in text. The inference component fills in gaps in text using the designed fill-in text before sending it to the text output module. Through control characters the knowledge engineer can heavily influence the style and format of the output of the system. If these formulations are absent, then the system will default to use less elegant standard formulations.

For example, a desired output for a specific question is the form:

"How should workstation—1 be connected?"

The required definition would be:

```
question('workstation',RELORD,'connection',
('How should the workstation be connected?',
nl(1)).
```

With the aid of selection parameters to select items from a list, quite complicated formats can be described.

3.3.6 User Support Texts

By the use of additional fill text, the knowledge engineer can supply additional information for help texts to every questioned attribute. These are used by the inference component to aid the user when he uses the command "SUPPORT".

3.4 THE INTERNAL REPRESENTATION OF THE KNOWLEDGE BASE

3.4.1 The Internal Representation of Rules

The external representation of the rules is accessed by the Loader, and compiled into an internal form. At this time, the rule compiler adds rule triggers to the database whereby backward rules are indexed by their conclusion attributes, and forward rules by their trigger attributes. Furthermore, the compiler classifies forward, backward and self referential rules. All this enables the inference component to select rules more easily.

Self referential rules are a special case which are handled like backward chaining rules. A backward rule may be a self referential rule when, in the conclusion part, an object–attribute pair occurs that also occurs in the premise. The object—attribute pair is flagged by a special pointer. This is necessary as in the purest sense, rules cannot be allowed to form loops. In order to still permit this special case, the inference component checks these rule types only after all normal backward chaining rules are processed. Self referential rules serve to assign default values to attributes which could not be deduced otherwise.

3.4.2 Frames

Other forms of knowledge elements are represented as slots of object or attribute frames. Fig. 3.5 illustrates how the items of the external knowledge

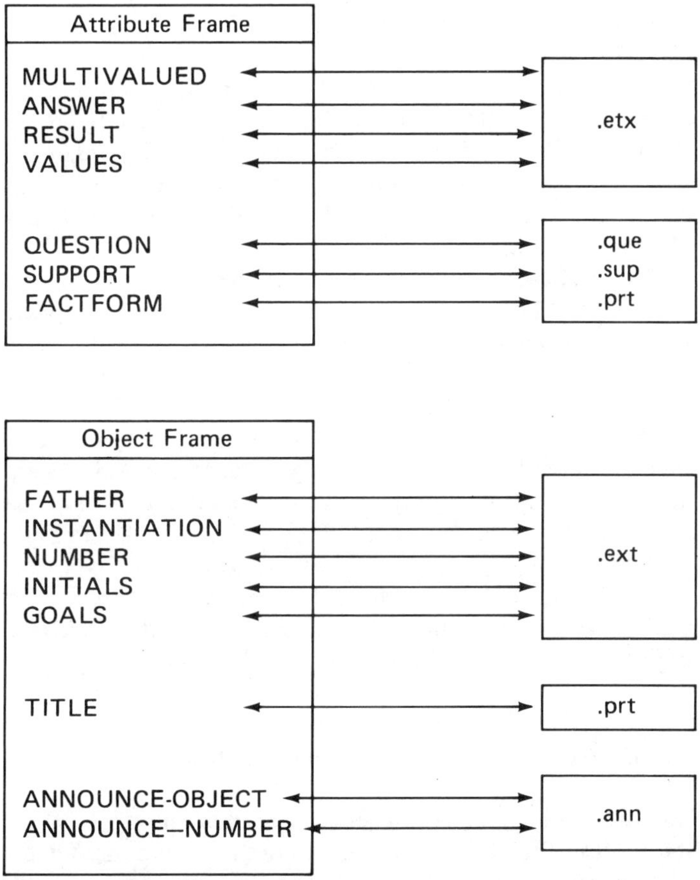

Fig. 3.5 — Relationships between TWAICE modules in the external knowledge base and the internal object and attribute frame design.

base are mapped to slots of object and attribute frames in the internal knowledge base.

3.5 OPERATION OF THE INFERENCE COMPONENT

3.5.0 Introduction

The main task of the inference component is the execution of the consultation and the control of the inference process itself. For this, the values of the goal attributes as selected by the knowledge engineer are determined.

This goal is achieved by the execution of a process called "attribute tracing". This attribute tracing is embedded in a process whose object is the determination of all goal attributes in an object instantiation, and is termed the "trace of an object instance". In turn, the trace of an object instance is part of a process that traces all instances of an object that are from the same parent instance in the dynamic tree configuration (for example, all keyboards allocated to workstation–1). This process is termed the "object trace" process.

The inference component begins the consultation by examining the object which has been defined as the STARTOBJECT by the knowledge engineer. The STARTOBJECT must be an offspring of the basic standard default object "root". In Fig. 3.3a, for example, in the domain of computer configuration advisor systems, the inference component would start with the object SYSTEM.

The tracing of attributes requires the use of the rules as defined by the user and the knowledge engineer. Before rules are applied, however, they must be verified. This is achieved by the procedure EVALHYP. From there, the examination of premises for the tracing of new attributes occurs in the procedure TRACEATTR.

If the attributes in the premise belong to objects not yet instantiated, then the tracing leads to the tracing of the relevant object and thus the object instance. Therefore the recursive process of backwards chaining is a three-level process in the tracing of objects, as illustrated in Fig. 3.6.

3.5.1 Implementation of the Inference Mechanism

The backward chaining inference mechanism in TWAICE is implemented in the kernel by two PROLOG procedures:

— TRACEATTR acquires the attributes
— EVALHYP evaluates the rule premises.

The basic principles of inference as implemented in TWAICE are coded in the routine TRACEATTR. The inference component determines the value of an attribute, in that it applies the strategies below in alternation:

1. apply backwards rule

OR 2. apply self referential rule with consultative premise NOTKNOWN

OR 3. user questions

OR 4. apply self referential rules with consultative premise UNANSWERED.

A detailed description of the flow in the inference component is illustrated in Figs 3.7 and 3.8, using the conventions that were devised for PROLOG procedures [cf. Clocksin and Mellish 1981, p. 170].

These figures illustrate that TWAICE also implements the well known inference principle from MYCIN termed "exhaustive evidence gathering".

```
>trace object- 1

    >trace all instances of object- 1

        >trace all goal attributes
        of instance object- 1

            >trace object- 2

                >. . .
                + . . .

            +object—2 traced

        +all goal attributes of instance
        object—1 traced

    +all instances of object—1 traced

+object—1 traced
```

Fig. 3.6 — Three-level recursive process for tracing an object.

This means that at the time of tracing an attribute, all relevant knowledge sources (rules) are taken into account. This enables a better focussed, less disjoint, consultation flow to take place.

3.5.2 Determination of the Level of Confidence

TWAICE uses a modification of the model of MYCIN for the determination of the confidence level [Buchanan and Shortliffe 1984, pp. 233–263]. In practice this means that if a fact is determined by a rule, the minimum level of confidence of the used premises is weighted by the level of confidence in the rule's conclusion. If a fact is determined by several rules, then the levels of confidence are accumulated in accordance with the computational formula:

(final confidence level) = (confidence level in rule 1)
+ (1000- [CLR1]) * (confidence level in rule 2)/1000.

A premise is only satisfied when the final confidence level exceeds a certain threshold level, which may be set by the knowledge engineer.

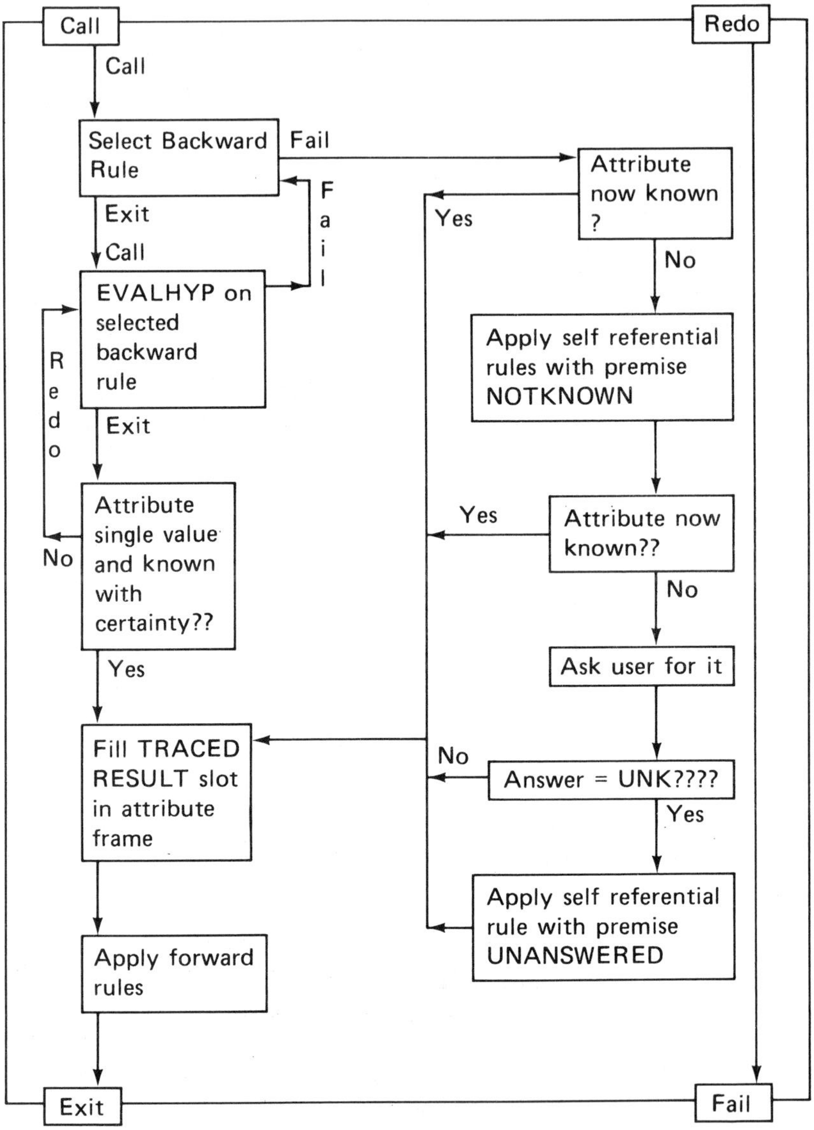

Fig. 3.7 — Flow chart of the procedure TRACEATTR (box model).

3.6 APPLICABILITY OF TWAICE

As TWAICE is based on the MYCIN paradigm, as a result of the design decisions, it is clear that it is currently limited by the same constraints as other systems developed within the same essential paradigmatic characteristics.

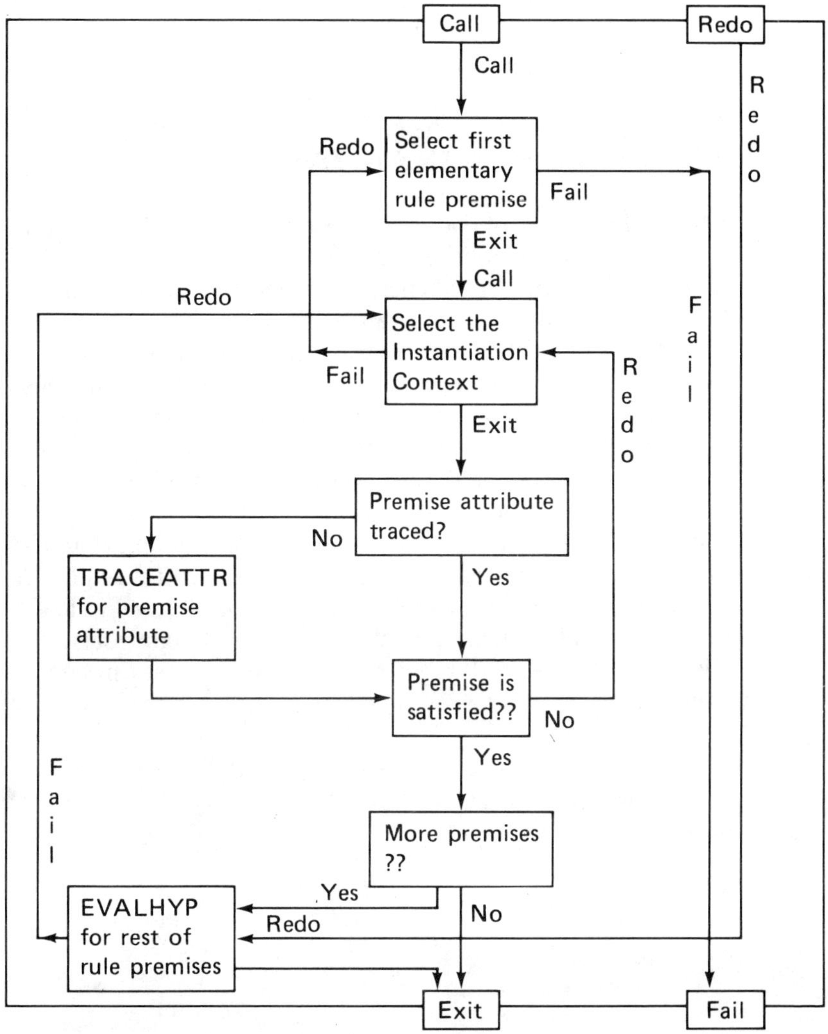

Fig. 3.8 — Flow chart of the evaluation procedure EVALHYP for rule premises (box model).

The methods and tools offered by TWAICE were not able to cope with the following types of problems; however, intermediate level features introduced in 1986 allowed those to be covered also [see Savory 1987].

3.6.1 Monitoring and Process Control Situations (Temporal Reasoning)

A fundamental requirement for these systems is the time variability of data, and the comparison of data from different time slices. This topic is examined in greater detail in a later chapter which demonstrates that despite this weakness in TWAICE, there are other systems that possess the required functionality. TWAICE already has, in the form of forward rules, a representation of event driven inference. However, currently there is no explicit representation of time, and no facilities for the analysis of time-varying data, or time series. TWAICE could only handle situations that deal with one instant snapshot. Use of multiple instances, however, enables finite differential equations to be calculated, thus enabling real-time monitoring to be performed in TWAICE [see Savory 1987].

3.6.2 Planning with Global Boundary Condition (Constraint Reasoning)

Global boundary conditions are those that cannot be described through the representation of dependencies between individual taxonomic elements. Global boundary conditions are usually found in optimisation problems, such as GOAL: define a network for *N* computers such that they are interlinked, but keep the networking operational and installation costs to a minimum; or GOAL: prescribe the medication that will cover all the symptoms, but minimise the number of individual items in the prescription.

Planning problems require a more sophisticated planning component, that generate, on the basis of a simple structure, sets of hypotheses that are tested against the global constraints (so-called "generate and test"). As long as this is not available as an integral component of TWAICE, the only way of representing this is via extensive applications of procedural knowledge, but this is in conflict with section 3.1.2, the design goals. Release 3.0 of TWAICE, made in 1987, covers planning situations via "worlds" [see Savory 1987].

3.6.3 The Representation of Deep Knowledge

The relationships described in IF–THEN rules may be interpreted in different ways. A rule could be one of the following:

— a correlation
— a heuristic
— a definition
— a causal relationship.

The knowledge represented in such a rule is "flat", i.e. all at the same level and not forming an obvious hierarchy of some application specific theory, or some highly structured solution strategy. The hierarchical criteria used to describe the static object tree is not always unambiguous; there are variations in interpretation depending on the problem domain. There is probably no single overall structuring criteria applicable to the static object tree, and this limits the possibilities for high level explanation capabilities. Work is commencing to allow frame representations to co-exist with production rules, which would allow different formalisms for the description of knowledge—whichever is best suited in each case [Aikins]. The increased power of expression with frames is balanced by a loss of simplicity of design. Knowledge representations with the expressive powers of programming languages are very powerful, but inherently difficult to test, extend and edit.

The search for a suitable knowledge representation formalism and the solution of the trade-off imbalance (expressive power vs. simplicity) are a major focus of research in expert systems today.

3.7 EXPERIENCES

Experience from the families of expert systems that also emerge from the stable of MYCIN suggest that TWAICE is well suited for the solution of analytical problems with a finite (enumerable) solution space, such as diagnosis and classification problems.

Experience with the configuration system CONAD also suggest that it is possible to use TWAICE to solve bigger problems, as long as these can be compartmentalised into sets of sub-problems. This is the case in the modular structure of the Nixdorf computer family, which was the target application for it.

4

PROLOG—Implementation Language of Artificial Intelligence and of TWAICE

Jon Young
St Cross College, University of Oxford, UK, and
Bernhard Mescheder
Nixdorf Computer AG, Paderborn, FRG

4.0 INTRODUCTION

PROLOG (PROgramming in LOGgic) is a non-algorithmic language typical of the new generation of computer languages that are especially suited to non-numeric calculations such as symbol manipulation. Alain Colmerauer and his group originally devised PROLOG about 1970, based on the formal concepts of predicate calculus developed by Kowalski [see Carnaghem, N. 1982]. It was first implemented in Marseille University by Colmerauer's group in 1972. The advanced centres of artificial intelligence research in France, in the UK at Edinburgh University [Warren 1980, van Emden and Kowalski 1976], in Budapest and at the University of Lisbon quickly adopted the language for AI work [Clark and McCabe 1980]. The 1980's and the advent of the Japanese Fifth Generation project brought a new lease of life to artificial intelligence research and thus PROLOG. Today, PROLOG is available in a wide range of implementations from small personal microcomputers to PC compatibles and mainframes [Campbell 1984, Noelke and Savory 1984].

The first objective of this chapter is to give the reader a short introduction to the language itself.

The second objective of this chapter is to relate how the language PROLOG was used in the development of the implementation of TWAICE, with emphasis on how the features of the language contribute to the goals of the implementation.

Finally, some of the problems that arose during the work described here and in other sections of this book are described, with accounts of how these were handled.

4.1 PROLOG PROGRAMMING

4.1.1 Rationale

PROLOG is suited to applications that require extensive symbolic processing, like expert systems. One of the earliest application systems written in PROLOG was the "Orbi" system at the University of Lisbon [Pereira and Warren 1980]. Use of the language was critically examined for the project, and PROLOG was found to be suitable for three reasons:

— The components of the system could all be expressed in the same formalism, allowing a uniformity for:

  — natural language processing
  — knowledge base
  — explainer
  — levels of knowledge representation
  — relational database
  — specialised control structures.

— The forms of expressions are very compact, and the programming may be implemented efficiently (even if execution efficiency awaits the advent of parallel processing). It is therefore a realistic means to express significant problems.
— The semantic duality of procedural and declarative functionality allows the development of meta-knowledge within the same formalism.

PROLOG differs from conventional procedural languages such as C, Pascal and Ada in two fundamental respects:

— The operations are not just assignment and comparison with numerical calculations of finite precision, but pattern matching and symbol structure processes
— The basic data elements are not numeric only, with some comparison keys, but may be arbitrary structures of symbols and relationships between them.

4.1.2 Terminology in PROLOG

Anonymous Variable.
This is a variable which will never need to be instantiated.

Arguments.
Names of objects enclosed within round brackets, "(" and ")". The use of the word arguments in PROLOG is closer to the semantic meaning of the word (i.e. debate, discussion, etc.) than that used in other computer languages as a variable transferred from one compilation unit to another. There may be any number of arguments in a relationship, and their ordering is significant.

Atomic Constants.
Atomic constants are normally only made up of symbols. They are usually not sensibly decomposed further.

Backtracking.
This is a method of searching the database to satisfy the goals. It is called backtracking as the database is searched and partial goals may be achieved, but if there is a later failure, then the search has to backtrack to the last success and proceed forwards from there via another route. If all routes are exhausted and the goal is not matched, then the goal is not reached.

Characters.
Characters are the alphabet of PROLOG. The alphabet of PROLOG includes the upper case letters A–Z and their lower case counterparts, the digits 0–9 and the arithmetic operators, as well as some special symbols.

Clause.
A clause is one complete PROLOG statement.

Conjunction.
Conjunction is a means of forming more complicated relationships and questions. For example, do John and Mary like each other may be written "likes(john,mary), also-likes(mary,john).". Conjunctions are be processed from left to right as a clause is parsed, until one goal is not satisfied.

Constants.
Constants are specific objects or relationships. They are either atomic or integer constants.

Database.
A database is a collection of facts and rules.

Definitions.
A definition is a group of facts and objects that define a larger entity. For example, a "family" may be defined as a man, a woman and one or more children if the man and the woman are married—to each other.

Facts.
Facts allow you to express arbitrary relationships about objects.

Integer Constants.
These allow integer arithmetic to be included in PROLOG. The use of numbers is limited in most PROLOG implementations, as it is primarily intended to be a symbol manipulation language.

Knowledge Base.

Sometimes used synonymously with the term database.

Lists.
A list is an ordered set of elements of some length.

Matching.
Two facts match if the predicates and arguments match perfectly.

Operators.
Operators are symbols that have a defined operation on their arguments. For example, 5 plus 5 is written usually as 5 + 5, where "+" is the addition operator in mathematics.

Ordering.
Ordering implies that the sequence of appearance matters. In an ordered list, it would be significant whether one item appeared before or after another.

Precedence.
An ordering of operators that is defined in the implementation.

Predicate.
A predicate appears just before an argument, and is a description of a relationship that may be a property of the related argument. For example, if John liked Mary, then a predicate "likes" may be defined, and the fact that John likes Mary may be expressed as

```
likes(john,mary).
```

The ordering is significant. Based on the above definition,

```
likes(mary,john)
```

implies that Mary likes John—not at all a foregone conclusion! A second predicate "also-likes" may be needed in such a case. A predicate may have any number of arguments, but the order in which they appear is significant.

Question.
A question, normally written as "?", is an expression that indicates that the database is to be searched to answer a query.

Rules.
Rules are general expressions stating that a fact depends on one or more other facts or objects in a definite relationship. For example, if "it is cold outside" then "wear a coat" when going out. Definitions can also be expressed using rules.

Structure.
A structure is an object in PROLOG that itself consists of several other objects or components. An entry in the Bibliography in this book may be thought of as a structure—it has authors, name, source and date collected together to be termed a "reference".

Success.
In PROLOG, success is the satisfaction of one or more goals in conjunction.

Syntax.
Syntax is the set of rules to fit the components of the language together.

Terms.
Terms are either constants, variables or structures. Each term is written as a sequence of characters.

Variable.
A variable in PROLOG is a means of deferring a decision about an argument. A variable is only instantiated when an object exists that the variable stands for. A variable remains uninstantiated when what the variable stands for is still unknown. In the English language, the pronoun may be thought of as a PROLOG variable equivalent.

For a more detailed explanation of terms, see Clocksin and Mellish [1981].

4.2 A PROLOG PRIMER

4.2.0 Introduction

Programming in PROLOG may be thought of as consisting of three basic elements:

— specifying facts about relationships and objects
— specifying rules about the above category
— querying the above two categories.

The program itself acts on a database of facts and rules, often called a knowledge base. The problem to be solved is presented as a query. PROLOG can be a conversational programming style ("interactive").

4.2.1 PROLOG and Logic Programming

The next section will aim to give a short introduction to PROLOG. It will become apparent that the language is based on the idea of theorem proving. PROLOG programs are rather like hypotheses about a situation, and questions may be thought of as theorems which have to be proved or disproved. The key to using PROLOG to maximise the advantages of logic programming is to isolate the use of the non-logical components into a small set of clauses. Concepts like the "cut", not developed here but causing a discontinuity in logic flow if executed, can be optimised by one use of the cut predicate, and replacement of other occurrences by the "not" predicate, thus maintaining a large part of the underlying logic of a program. "Asserts" and "retract" are another set of predicates that require isolation.

So the ultimate goal of full logic programming is not reached by PROLOG, but it does provide a programming system of some use and clarity that a general purpose logic programming language would also need to offer.

4.2.2 Facts in PROLOG

The facts in PROLOG are relationships between two objects. For example,

"John owns the book"

is a declaration that a certain relationship (in this case the property of ownership) exists between one individual object in the relationship ("John"), and another object ("book"). The order of the objects in the fact is significant. "John" owns the book, the book has no ownership relation to John. The book has the relationship "is-owned-by", which is different (the semantic negation of the relationship in the initial ordering). When trying to establish a relationship, though, a confirmation is sought:

"Does John own the book?"

In common PROLOG notation, the fact used above as an example is expressed as:

```
owns(john,book).
```

Using this notation, all relationships and object names are written in lower case letters. The objects are separated by commas, and the order in which the arguments appear is significant. This order must be maintained for sensible use of the database of facts. The relationship is called a "predicate", and the objects just "arguments".

Taking another common example, that of "John liking Mary", which is often quoted. This fact may be written as

```
likes(john,mary).
```

If written

```
likes(mary,john)
```

then the implication that "Mary likes John" may be reasonable in the light of other knowledge, but is not correct unless established as a fact in its own right; "Mary likes John".

4.2.3 Questions in PROLOG

Once a number of facts have been collected together in a database, questions may be asked to the database about the domain related to the facts known to it.

Consider an example of a database of friends in a group and their likes:

```
likes(john,mary).
likes(john,fred).
likes(mary,fred).
likes(fred,john).
```

So this example has three objects, John, Mary and Fred, and there are four facts about them. In PROLOG, a question is formulated by the question mark and then a hypothesis. For example:

```
?- likes(john,mary)
```

is a valid PROLOG question. In order to answer this question, which is the question "Does John like Mary?", the database is searched to see if the fact is known to the system. If a match is found, i.e. if the predicate and arguments of the question match the predicate and arguments of a fact exactly, then the question may be answered as "yes". However, if the question is:

```
?- likes(john,alan)
```

and following the same algorithm described above, no match will be found, and the question to the system will be answered as "no". This may be very misleading, as in fact the question cannot be answered as there is no knowledge about "Alan" in the database. In fact the correct response should have been "unknown". Sometimes, then, PROLOG assumes that if the fact cannot be proven, then the opposite is true, when in the situation of a complete world model the facts may actually be absent. Using a chain of reasoning that involves this sort of conclusion will inevitably give misleading responses.

4.2.4 Variables in PROLOG

Instead of only using specific objects as arguments, these can be replaced by variables. A variable is usually written in capital letters, and it represents a fact that is not instantiated at the time. In many other computer languages, such as FORTRAN, a variable is used in a strictly erroneous manner, in that it is possible to assign a value to it and write such algebraically meaningless statements as

$$I = I + 1$$

In PROLOG, a variable is used more in the sense of an algebraic variable—

to represent a quantity that is unknown at the time. In particular, variables may not be assigned to, but one may assert equality relationships among objects that can include variables. Variables may appear as arguments in terms. They may be regarded as partially specified data structures that will be instantiated fully only later. This allows formulation of more general queries, such as:

"is there anything John likes ?"
?- likes(john,X).

Based on our example "likes"-base, two facts match this question. If the facts above appear in the database in the same order, then the system will respond with the reply:

X = mary

The system may then be prompted to continue searching, in which case a second reply is obtained:

X = fred

If further searching is then prompted, the system will respond with

no

when all facts in the database have been searched in relation to the question. "no" implies there are no more matching facts, not necessarily that John likes only Mary or Fred to the exclusion of the rest of mankind!

4.2.5 Conjunction in PROLOG Questions

Conjunctions are a method for the formulation of more complicated questions. A number of simple questions can be asked together, separated by a comma. The question "Does Mary like John and Fred?" can be formulated:

?- likes(mary,john),likes(mary,fred)

and the answer "no" would be obtained. "Do John and Mary like each other?" is written as:

?- likes(john,mary),likes(mary,john)

and again based on the facts base, the response would be "no".

Using variables and conjunction, even more powerful questions can be asked, such as "Does John like anyone who likes John?":

?- likes(john,X),likes(X,john)

to which the response would be:

X = fred

In the initial goal of the above question, X is unknown at the time of formulation of the question—it is not instantiated. While executing the instruction, though, PROLOG may find a match, in this case "mary". From the instant where the variable X has been instantiated to "mary", the other references to "X" will be treated as references to "mary". Now there is an attempt to match the second goal, which now reads:

likes(mary,john).

This fails, however. Therefore the first goal is retracted (backtracking) and another attempt is made to find a possible value of X that is not "mary", but some other fact. In fact, "fred" also meets the first goal, and thus X is now instantiated to "fred".

The basis of backtracking is an alternation successively between two neighbouring goals in a conjunction. An arbitrary number of conjunctions may be processed this way in a single statement.

4.2.6 Rules

Very often it is possible to express a relationship in terms of rules much more succinctly than an enumeration of possibly an infinite set of instantiations of a fact. In the above examples, it is preferable to store a rule about what john likes, rather than list all the things john likes. Suppose john likes anyone who likes wine. The rule head and body would be written thus:

likes(john,X) :- likes(X,wine).

The head relationship is "likes(john,X)". The body is likes(X,wine). Combined they express the fact that john likes anyone who likes wine.

Rules may be entered in the same way as facts, and often appear mixed within the facts base. Facts and rules are called "clauses" in PROLOG. When PROLOG encounters a rule when searching the database for a clause matching a question, it attempts to match the head of a rule with the goal in the question. If the two match, then the body of the rule contains subgoals that must be satisfied in order to satisfy the original goal—which is attempted using the match and backtrack method.

4.2.7 An Example with Rules

Consider a rule about "sisters" as an example. There are two people called "X" and "Y". X is a sister of Y provided that:

X is female AND
X and Y have the same parents.

This may be written in PROLOG as

```
sister(X,Y) :- female(X),
               parents(X,MOTHER,FATHER)
               parents(Y,MOTHER,FATHER).
```

which may be read as:

> It is a fact that X is a sister of Y if
> X is female and if
> the parents of X and
> the parents of Y
> are the same.

Other facts that would help establish this rule would be of the sort:

```
female(alice).
female(victoria).
female(anne).
male(albert).
male(edward).
parents(edward,victoria,albert).
parents(alice,victoria,albert).
```

There are seven facts in the database now, three relating to which persons are female, two about who is a male, and two about who is a parent to whom. Questions can now be asked of the facts above, for example:

```
?- sister(alice,edward).
yes
?- sister(albert,edward).
no
?- sister(alice,anne).
no
```

Therefore, it is a fact that Alice is a sister of Edward. Other questions may be formulated thus:

```
?- sister(alice,alice).
yes
?- sister(alice,X).
X= edward
?- sister(X,Y).
X= alice, Y= edward;
X= alice, Y= alice;
?- sister(X,X).
```

```
X= alice
?- sister(X,Y),parents(Z,_,Y).
no
```

Note the use of an underline "_" character where a variable is usually expected—the anonymous variable.

The last question asked above is "is X the sister of Y who is the father of Z"; and the database gives the answer NO. This merely means that there is no fact in the seven-fact database that satisfies the above. The two facts about the males are never used; they are quite redundant, but their appearance does help reinforce completeness. There is one error in this example, i.e. that a person can be a sister of herself. To avoid that, the rule must be modified to exclude that condition, i.e. NOT (X=Y).

4.2.8 Backtracking

Backtracking is the method by which the PROLOG question goal is evaluated. Reconsider the question:

```
?- sister(X,Y),parents(Z,_,Y).
```

The two goals are connected by a conjunction, therefore both goals have to be satisfied. Each sub-goal in the conjunction is satisfied (or at least attempted to be) in a sequence from left to right in a composite expression. In this case, the "sister(X,Y)" condition is tested by running through the facts base literally from start to end. The rule for sisters is found, and the body of this rule now becomes a new set of goals to be met, and the left to right evaluation of:

female
parents and
parents

proceeds. Iff (meaning If and only If) the "sister" goal is satisfied, the next step "parents(Z,_,Y)" is attempted.

If all the goals in a clause succeed, then the question succeeds. If any goals fail, an attempt is made on its left neighbour to resatisfy a goal there by locating another possible answer. If a failed goal runs out of left-hand goals to resatisfy, then the whole goal has failed.

4.2.9 Arbitrary Data Structures

Arbitrary Data Structures are represented as terms that can have any number of components. For example, suppose in a database, a printer has to be described. A printer consists of a number of components, such as paper feed mechanism, buffer memory, print heads, case types, power supplies, etc. It is possible to define a printer structure so that the various levels of detail can be handled like one composite object.

Clauses (i.e. facts and rules) are also represented as structures, and therefore programs are written using the same data structures, a feature PROLOG shares with LISP.

4.2.10 Lists in PROLOG

As in other languages used in artificial intelligence research, the data structure "list" plays a major part in PROLOG programming. The "list cell" in PROLOG is represented by the predicate ".", and has a "head" and a "tail". Lists are binary trees constructed from list cells. However, the "dot" notation can be cumbersome, so terminal nodes of lists are written separated by commas, and all the list is enclosed by square brackets thus: "[... , ...]".

The empty list is written as [].

Examples of lists are:

```
[1,2,3,4,5,6,7,8,9,0]
[a,b,c,d,e,f,g,h,i,j,k,l,m,n,o,p,q,r,s,t,u,v,w,x,y,z]
[a,e,i,o,u]
[the,cat,sat,on,the,mat]
[l,m,n,o,p,q,r]
[[this],list(is,made + of),[several],structures]
```

The notation [a | b] denotes a list whose elementary head is "a", and whose tail is "b". This is used heavily in pattern matching. Suppose a predicate is defined that succeeds if its first argument is in the list given as the second argument. This is decomposed to two clauses: is the argument in the head of the list, or is it in the tail of the list?

This may be written in a procedure as

```
member(X,[ X | _ ])
member(X,[ _ | L ) :- member(X,L).
```

PROLOG clauses are being employed to write the program, but it looks the same as an entry in the database. An example based on the above is:

```
?- member(darwin,[marx,darwin,freud]).
yes
?- member(X,[marx,darwin,freud]).
X= mark;
X= darwin;
x= freud
```

In the first example, the predicate "member" was just used to establish if an item was in a list. The second example defined a variable which was in turn instantiated to all elements of the list.

This suggests how to use this to check if two lists differ, for example. In order to find if one list has an element that another list may not have:

```
differ(X,Y) :- member(Z,X),not(member(Z,Y)).
```

In order to evaluate this expression, PROLOG jumps between the two member goals, until both are satisfied or fail. The goal "not(X)" is considered to have been reached if its argument X fails.

4.2.11 Symbolic Differentiation by Pattern Matching

Pattern matching can be used, for example, in the conversion of arithmetic expressions or in compilers such as the Edinburgh University DEC-10 PROLOG compiler.

Consider the problem of symbolic differentiation (and for that matter, integration as the inverse of differentiation), which is often taught as a number of rules to apply to terms in an expression to be integrated. These rules translate into PROLOG very easily. Using the functors +, −, etc., to represent non-terminal nodes of expression trees, they have a built-in syntax declaration as right-associative infix operators with the usual precedence relationship.

The predicate "diff(X,Y,Z)" is defined as "the derivative of X with respect to Y is Z". Some examples are listed below(the symbol ^ means "to the power of"):

```
diff(X,X,1).
diff(X^N,X,NX^(N-1)).
diff(C,X,0) :- atomic(C).
diff(U+V,X,A+B) :- diff(U,X,A),diff(V,X,B).
diff(U-V,X,A-B) :- diff(U,X,A),diff(V,X,B).
diff(C*U,X,C*A) :- atomic(C),C =|= X,diff(U,X,A).
diff(U*V,X,B*U+A*V) :- diff(U,X,A),diff(V,X,B).
```

Based on the above, a working program could take the query

```
?- diff(x*x - 2, x, A)
A= 1 * x + 1 * x - 0
```

The goal "atomic(Z)", whose definition is built into the PROLOG system, succeeds if its argument Z is an atom or an integer, and fails otherwise. In this case it is used to find if the problem is to locate the derivative of a constant. The operator "=|=" operates as "is not the same as"—it succeeds unless its two arguments match! The answer may not be in a commonly used format, but it portrays the way in which the result is derived.

Using some straightforward facts about algebra as described below easily reduces the clumsy form above to one more commonly used.

4.2.12 Simplification of Algebraic Expressions

The predicate "simp(X,Y)" is defined as one where the expression X is simplified in the algebraic sense to give the expression Y. A number of facts are needed to achieve this:

```
 1 simp(E,E):- atomic(E),!.
 2 simp(E,F):- comp(E,Op,L,R),
               simp(L,X),simp(R,Y),
               comp(S,OP,X,Y),
               s(S,F).
 3 comp(X+Y,+,X,Y).
 4 comp(X-Y,−,X,Y).
 5 comp(X*Y,*,X,Y).
 6 s(X*1,X).
 7 s(X*0,0).
 8 s(X+0,X).
 9 s(X−0,X).
10 s(1*X,X).
11 s(0*X,0).
12 s(0+X,X).
13 s(X+N*X,(N+1)*X)
```

Clause 1 states that an atom simplifies to itself, and there are no more solutions beyond that. Clause 2 decomposes an expression tree into a node and two branches using the "comp" predicate, then simplifies each branch separately and finally reconstitutes the expression with simplified branches called "s". There are pairs of clauses for addition and multiplication to account for commutativity. It works as follows: in order to simplify an expression E using the s clauses, simplify the left-hand argument, then the right-hand argument and see if the results are in the table. As the simplification is recursive, eventually the leaves of the tree will be populated by integers or atoms. They are simplified into themselves by clause 1.

The differentiator and simplifier can now be used as embedded goals in a procedure, for example:

```
differentiate:-
        write('Type the expression to be differentiated:'),
        read(Expression),
        diff(Expression,x,Deriv),
        simp(Deriv,Simplified),
        write(' the derivative of '),
        write(Expression),
        write(' with respect to x is '),
        write(Simplified).
```

When executed, it could look like this:

```
?- differentiate.
Type the expression to be differentiated:
x*x - 2.
 the derivative of x*x - 2 is.
2*x
```

4.2.13 Implementation Aspects of PROLOG

PROLOG is fast turning into a very powerful tool in the software development environment. The design of the code into which the PROLOG clauses are compiled is often based on an abstract virtual machine. It is the inability to implement these virtual machines in the world of classical von Neumann architectures that has been the main reason why PROLOG has not found wider use, and early implementations were not noted for their run time efficiency.

Some of the specific functionalities required by an implementation are:

- goal invocation
- stack housekeeping
- backtracking
- unification in contexts
- construction of arguments for sub-goals.

In executing a program, most of the Central Processor Unit (CPU) time is used by unification and backtracking. Each unification step must be generalised, as the terms to be matched are only known at run time. If at least one of these is known at compile time, 10 to 20 fold speed increases can be obtained as the unification can be optimised. With emphasis placed on the rapid selection of appropriate clauses, use of special indexing code may also help: it reduces wasteful unifications and reduces memory requirements.

The database management is complicated by the fact that it is not just a static array, but a real relational database. The data structure is almost certainly to be changed dynamically. It can be handled by holding the dynamic clauses in an interpretive section, while compiling the static ones. SD-PROLOG, developed by Systems Designers (UK), combines threaded code with an incremental compiler to allow even fully compiled clauses to be modified, deleted and listed as if they were being interpreted rather than compiled.

4.2.14 Characteristics of Implementations

There are many different implementations of PROLOG now available [Campbell 1984]. Acquisition of a compiler or interpreter should be carefully considered in the light of an application and a number of other criteria [Clocksin amd Mellish 1981] which may include:

Syntax.

Is it friendly, readable and maintainable?

Bounded Numbers.
What is the limit for integers; are real numbers permitted?
What is the limit on the number of arguments?
How many characters are allowed in an atom?
How many clauses are allowed in a predicate?

Debugging.
What facilities are available for debugging, and are they sufficient?

Environment.
What DP support environment does it need, and what resources will it take when used in the most likely scenario (possibly 20 students simultaneously in a university environment)?

Compilation, Interpretation.
Which is on offer, or are both possible? What are the relative advantages and disadvantages of each in the environment in which it will be used?

Special Predicates.
Virtually every implementation has its own variation of predicates, and these characterise the system being considered. If an existing implementation is in use, the conversion problems should also be considered.

Cost.
What is the cost of what is offered, and can it be purchased or leased, and are multiple copy options available?

Documentation.
Is the documentation adequate for the purposes to which the software will be employed, or is more needed?

Maintenance.
Is this available for the software, updates and documentation?

Extendability.
Can the software be easily extended, or would this mean editing the basic software purchased, and invalidating support and documentation?

The rest of this chapter is all in the context of the PROLOG implementation used in TWAICE.

4.3 THE USE OF PROLOG IN THE IMPLEMENTATION OF TWAICE

4.3.0 Introduction

In the previous part of this chapter, the emphasis has been on looking at features of PROLOG from the perspective of generalities of a declarative language from the logic programming paradigm. The remainder of Chapter 4 will deal with specific implementation details and examples, as relevant to the implementation of TWAICE.

The characteristics of PROLOG relevant to TWAICE are demonstrated via examples, and build upon the related sections in Chapter 3 on the functionality of TWAICE.

4.3.1 The Internal Representation of Knowledge in TWAICE

The most important internal representation of knowledge in TWAICE is the production rule. The most important inference mechanism in TWAICE is that of backward chaining. In addition to this, taxonomic knowledge is stored using a frame structure (see section 3.5).

The implementation of the design decisions described in the previous chapter are effectively supported by PROLOG. The external form of a production rule can be mapped directly onto a Horn clause which can be directly interpreted by PROLOG. The backward chaining inference mechanism can be explained by PROLOG's goal oriented evaluation strategy for the clauses. However, the evaluation of production rules cannot be accomplished directly by PROLOG interpretation. Apart from the pure clause evaluation, other tasks occur during execution, such as:

— determination of instantiation contexts
— entry of facts in the dynamic database
— the use of forward rules
— annotation of trace information
— gathering of knowledge for explanation.

Therefore a special rule interpreter is built on top of PROLOG. It is a part of the inference component in TWAICE.

Object and Attribute Frames can be represented in PROLOG. This is through individual slots with PROLOG facts of the form:

```
slotname(frame name,slot value).
```

For example, in the configuration advisor CONAD, the frame "PRINTER" could be represented thus:

```
expect('printer',
Order ['cover','description','paper_transport',
'Order-No','type_face'] ).
statson('printer','workstation').
```

```
goals('printer',['configuration']).
initialdata('printer',[])
instype('printer',rulebased)
etc.
```

4.3.2 Decomposition of Elementary Rule Premises by Unification

In the evaluation of rule premises, every term has to be decomposed analytically into its constituent parts. In the expert system shell MYCIN, which is implemented in LISP, this is accomplished by so-called templates. These templates describe the internal premise representation of every premise type that is to be decomposed [Davis and Lenat 1982, p. 254]. For example, in MYCIN the elementary premise

site = blood

has the internal LISP representation

(SAME CNTXT site blood).

The identification of the various components of the premise (i.e. type, object, attribute and value) is controlled by the following MYCIN template entry:

Premise Type	Template
SAME	(SAME CNTXT ATTRIBUTE VALUE)

In PROLOG, the situation is much simpler, as templates are not required. In TWAICE, attributes are always referenced together with the respective object. Taking the above example (the premise culture.site = blood) from MYCIN, it would be written in TWAICE internally as a PROLOG clause:

evalsame(culture,INST,site,[blood])

where INST is the instantiation variable that is defined by the inference component with the aid of the dynamic object tree. These premises are unified by the inference component with the term:

evalsame(OBJECT,INST,ATTRIB,VALUELIST)

Through the binding of the variables OBJECT, ATTRIB, VALUELIST to the constants "culture" and "site", and the list [blood], a direct analytical decomposition of the premise into its component parts is achieved.

4.3.3 Evaluation of Rule Premises via Backtracking and Recursion

In TWAICE, the implementation of the evaluation procedure of the rule premise (EVALHYP) is dependent on the PROLOG looping mechanism of recursion, and backtracking. Fig. 4.1 shows a complex rule premise being

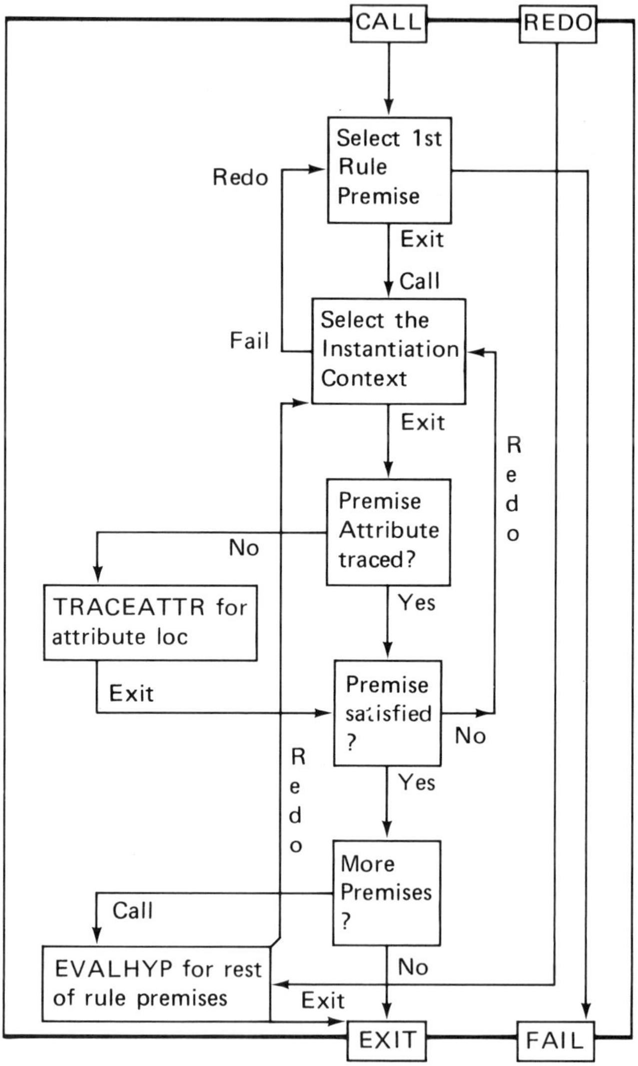

Fig. 4.1—Flow diagram for the evaluation procedure for rule premises: EVALHYP (box model).

evaluated.

The evaluation proceeds by the evaluation of the first component or term, followed by the remainder of the expression. The selection of alternative premises, as well as alternative instantiation contexts, is made via the process of backtracking. This is represented in Fig. 4.1 by the "REDO" entries in the procedures:

"select instantiation context"
"select first rule premise"
"EVALHYP for rest of rule premises".

4.3.4 Unification of Incomplete Data Structures by Table Calls

A table in TWAICE is represented by a PROLOG fact in the form:

table_name(entry-1,entry-2,...,entry-n).

A table call can be realised quite easily using unification, in that the procedure "table_name" is executed. The rule compiler generates the following format for the table call (with variable arguments):

table_name(ENTRY-1,ENTRY-2,...,ENTRY-N).

Also, a number of pairs are generated that bind the entry parameter in the table call to value lists. These are of the general form:

(ENTRY-M,VALUE_LIST)

In addition, the exit parameter is indicated.

4.3.5 An Example

A Table is assembled in the module .tab, and referenced through an entry in a data dictionary which describes the interface between the knowledge and the inference component in an explicit (thus independence is assured) manner. This allows the relatively easy addition of databases as knowledge sources to TWAICE. An example from the configurator advisor system is given by the following extract from a table describing computer display types:

Type	Inventory Order-No.	Article type	Size m^3	Power Watts
NX123	DPY-4	CRT	1.2	250
NX124	DPY-7	CRT	0.8	150
NX123S	DPY-5	CRT	1.2	200
9"CRT	DPY-0	CRT-RGB	0.9	175

The table is called "Dpy_Data". The external form of the conclusion is:

Display.Order_No = LOOKUP(Dpy_Data,display.type)

The internal form of the conclusion is:

```
lookup('Display',INST,'Order_No','Dpy_Data'(
        E1,E2,E3,E4,E5),[(E1,VALUE_LIST1)],E2).
```

where arguments have the following significance:

1–3 conclusion attribute
4 format of the table call
5 binding value of the entry parameter
6 exit parameter.

The implicit binding of variables in this manner allows for an easy realisation of the table call. The inference component needs merely to bind the variables of the entry parameter to elements in the value list prior to executing the compiler-generated table call directly.

4.3.6 Syntax Analysis by Grammar Rules

The syntax of production rules and of user commands can be easily described in PROLOG using grammar rules. Grammar rules relating to user commands in TWAICE consist of three arguments:

— The first argument is the list of words from the user input that have to be parsed, and is forwarded to the syntax analysis procedure.
— The second argument is the remaining list of unparsed words that remain after a successful syntax analysis step.
— The third argument is the internal representation of those parts of the input that have been parsed successfully.

Grammar rules in PROLOG are a very compact form of representation for the description of sentences in a language [Clocksin and Mellish 1981]. The evaluation strategy implemented in PROLOG for procedures makes the implementation of a parser as a separate piece of software unnecessary. A parsing problem of the form:

```
syntax_command([then,'Order_No',of,'System'],[],COMMAND)
```

is resolved directly in PROLOG via the interpreter using the grammar rules. The grammar rules are expanded by the PROLOG evaluation strategy dynamically to a syntax tree.

An Example: Syntax description of a command "then" in the knowledge analyser.

A Possible Syntax:

```
then ⟨object⟩ . ⟨attribute⟩
then ⟨attribute⟩ ⟨preposition⟩ ⟨object⟩
```

PROLOG Grammar Rules:

```
syntax_command(then.F0,FN,then(OBJ,ATTR)) :-
        syntax_attr(F0,FN,attribute(OBJ,ATTR)).
syntax_attr(F0,FN,attribute(OBJ,ATTR)):-
        syntax_name(F0,F1,OBJ),syntax_dot(F1,F2),
        syntax_name(F2,FN,ATTR).
syntax_attr(F0,FN,attribute(OBJ,ATTR)):-
        syntax_name(F0,F1,ATTR),syntax_prep(F1,F2),
        syntax_name(F2,FN,OBJ).
syntax_dot('.'.FN,FN).
syntax_name(NAM.FN,FN,[NAM]).
syntax_name(NAM.F0,FN,NAM.NAMR) :-
        syntax_name(F0,FN,NAMR).
syntax_prep(PREP.FN,FN) :- preposition(PREP).
preposition(of).
preposition(in).
preposition(on).
etc.
```

4.4 PROBLEMS IN USING PROLOG

4.4.1 Size of the Implementation

In the version of TWAICE described here, there are about 1100 PROLOG procedures with about 2100 clauses. The knowledge engineering tools (i.e. the TWAICE implementation without a knowledge base) requires an object file of about 0.8 Mb. There are parts of TWAICE that are functions which are atypical for expert system shells, but are more in the realms of traditional programming requirements, such as:

— dialogue control
— output routines
— menu handlers.

Whereas PROLOG supports TWAICE kernel mechanisms very well and efficiently, the programming of more traditional algorithmic sequential flow is quite difficult. It is here that the total lack of language features for the control of execution becomes painfully obvious. Also, an absence of an integrated PROLOG implementation into the surrounding software and systems environment becomes evident. Because of these requirements, some PROLOG implementations offer interfaces to other, more traditional

3rd and 4th generation languages, so that the functionality and power of traditional programming becomes available to the PROLOG based application if required.

4.4.2 Computational Resources

A second problem with PROLOG implementations is the high requirement for CPU power, requiring very fast (and thus expensive) machines: or ordinary machines lead to unacceptable response times. Also, due to the database structure, a high primary memory requirement is a common feature of PROLOG programs. A typical consultation for the configuration advisor CONAD with eight workstations consists of 73 questions deducing 380 facts. The CPU requirement for this was 600 seconds of dedicated time. This implies a processing rate of only 0.6 facts per CPU second. Furthermore, CONAD consultations require 2 to 3 Mb of virtual memory.

The run time demands are due in part to the large and extensive search spaces that PROLOG programs tend to have to execute. A second reason for the slow overall speed is the delay caused by procedures that edit part of the dynamic database.

4.4.3 Information Transfer

An example of how information is transferred between procedures illustrates some of the problems that arise. The two means by which information transfer is possible between two PROLOG procedures are:

— through unification of variables
— through the dynamic database, with "assert" and "retract".

There are PROLOG implementations where information transfer is possible by variable assignment, if the information itself is free of terms (e.g. "set" or "cont" in MPROLOG). Running some tests on MPROLOG on a VAX 11/780 gave the following run time measures for one information transfer:

using unification	0.27 ms
via dynamic database	4.89 ms
variable assignment	0.98 ms.

Therefore information transfer via unification is nearly four times faster in this environment than variable assignment, and twenty times faster than going via the dynamic database. Therefore, whenever possible, PROLOG programs should be written free of side effects (i.e. without changing the dynamic database). Desirable as it is, though, it is not always possible. Cases where "assert" and "retract" cannot be dispensed with include:

— administration of symbol tables
— administration of run time variables
— memory accessed facts

— storing of protocol information
— setting of consultation options
— backtracking.

In backtracking, all variable bindings are cut, and therefore reasons for failure of rules or similar information can only be recorded via entries in the dynamic database.

The next improvement in the execution of PROLOG programs will come from the hardware/architectural side where better support for unification and resolution will be supplied, most probably with the use of quite high levels of parallelism.

5

The Essence of Knowledge Engineering

Uwe Noelke
Nixdorf Computer AG, Paderborn, FRG

5.0 INTRODUCTION

Expert Systems are knowledge based systems that contain an inference component and a knowledge base (see section 3.1.1). The knowledge base contains knowledge that is required to solve problems which usually require a measure of (human) intelligence. Knowledge Engineering is that discipline which acquires the knowledge of an expert, or from some other source, and represents this in some form in the knowledge base of the expert system. Knowledge acquisition and knowledge representation are in the forefront of this activity. Sources of knowledge may include such diverse media as:

— human experts
— technical books
— encyclopaedias
— other data or knowledge bases
— audio-visual sequences
— multi-media variants on the above.

This section restricts its considerations to the knowledge engineering associated with the first category in the list above—that of acquisition knowledge from a human expert. The objective of this section is to develop a staged concept. The development described here has five major phases, and these are explored in greater detail, with practically oriented check lists that a knowledge engineer can actually use during an engineering exercise. This is to be found in sections 5.3.1 to 5.3.5 of this chapter. In section 5.4 a number of practical hints will be listed for a productive interview with experts. This chapter ends with two methods used by Nixdorf Computer AG to come to terms with the objectives of knowledge engineering.

5.1 GENERAL KNOWLEDGE ENGINEERING AND TWAICE

The general guidelines to the techniques of knowledge engineering are valid independently of the development environment in which the application is being built into an expert system. Those sections that are technically more detailed take into account those possibilities (and those limitations) encountered by the use of the Nixdorf expert system shell TWAICE, which is domain independent. The support offered by TWAICE also plays a role in the selection of methods and tools to be used at times, but this is usually recognised as a pragmatic solution for the particular circumstances.

The vast bulk of the knowledge engineering literature is of a predominantly theoretical nature. The practical technology of knowledge engineering with which one could contemplate an actual knowledge engineering exercise has been quite neglected. The principal authors of this book have attempted to review the available material and systemise it into a model of knowledge engineering behaviour. Two areas of expertise were considered especially important:

— error analysis/fault diagnosis
— computer systems configurations.

There are established, operational knowledge bases available for these domains, and this chapter attempts a systematic report of experience gained in the process of creating a similar system.

5.2 GENERAL ISSUES OF KNOWLEDGE ENGINEERING

The expert that makes his knowledge available for the filling of an expert system is usually a specialist in a narrow section of some technology or process, called his "domain". His specialist knowledge is separable from his general knowledge (i.e. common knowledge about the world outside the specialist domain). The expert's specialist knowledge consists of a number of categories of knowledge, including:

— definitions
— references
— facts
— procedures
— algorithms
— strategies
— heuristics/"rules of thumb".

The knowledge engineer's principal responsibility in the development of an expert system is to prevent the bottleneck of knowledge acquisition becoming too tight. He is required to extract the domain related knowledge from the expert, usually by means of a two-way dialogue.

This knowledge then has to be formalised in terms of the representation available and entered into the expert system. Until some knowledge is entered into the expert system, it is a useless shell, a lifeless skeleton. The quality and scope of the knowledge with which it is populated is crucial to the eventual quality of the system. The schematic activity plan is shown in Fig. 5.1.

The most difficult aspect of this work is that the knowledge engineer has to help the domain expert identify the domain and application knowledge, to structure it, formalise it into some form of knowledge representation, and then to group this acquisition knowledge into concepts (groups of related knowledge). The knowledge engineer has to analyse the utterances of the domain expert very carefully, to try to think like him, and to understand the nature of the expertise that the expert possesses in some detail. This task should not be underestimated. While it is in progress, the knowledge engineer has to learn a lot about the domain and the expert, while the expert has to grasp the concept of an expert system so he can assist the task by structuring his knowledge a little to aid the knowledge elicitation process. During this time there is a high intellectual demand on both parties.

The knowledge base that is created incrementally from the knowledge acquisition process is refined by continuous use. The process can be represented by a cycle as shown in Fig. 5.2.

More explicitly, the six steps are as follows:

(1) The knowledge engineer structures the domain knowledge with the expert, and discusses with him which rules are to be edited or added to the knowledge base.
(2) The knowledge engineer edits or extends the knowledge base.
(3) The knowledge engineer selects some test cases (case data) from the test case library to check for consistency in the knowledge base.
(4) If the test cases above give rise to problems, the knowledge engineer analyses them together with the expert to try and locate a solution, prior to restarting at step (1).
(5) The expert tests the modified system, until the next problem is encountered from the set of test cases.
(6) If no more problems are located from the test case library trials, then the current edit or extension to the knowledge base has been successful. If more knowledge is to be included, restart at step (1).

This shows that once a prototypical shell implementation is available, then through the cycle of extract–edit–test–refine cycles the knowledge base gradually grows in both depth and width/scope.

For the largest part of the development cycle, the knowledge engineer is in close contact with both the expert and the expert system, and frequently acts as a direct interface between the two parties. The communications gap to be overcome is often formidable—the knowledge engineer is a novice in the specialist domain, and the domain expert a novice in knowledge engineering and expert systems technology. An essential step for the initial understanding between the two experts and the system is for the domain expert to become familiar with the terminology of the expert system and the knowledge engineer to become familiar with the terminology of the expert's domain, leaving any other difficulties to be resolved as and when they arise during knowledge elicitation. Currently, only a few tools exists that aid the knowledge engineer in the acquisition task.

The expert's knowledge may be split into two different forms:

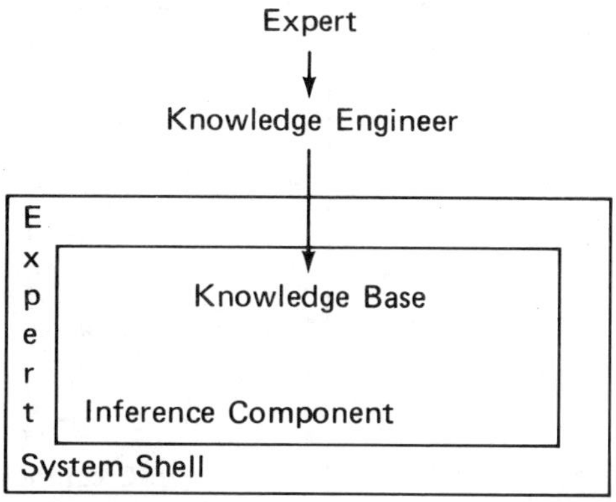

Fig. 5.1—Area of activity of a knowledge engineer in the framework of an expert system.

— the structural or factual knowledge that determines which problems are to be solved
— the strategic knowledge that shows how the expert would solve the problem and what factual and structural knowledge he would use for doing so.

As mentioned at the beginning of this chapter, expert knowledge may also be supplemented by knowledge from text books and manuals about the application domain.

5.3 THE FIVE STAGE CONCEPT FOR KNOWLEDGE ACQUISITION

5.3.0 Introduction

The task of knowledge engineering has to be accomplished in conjunction with all parties involved—the knowledge engineer, the domain expert and the eventual end users.

It may be split into five sub-tasks. It is usually necessary during the execution of these five tasks that the expert at least is taken off his daily tasks and allowed to concentrate full time on the elicitation task. This is important for the customer to realise, as it may mean an extended absence of the often leading expert.

In order to clarify the terminology, an expert in this sense is the domain expert who makes his knowledge available for the knowledge engineer to work on, whereas the term "user" is reserved for the eventual end user of the system once filled with knowledge. The user does not have to be an expert on the technical domain, though he is generally familiar with the terminology and problems of the area as a whole. Users have important input on the design of the user interface and how the system will eventually be used to support them in their daily routine usage.

Prior to commencing the initial step of knowledge engineering, the

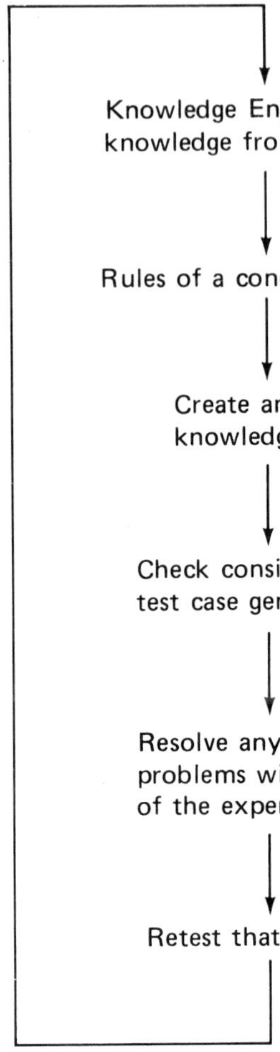

Fig. 5.2—Creation and refinement of the knowledge base.

future customer must have obtained a wide overview of the techniques and application possibilities of expert systems generally. A view of the practicability of the whole exercise should be gained before commencing at all.

The five phases of knowledge engineering are essentially:

(1) In Step 1, "problem definition", the knowledge engineer allows himself to be initiated by the domain expert about the technical domain in which the problem resides. The expert allows himself to become acquainted with the environment and properties of expert systems in general. The knowledge engineer should arrange at least a generally comprehensible demonstration of the knowledge base. After this familiarity has been gained, the goals of the expert system are defined, the "problem definition".

(2) In Step 2, "conceptualisation and formalisation", the knowledge engi-

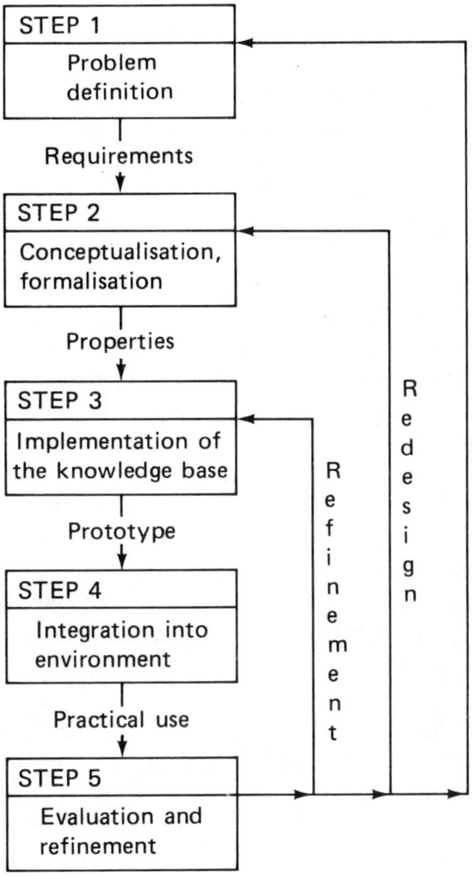

Fig. 5.3—The five essential phases of knowledge engineering.

neer attempts to elicit the knowledge of the expert by interviews. Once having elicited the knowledge, the knowledge engineer must try to formalise it with the knowledge representation choice he has available. Included in this phase is the clarification of terminology and creation of a taxonomy. It should be possible at the latter stages of this step to create a mini-prototype based on just a few rules.

(3) In Step 3, "implementation of the knowledge base", the expert and knowledge engineer create and debug the emerging knowledge base of the expert system. Possibly the expert can perform parts of this autonomously, especially if the expert is also selected to be the eventual maintainer of the system after installation.

(4) In Step 4, "integration into the environment", the expert and the knowledge engineer integrate the expert system in the environment, referring to both the computational environment where the application

is to perform, and the social/organisational environment where the users reside and the system will encroach.

(5) In Step 5, "evaluation and refine", the knowledge engineer and expert, possibly assisted by other experts at this stage, evaluate and refine the expert system as created by the previous incremental processes. The task of knowledge maintenance is given over to a trained expert or group of experts, depending on the size and scope of the system to hand, and the dynamics of the knowledge—the frequency of external editing required and similar parameters.

5.3.1 Step 1: Problem Definition

5.3.1.0 Introduction

This section describes the activities to be performed under step 1 by the knowledge engineer. The order of appearance of the activities should be adhered to when executing this step in an actual exercise.

Initially the knowledge engineer should browse through newspapers, journals and technical reports and have broad discussions with the expert. This is so that he may gain a broad understanding of the domain, its basic characteristics and unique points. The organisational environment in which the expert system has to operate eventually should also be analysed at this time. During this phase the knowledge engineer must grasp the major issues and interrelationships of the domain, as well as being able to transform these to the representations available via his expert system tool kit.

5.3.1.1 Introducing the Expert to Expert Systems

The second phase in step 1 is when the knowledge engineer introduces the domain expert to the general technology of expert systems. The essentials and the functionalities should be covered at this stage. The knowledge engineer should attempt to point out possible applications in the domain, having now grasped the essential problems of the domain. Some introductory texts about expert systems should be distributed for studying off-line. At this point, the knowledge engineer should prepare a demonstration of a real expert system, but in an application domain that is generally comprehensible with a reasonably useful knowledge base — not just a "toy" system, as is often used.

5.3.1.2 Problem Definition

The knowledge engineer and the expert are now in a position to postulate meaningful objectives of the expert system, with an understanding of each other's technology and terminology. The following questions should be asked critically:

— which problems are to be solved?
— where will the expert system be installed?
— what is the organisational environment like?

Having some concept of what the answers to the above questions will look like, the knowledge engineer must now attempt a detailed project planning exercise. A first step is the establishing of the "requirements expression" for the expert system. This step can proceed in parallel to other following activities. The requirements expression document should have at least the following sections included within it:

— organisational environment
— requirements of the expert system
— user interface requirements
— taxonomy of the domain.

The knowledge engineer must by now be familiar with the terminology of the expert's domain, via study and interview with the expert.

5.3.1.3 Scripts

The expert and the knowledge engineer design scripts that deal with about three simple cases from the domain. This serves to make the knowledge engineer familiar with his new "expertise", and allows the expert to consider the structure of knowledge in his specialist area, particularly that part that is procedural. The scripts should describe the instantaneous state of a solution by the expert, showing typical detailed terminology, and hints from the expert about which strategy is to be applied at each moment in the solving process. Both expert and engineer should use the scripts as annotation pads, recording all their experiences. These scripts will eventually serve to be a base for the taxonomy and rules of the initial mini-prototype.

Now the fundamental strategies, with which the expert solves his problems, have to be elicited. This is again accomplished through detailed interviewing. The most important questions to be answered in this phase are:

— which facts does the expert attempt to ascertain first?
— which question does the expert pose first?
— under what basis does the expert hypothesise?
  — with incomplete knowledge?
  — only with complete knowledge?
  — with certain items of knowledge present?
— how does the expert confirm a hypothesis?
— in which order does the expert process sub-problems?

In addition to the "what" in the above, the supplementary question "why" is also to be raised. "Why" one approach rather than an alternative approach at any stage is very useful detailed knowledge to possess.

5.3.1.4 Taxonomy

The knowledge engineer has to explain the concept of a taxonomy to the expert now. The expert has become familiar with the taxonomy elements of object/attribute/value triples. However, the expert does not need to know details of the methods of operation of the inference component, nor create any rules. A good understanding of the taxonomy of a domain by the expert will lead to better structured knowledge, and thus easier consistency and plausibility checking (see the section on taxonomy knowledge in Chapter 3, section 3.3.1).

The expert will probably need assistance to enable him to structure his deep specialist knowledge into a number of sub-tasks and components that are connected by a clearly established relationship, and consistent.

The expert and the knowledge engineer must now propose various dependencies between the components in the domain using the tree structure developed in Chapter 3 (section 3.1.3). However, at this stage it is not required to establish the precise rules of dependencies, nor how they are handled by the inference component.

5.3.1.5 Summary of Step 1

By the end of phase 1, "problem definition", the expert should have supplied the answers to the following questions:

— what is the nature of the problem to be solved?
— how can the problem be defined?
— what is the broad shape of the solution?
— what concepts are to be used?
— what are these concepts called?
— are there sub-problems, and are they enumerated?
— what are the most important concepts?
— how are the important concepts related?
— can the causal relationship be represented in hierarchical tree structures?
— what data are available?
— what is the related information flow?
— what aspects of the human domain knowledge is important for the problem's solution?
— what general knowledge aids the problem solving in humans?
— what domain specific knowledge aids the problem solving in humans?
— what situations may prevent a solution to a problem?
— how are any obstacles overcome in the expert system?
— how do the problems influence an expert system?

Equally, the expert has gained knowledge about:

— expert system technology
— structure of knowledge in his domain
— taxonomy.

The knowledge engineer has gained knowledge about the domain also.

5.3.2 Step 2: Conceptualisation and Formalisation

5.3.2.0 Introduction

Step 2 can only be sensibly commenced when both the expert and the knowledge engineer have some detailed knowledge about their respective areas of expertise, when the requirements of the expert system are established and when the problems that have to be tackled are well defined. In this step, the knowledge engineer has to explain a number of items to the expert, and further work revolves around the scripts developed in step 1.

The expert should now begin to understand the following, by training with the knowledge engineer:

— functionality/operation of the inference mechanism
— incremental construction techniques
— rule syntax.

5.3.2.1 Further Work on Scripts

The scripts developed in step 1 are incomplete, and at best represent snapshots of the state of the system or the expert's thinking. These scripts are also usually still idealised. The expert must now add his own requirements for the expert system, and the requirements for the user interface (i.e. the dialogue structure) with regard to the capabilities of the expert system shell and its development tools that would be reasonably expected to be available. The knowledge engineer should note that it is unrealistic to expect the expert to be able to design a realistic dialogue structure at this stage of his knowledge about expert systems, unless he is also an experienced data processing practitioner. It is the task of the knowledge engineer to steer the expert towards realistic objectives for the user interface while retaining maximum flexibility and user friendliness without sacrificing too much performance.

5.3.2.2 Formalisation

The dependencies of the domain knowledge that have been gathered in step 1 now have to be so configured that they are suitable for processing by the inference component (see sections 3.1.3 and 3.3.1). This task is usually completed by the knowledge engineer more or less in isolation. During the formalisation/reconfiguration phase, the first rules are developed also.

If appropriate, additional knowledge may now be taken up from sources such as textbooks, journals, etc. These should be facts that are reasonably clearly structured and well defined.

5.3.2.3 A First Prototype

The knowledge engineer implements a mini-prototype with a few rules and only a part of the taxonomy. This serves the purpose of introducing the expert to his future tools via a meaningful entry and thus hopefully motivates future co-operation. The scripts used for this are those developed in the earlier sections. If the test cases have been well chosen, it should be possible to tell from the implementation of this prototype whether the correct basic solution strategy has been selected. Another very important aspect of this mini-implementation is that it gives the expert the first opportunity to see some results of the work to date. As such, it can serve as a valuable feedback loop from the expert system via the expert to the knowledge engineer.

The work begun in step (1) on the requirements expression document must now be completed.

The expert and the knowledge engineer now construct rules with which the knowledge base will be populated. The taxonomy of the domain is a useful tool for the knowledge engineer at this time. This greatly facilitates checking the knowledge base for completeness. There is a tool available in the TWAICE development environment that supports the detection of illegal concepts (i.e. those that are inconsistent with the taxonomy) and syntactic correctness of the rules (see Chapter 3, section 3.2.6).

By repetitive re-examination of the details of the expert interview(s), the knowledge engineer has to:

— detect and close all gaps in the knowledge base
— detect and resolve rule conflicts
— detect and resolve incorrect or incomplete knowledge.

This section has to be completed while the knowledge engineer still has rapid access to the expert, in case the interview fails to yield a solution to any of the above problems.

5.3.2.4 An Extended Test Case Set

Once the above items have been resolved, the basic decisions taken to date become characteristics of the implementation. They are fundamental to the nature of the system. The approach should also have been validated by now to the extent that it has withstood some rigorous testing on a small test case set.

In order to get a feel for scaling problems, and to see how the system will cope with an extension of knowledge of a fairly large order at this stage, the expert in association with the knowledge engineer should now assemble a test case set of about 40 examples. These can be scripted like previous ones. The actual cases can also be used later during the testing and debugging phase. The greatest care should be taken to include realistic problems, as well as partially defined ones. Trivial or "straightforward" cases are unlikely to lead to a real learning stress on the system at this time, and may give misleading performance indications later. Within this test case knowledge base, the expert system must be exercised to its operational limits.

5.3.2.5 Conclusion for Step 2

By the end of the step that covers conceptualisation and formalisation, the following open questions must have been resolved :

— what is acceptably completed?
— what requires further detailed analysis?
— what requires an alternative approach?
— how are the objects in a domain related?
— which processes contribute to solving problems?
— what are the limiting factors for the activation of a process?
— what data are available and how?
— are data associated with uncertainty?

— is any uncertainty in the data quantifiable?
— is the logical interpretation of data dependent upon a sequence of events, or on time?
— what resources will be consumed by data acquisition?
— what questions have to be posed to acquire the data?
— are the data precise and reliable, or unreliable and fuzzy?
— are the data complete and consistent for the solution process?

5.3.3 Step 3: Implementation of the Knowledge Base

5.3.3.0 Introduction

In the third step the knowledge engineer and the expert continue with the implementation of the knowledge base. This should be accomplished by direct use of the mini-prototype built in the earlier step. While implementation continues, debugging proceeds with the aid of the test case library developed for the second step. In order to complete this step as described, the following activities are recommended.

The expert and the knowledge engineer develop further rules and thereby extend the knowledge base. The partial problems developed in step 1 are followed through in a logical sequence.

5.3.3.1 Extend and Test the Knowledge Base

At this stage, the expert should be competent enough to develop further rules and introduce these to the knowledge base in order to extend, test and debug it, without the explicit aid of the knowledge engineer. In the TWAICE environment, there are some tools available to support this operation, in the shape of capture and editing tools for rules and the object/attribute/value triples. This is also referred to in section 3.3.4 on the knowledge acquisition component of TWAICE.

The knowledge engineer decides if "attached procedures" are required so that the final expert system may meet the most relevant concerns of the expert, including covering procedural knowledge also. After a major incremental step for the extension of the knowledge base has been taken, the knowledge engineer should gather the results generated by the expert system, along with its explanations, and expose them to other experts (not the domain expert with whom he has been working most closely). These experts should then work through the cases in isolation, then collectively review the correctness and consistency of the solutions and explanations presented by the expert system. These experts may also wish to further test the system with real and purely hypothetical test cases. This may lead to the generation of new test cases which will be useful in the downstream testing phases, and as such they should be documented and added to the scripts previously prepared.

5.3.3.2 Blind Testing

For a part of the testing phase, the experts should test the system out of sight of the user. When the user is presented with an output, he should not be aware of whether it is generated by the expert system or the human expert.

This has overtones of the "Turing Test" for possession of the property of "artificial intelligence" [Forsyth and Rada 1986, Hodges 1985].

In a "blind test and evaluation", both expert and expert system are given the same test case problems, but separately. Both sets of outputs are then evaluated and checked for consistency and accuracy by the other experts—without knowing the precise source of the output, of course.

In this phase of the testing and evaluation, the future users of the system once it is installed in the field should also be involved. The wishes and requirements of the end user must be taken into account as much as is practical for an efficient system. The user also begins to see the capabilities and limitations of the evolving system.

5.3.3.3 Test and Debug

At every major modification stage (e.g. the resolution of a new rule which gave rise to inconsistencies) all test cases from the test case library (see section 3.2.7) should be run and tested for the absence of known errors and, as far as possible, the absence of new errors (i.e. inconsistency with the existing knowledge base). The principal reasons for insufficient capability in an expert system that may begin to arise at this stage include:

- inadequate input or output, e.g.
  - imprecise question formulation
  - difficult queries
  - unsuitable input media
  - too sparse explanations or conclusions
  - too verbose explanations or conclusions
- unsuitable and erroneous rules, e.g.
  - incorrect premises
  - inconsistent premises
  - incorrect conclusions
  - inconsistent conclusions
  - improper ordering/partitioning of rules
- incorrect control strategy, e.g.
  - sub-problems in an unnatural sequence
  - unsuitable inference mechanism
- inadequate test cases, e.g.
  - too simple cases
  - conflicting cases
  - erroneous cases
  - ambiguous cases
- incompetent problem solution, e.g.
  - knowledge insufficient for solution of problem
  - rules inadequate for problems scope

— overspecialised problem solution, e.g.
  — knowledge base is too specialised
  — domain of experience too narrow
  — insufficiently broad boundary conditions.

5.3.4 Step 4: Integration into the Environment

The fourth step is in many ways the most crucial, in that it exposes the system seriously to the end user. This phase requires a great deal of "sensitivity", and serious mistakes in this phase may easily nullify all the previous work. The following tasks have to be undertaken in this fourth step:

— integration into the organisational environment
— integration into the existing computer environment
— acceptance of the new system by the users in steps.

In each case, the main issue is the non-disruption of the existing processes, and the creation of a positive attitude towards the introduction of the new system at a low resistance level. Education is a major weapon in the integration armoury.

5.3.5 Step 5: Evaluation and Refinements

5.3.5.1 Joint Evaluation and Refinements

Several months after the deployment of the expert system as developed above, the fifth step commences. This is an exchange of views and experience between the knowledge engineer and the users and experts relating to the performance of the system. The following aspects could be taken into account:

— Independent experts should evaluate the system in parallel, using it in their everyday tasks, and offer evaluations based on predetermined criteria in order to allow comparative assessments.
— Users (especially non-expert users) should be asked in depth about their everyday experience in using the system. A large sample size of users should be questioned in order to obtain a balanced view of the possible extension that may be made in a revision of the implementation. Users are an essential part of the feedback loop, and note should be taken of their suggestions for possible future implementation.

Finally, the knowledge engineer and the expert write a concluding evaluation. This must include a cost/benefit analysis and also a list of required extensions and refinements to be implemented should further work be done on the development.

5.3.5.2 Evaluation by the Knowledge Engineer

The evaluation of the expert system carried out by the knowledge engineer alone essentially concerns conclusions about the completeness and the consistency of the knowledge base. Another aspect is the correctness of the advice and inferences the system generates during use.

The knowledge engineer must train one or more local (i.e. customer staff) personnel in the art of maintaining the knowledge that the expert system will gradually accumulate through frequent use. He must be able to judge the eligible personnel for the capabilities of performing this often difficult task. It is a task not unlike that of a database administrator in classical applications. Bad knowledge base maintenance will soon make the expert system unusable and often the system is rapidly discarded as a direct result.

5.3.5.3 *Evaluation by the User*

Users may evaluate the expert system on a number of criteria which are relevant to their own efficiency:

— degree of difficulty of use (Man–Machine Interface (MMI))
— comprehensibility of output
— acceptability of output
— efficiency of expert system
— response times
— reliability of expert system
— breadth of scope of knowledge available.

5.3.6 Summary of Important Criteria in Evaluation

An expert system may be evaluated on a number of criteria, and each application may place a different emphasis on them, which may be in part driven by the complexity of the application, and the intended user. Important criteria include:

— quality of the system's decisions
— quality of the system's advice
— a good user interface (Man–Machine Interface)
— run time behaviour
— cost/benefit analysis
— organisational integration.

5.4 INTERVIEW OF EXPERTS

The interviews between expert and knowledge engineer are the single most important knowledge acquisition method. They should be carefully planned and executed with maximum insight into the problem domain. The main problem is to ensure that the knowledge so elicited is the complete knowledge for that specific domain of problems to be solved. Both parties have to be aware that each other's terminology is unfamiliar to them, as at the outset there has been little mutual exposure other than independent preparation for the work ahead.

Interviews are difficult interaction mechanisms to predict, but a number of recommendations may be made based on experience gathered by the TWAICE team in the development of test cases. These include:

— create a productive atmosphere
— listen to the expert
— attempt to summarise the expert's opinions into a clear and precise set of statements with which the expert can agree
— differentiate between general and specific knowledge of an expert
— focus on certain examples and objects
— follow reasoning chains through to conclusions
— let the expert itemise sub-goals where they exist
— group related sub-goals together, with the expert
— be aware of the dangers of premature conclusions
— do not oversimplify too early, before the domain is understood fully
— give the expert some idea of how the eventual dialogue with the system will look
— arrange at least one demonstration for the expert
— do not force answers from an expert if he is not certain
— note where knowledge of the expert is incomplete
— attempt to see the interdependencies of the expert knowledge
— draw a tree structure of the knowledge and discuss with the expert and seek to obtain his agreement
— attempt to extract rules from the verbal output of an interview
— attempt to see where rule knowledge is complete, and fill in gaps by steering the dialogue to that part
— where more than one expert is involved in the interview process, attempt to act as arbitrator between them
— where multiple experts are involved, attempt to get a common view.

More detailed planning for conducting interviews is found in Breuker and Wielinga [1984]. Strategies for interviewing and for the interpolation of verbal data are discussed.

5.5 KNOWLEDGE ENGINEERING AT NIXDORF

5.5.0 Introduction

Nixdorf pursues a number of ways whereby the task of knowledge engineering may be carried out for a specific customer in the implementation of TWAICE:

— customer supplies the knowledge engineer
— Nixdorf supply the knowledge engineer
— Nixdorf supply the knowledge engineer and trains the expert
— third party knowledge engineer.

5.5.1 Customer Supplied Knowledge Engineer

The customer selects an appropriate employee (who may be the domain expert himself), and sends him to specific training on site at Nixdorf. The training is for the task of knowledge engineering. It must be said that not every employee is capable of performing the task, nor that the training or retraining effort is at all trivial. The time required for an adequate training spans a considerable number of weeks.

Once trained as a knowledge engineer, the employee returns to the customer's site and develops the previously described tasks with his in-house experts. This may be a possible route when the knowledge is so highly specialised that a trained knowledge engineer may not comprehend the domain, or where the rules are embodiments of some confidential details that the customer does not wish to expose (e.g. some new chemical process). The Nixdorf knowledge engineer in this case only supplies support to the expert system shell TWAICE and its tool kit, not for the specific knowledge in the knowledge base.

5.5.2 Knowledge Engineer from Nixdorf

The knowledge engineer is supplied by Nixdorf. He interacts with the customer's expert(s) and, being fully conversant with the use and ability of the tools, acts as an interface between the expert and the expert system during the entire development phase. This may be the fastest method, but it involves the lowest level of technology transfer to the customer, and leaves the customer often wholly dependent upon further support as the expert system goes into service.

5.5.3 Knowledge Engineer from Nixdorf trains customer

This is essentially as section 5.5.2, but during the prototype development phase, the knowledge engineer makes it a specific function of that phase to train the customer's experts to such a degree that once the engineer leaves, the expert is able to support the day-to-day maintenance of the knowledge base. Nixdorf would continue to supply system support for the tools as before.

5.5.4 Third Party Knowledge Engineers

It may be that the customer prefers independent experts to populate their system. There are so-called knowledge houses now being established that specialise in this sort of task. However, in this industry at this time, most of these houses are associated with some product or other. It is highly unlikely that they will have extensive experience of the specific expert system shell being used by the customer—and certainly not to the depth of the vendor of the expert system. This may seem an attractive method, but is possibly the high risk strategy at this time, bearing in mind the immature state of the technology. There is some justification in complementing the team with such a third party independent expert who may be helpful, especially in multiple expert situations.

6

Knowledge Acquisition and Machine Learning

Lothar Fohmann
Nixdorf Computer AG, Paderborn, FRG

6.1 THE PROBLEM

6.1.0 Introduction

The objective of this chapter is not to define the set of problems in the domain of learning systems in general in artificial intelligence, but to concentrate on those issues relating to knowledge based systems, and then from the viewpoint of the bottleneck of knowledge acquisition.

6.1.1 The Dimension of the Problem

Therefore, based on the above, the major considerations will focus on:

— whether, and to what degree, learning systems may be used to overcome this characteristic bottleneck in the application of knowledge based systems
— whether, and to what degree, learning systems may actually be used to improve knowledge acquisition qualitatively, or at least to make the process of acquisition more efficient and more effective.

6.1.1.1 Knowledge Based Systems and Artificial Intelligence

Knowledge based systems are programs that consist of at least two active components: a knowledge base and a so-called "inference" engine. The concept of a "program" initially was that of a series of instructions. This classical von Neumann computational schema concept lacks the ability to distinguish context dependent situations, and with its inherent linearity proved to be unsatisfactory practically. Therefore some subsequent developments of programming paradigms developed dual programming concepts.

One concept arose out of the mathematical differentiation between operators and operands. It should be useful to distinguish, in the programming paradigms, between the algorithm and the data structures of a problem. A typical member of a group of languages that represent data structured oriented programming (i.e. algorithm plus data structures) is

PASCAL. The conceptual split of the algorithm and the objects on which the "instructions" act led to a development which terminated in a certain degree of data independence, in that the data structures were removed (or "hidden") from the program itself. It was this development that led the way to the development of database systems. This concept is taken further in the new procedural language Ada, which is about to become an ISO (International Standards Organisation) standard for wide use in real time systems.

Another concept imported its principal ideas from the first order predicate logic and draws a distinction between the descriptive (factual) logic of a program and the algorithmic control functions. The language PROLOG (PROgramming in LOGic) is based on this programming concept. It is frequently used in Europe for the implementation of intelligent systems, and is the base implementation concept of the Japanese 5th Generation Project "KLn" (Kernel Language version "n").

Yet another viewpoint is represented for the research domain of artificial intelligence in the equally significant language SMALLTALK. This is based on the abstract datatype (an abstract datatype is composed of an abstract data structure and an associated access function). A program of the SMALLTALK paradigm consists of a number of objects that are composed of (local) procedures as well as (local) data. The execution of a program conceived in this style consists of a form of action by program objects so that objects send or receive communications from other objects, called "message passing". This object oriented programming concept consists of a set of objects in the form of (data,procedure) couples. In this object oriented programming paradigm, the conceptual duality is hidden by the concept of the object—but the program behaves as if it were explicitly incorporated.

The most recent duality concept arose in artificial intelligence—that of the knowledge based program. This consists of a knowledge base and the inference component. The knowledge base can contain descriptive and/or procedural knowledge for the solution of problems. It is the function of the inference machine to instantiate the knowledge base to the problem at hand, i.e. to interpret the problem in the context of its knowledge about the problem domain. Exactly which formalism is used to represent the knowledge (for example: predicate logic set rules, specific rules and facts, graphs, trees, nets, frames or procedures) is, for the conceptual level of the knowledge based system, without significance (for references on this topic in knowledge based systems see Waterman and Hayes-Roth [1978]).

One group of knowledge based systems are the so-called "Expert Systems". They are characterised by their operational characteristics to simulate a solution to a problem and perhaps also the behaviour of a (human) expert (for introductory texts on Expert Systems see Hayes-Roth *et al.* [1983] or Michie [1982]. Based on the representation formalism employed, it is practical to distinguish between production systems and knowledge based systems in general. Production systems are systems where at least a part of the knowledge in the knowledge base is formulated by production rules (for Production Systems see Nilsson [1982] p. 17 *et seq.*).

Production rules are implicative statements, where an action is implied within the rules.

However, in the 1950's there was a preconception dominant in artificial intelligence research that it was sufficient that problem solving systems would contain general, domain independent, knowledge coupled with very powerful problem solving strategies which would give qualitatively satisfactory results. Practical experience, however, conflicted with this preconception.

Since the mid 1960's, and reinforced in the 1970's, the above directions were replaced by recognition of the fact that the construction of problem solving knowledge based systems that give satisfactory performance requires emphasis on precisely the previously neglected aspect—to highlight domain specific problem solving knowledge. Therefore the new concept of knowledge based systems emerged—a domain specific knowledge oriented system paradigm. This concept has now percolated all artificial intelligence activity in this area (for the history of the move between paradigms see Hayes-Roth *et al.* [1983], p. 6 *et seq.*).

6.1.1.2 Learning Systems in Artificial Intelligence

In the context of the material presented below, learning systems are understood to be machine based systems that can modify themselves so as to increase their performance (either capability or effectiveness).

In conceptual terms the relative positions of knowledge based systems and "Machine Learning" systems are such that there are quite significant overlaps. There are, at least on conceptually based grounds,

— knowledge based learning systems
— knowledge based non-learning systems
— learning non-knowledge based systems.

The last class, which is scientifically the oldest type of system, have been entirely replaced by the development of artificial intelligence in the 1970's.

6.1.1.3 The Expert System Shell TWAICE

The final coordinate to the state of the art in the topic under discussion here is that relating to the expert system shell TWAICE. This product from Nixdorf AG is the most recent addition to the family of systems that originated from EMYCIN [Mescheder, Chapter 3 of this book]. Therefore learning systems in this context are only examined insofar as they could contribute usefully to a knowledge base built under TWAICE in the following areas, but compatible with the artificial intelligence related concepts:

— for creation and extension
— for qualitative improvement
— for better effectiveness

of the knowledge base.

However, in the development of the following general theories of learning knowledge based systems, the latter (i.e. the viewpoints taken in the expert system shell TWAICE) are deliberately excluded from consideration. The theory will have to cover the requirements of learning systems on the one hand and of knowledge based systems on the other, and from this a number of practical consequences may be drawn for learning in the TWAICE environment. Therefore a dual research and development strategy is followed. However, aside from the probably necessary reiteration of the general theoretical aspects, practical aspects of implementation follow.

6.1.2 The State of the Art in Knowledge Acquisition and Learning

6.1.2.1 Knowledge Acquisition

Knowledge acquisition or the construction (and filling with "information") of knowledge bases in knowledge based systems represents, from the theoretical as well as the practical viewpoint, the single most difficult facet of the total problem domain of knowledge based systems. Useful introductory material is in Quinlan [1982], and, taking more of an overview, Buchanan *et al.* [1984] and Noelke [in chapter 5 of this book]. The state of the art in the knowledge acquisition area is currently characterised by the following drawbacks:

— the singular theories of knowledge acquisition are often not regarded as portable enough for the practice of knowledge acquisition on a day-to-day basis
— the experience base of knowledge acquisition is currently still small and superficial, preventing significant validation of the methods and theories developed for knowledge acquisition in the large.

6.1.2.1.1 On the Theories of Knowledge Acquisition

In order to be able to represent the knowledge required to problem solve in the appropriate domain, it is necessary to develop a mathematically formal conceptual model of the application domain that is capable of machine interpretation. The insight to develop these models for knowledge acquisition has wide-reaching consequences. The very nature of the knowledge acquisition process is that the elicitation of knowledge such as that necessary for the construction of the model is principally a creative, non-mechanical and openly practical activity or "craft" for knowledge engineers and experts. The model characteristics must also satisfy the requirements demanded by the knowledge acquisition process and respect the limitations of the theory as regards the elicitation process [Kirsch 1977, Vol. 2, p. 32 *et seq.*]. Therefore, in this context, the model theory of knowledge acquisition is the approach that develops a mathematical model of the process within which the elicitation/abstraction/representation of knowledge then takes place.

The model theory approach postulates formal, semantic and pragmatic requirements.

Formal requirements relate to the model characteristics as such, whereas semantic requirements affect the relationship between the model and the original process. Finally, pragmatic requirements relate the models to the original process, and the builders and users of the models.

At the formal level the model theory requires that in the current context of knowledge bases within knowledge based system, the model be consistent (i.e. it does not contain explicit contradictions) and capable of machine (i.e. automatic) interpretation.

At the semantic level, the essential requirement is that the model theory should ensure that there is a close relationship between the model and reality. This relationship requires a sufficiently close coupling so that a problem that occurs in the real world problem domain can be solved by manipulation of only the model. The fact that this requirement represents only a sufficiently close similarity and not an identical representation between the real world and the model stems from the fact that models can only include explicit concepts of parts of the original domain, while including more abstract representations of other components—often grouped for simplicity. For this reason a model that is identical to reality is generally not feasible. The overall achieved level of abstraction, however, is the essential function of the model in that it achieves a usability and computability in a highly complex domain by reducing the explicit complexity to essentials.

Similarly, the sense of a functional equivalence (i.e. the model can replace the original system) from the aspect of problem solving characteristics is, however, only achieved when the problem and the associated solutions are already available in the original system. This is in the sense that the problem and the solution are already well defined or capable of being defined within the operational framework of the real world domain. Models that deal with ill-defined real world domains are excluded from this semantic requirement, as it is not possible to meet the requirement through any type of formal model. In such cases this specific requirement may only be maintained on a very pragmatic level, and may only be weakly met, if at all.

Actual functional equivalence of the model and the real world domain is rare. Because of major differences in idealised models and practical reality, functional equivalence is only approached in such modelling situations where reality is idealised. Only in such idealised cases can model relationships be upgraded from being a bare similarity to possessing the real characteristics of a fully functional equivalence. In this case, basic differences between a model and its real world counterpart can be ignored at the functional level.

The requirement for a functional equivalence between model and real world can be split into two complementary partial requirements:

— correctness of the model
— completeness of the model.

"Correctness" in a model, relative to the process being modelled, is achieved only when all the cases of problem solving instances coincide with that in the original process. This is the situation where the problem solving capabilities of the model can mimic some of those of the real world system which the more abstract model aims to describe.

"Completeness" is a property of a model where, relative to the real world system, all individual possible problem solving instances of the real system agree with the outcome of the model under similar inputs. In this case the problem solving capabilities of the original system are less than or equal to that of the model's capabilities. The conjunction of these two partial requirements represents the overall requirements for functional equivalence between model and real world systems.

Pragmatic requirements are those that relate to the use of the model in some computational environment. They are generally introduced by the builders of the system or its eventual (human) end-user. A fundamental pragmatic question to be asked of every model in relation to the system it represents is whether, quite independent of correctness and completeness, in the view of the eventual end-user, it can actually contribute usefully to the solving of the real world system problem domain in which it is intended to operate. If it does not do so, with hindsight the pragmatic requirements must have been erroneously specified or interpreted. Almost assumed in many cases, but practically often not implemented, other pragmatic requirements are that a model should be:

— readable (understandable)
— communicable (between like-minded users for example).

At the formal and semantic level there are other limitations for the construction of models and thus for the acquisition of knowledge. These limitations cannot be ignored, nor overcome.

One formal limit is that of computability. Computable numbers are those that can be expressed by a Universal Turing machine or an equivalent formalism (for a definition of this machine in historical perspective see Hodges [1985]), such as production systems or first order predicate logic; or indeed any hybrid system composed of such a formalism. It does not follow that formally, correctly modelled numbers are always computable.

The semantic limitations on knowledge acquisition are far more important, however.

A generally applicable semantic limit is the fundamental nature of mathematics and thus the acquisition of knowledge within a classical mathematical model framework. Only dimensional scales can be handled in classical mathematics, being external characteristics of a symbol or set of symbols (such as classes). Symbolic content is lost as it cannot be mathematically manipulated. The availability of methods to process mixed numeric and symbolic structures defines the extent of this limitation at any time.

Though often confused with the Turing limit of computability, it is in fact a quite different problem and should not be confused with it.

Another generally valid semantic limitation to knowledge acquisition arises out of the circumstance that every (mathematical) model within an understood context is based on the understanding that it is based in on a real world domain with specific characteristics. Knowledge acquisition always takes place relative to only this original real world domain and the levels of abstraction above it—i.e. to various components of the domain only. This relatively obvious limitation, however, leads to the conclusion that there cannot be a general semantic (mathematical) world model, and therefore no general purpose, all embracing knowledge base. Finally, as a characteristic of the model is independent of content, there can be no expert system shell (or knowledge based system shell) that is equally suitable for use in any (i.e. an initially unspecified) domain.

If those individual results are assembled, and if one views Model Theory or mere Recognition Theory of Analytical Scientific Theory [Stegmueller 1973–74] then it comes as no surprise that the problems encountered by knowledge acquisition seem familiar. These problems are already known from the area of empirical theories in scientific theory, only in this case, an additional problem of automatic or machine interpretation arises. Even today the state of scientific theory discussions on the possible relative relationships between various empirical theories regarding:

— conflict
— complementarity
— duality
— specialisation
— revision

is still in a state of flux. Little wonder then that in the domain of knowledge acquisition there is currently no universal application model (world model), nor a satisfactory universal knowledge representation formalism. There is still a need for creativity and imagination in the construction of Expert Systems. It will be a long time before model construction consists of only completely deterministic methodologies!

Knowledge acquisition as an emerging science will have to live with the plurality of models and knowledge representations for some time, just as computational theory has to accommodate a set of computational formalisms such as Turing Machines, Markovian Algorithms, Partially Recursive Functions or Lambda Calculus.

6.1.2.1.2 Methodology and Practice of Knowledge Acquisition

Viewed from the methodological viewpoint, knowledge acquisition shells are characterised currently by the fact that the well-established Phase Model of the software development process is taken and transferred to the construction of knowledge bases. Knowledge bases are regarded as a special case of the general software development process, and hopefully only minimal changes have to be made [Buchanan *et al.* 1984]. Not least because of this unsatisfactory state of affairs, the recommended methodology and practical experience that follows are relatively autonomous from any established theory at this stage.

A model for knowledge acquisition that is frequently cited in the literature is that of Reformulation [Carbonell *et al.* 1983]. This model essentially has five phases:

— identification
— conceptualisation
— formalisation
— implementation
— test.

The first phase is "identification" of the characteristics of the problem, especially those that are localised to the specific application domain, and those that are more specific to the application itself.

"Conceptualisation" refers to the process of determining which concepts are to be used for modelling of the knowledge surrounding the problem, and the knowledge representation of the means to solve the problem.

"Formalisation" refers to the formulating of the concepts in a stricter semantic context under an abstraction of model semantics.

"Implementation" refers to the representation of rules and facts in a formal model, possibly (usually) in a method suitable for machine computational use.

"Testing" is the final phase of the model. The rules and knowledge contained in them are tested to validate them against a set of requirements, such as completeness, consistency and correctness.

A development methodology will only be employed in practice if there are a sufficient number of tools available to support a large part of the spectrum of the problems that arise in it. By reducing the workload of the knowledge engineer, tools become attractive to use. As automated tools perform more consistently (in theory) than fallible humans, the methodology used to produce them is gradually introduced into the whole technology. There are always components of the knowledge acquisition process, though, for which there are no tools and this is where the creative requirements arise in the knowledge engineer. The development tools act as links between practice and the often constraining methodology. Use of the tools also implies an acceptance of the methodology used in the tool implementation, even if only at a pragmatic level.

A significantly wider and deeper experience base in practical knowledge acquisition has to be developed. These gathered experiences have to be fed back to encourage theoretical and then methodological progress. Most significantly, more and better knowledge acquisition tools have to be developed and made available for general use.

6.1.2.2 Automatic Learning

In contrast to knowledge acquisition, automatic learning is tackled simultaneously from two sides. One approach is via the knowledge based system technology within the wider domain of artificial intelligence. The second approach is via the study of the human learning branch of psychology. It is therefore quite imaginable that the state of the art in the problem domain of the intersection of these two quite different sciences is not clear at all. Even today the concept of "learning", and what is and is not sensible in terms of research avenues to be followed, is the subject of heated debate [Simon 1983]. Within artificial intelligence, though, a terminology and a conceptual taxonomy have slipped into a vacuum and have been broadly accepted by many. There is nevertheless considerable variation in what different knowledge engineers see as conceptual contents, extent, and limitations: see [Carbonell *et al.*] [Buchanan *et al.* p. 131, p. 155] [Forsyth, Rada *et al.*].

Examples of the lack of agreement include:

— how learning and knowledge acquisition are related and how they should behave towards each other
— are learning and direct knowledge acquisition mutually exclusive, or is knowledge acquisition a sub-term of learning?
— what the criteria for learning are
— what the differences in criteria for different learning categories are
— how far different categories can be treated in common
— what is meant by
  — learning goals
  — learning categories
  — learning types
  — learning sources
  — learning objects
  — learning inputs
  — learning outputs
  — learning methods
  — learning agents
  — learning roles
  — learning resources
  — learning means
  — learning validation criteria
— and how the above learning parameters are interrelated to each other.

A comprehensive theory and methodology of automatic learning does not exist yet in artificial intelligence. The plurality of the learning parameters and the depth and breadth of problems and their rapidly increasing complexity are all responsible for this. Nevertheless, practical experimentation with learning systems is far advanced relative to any cohesive and comprehensive attack on the area of methodology and theory. For an introduction see Langley and Carbonell [1984].

Nevertheless a non-trivial but small section of the overall problem domain has been recently conquered. This is the area of inductive learning of classification rules by example. Theoretically and methodologically, it seems that this area is now largely understood. However, inductive logic concepts were not used directly, nor were the conclusions in conflict with them [Carnap and Stegmueller 1958].

Over and above this, it has been agreed within the artificial intelligence community since the 1970's that learning systems must contain two types of knowledge if they were to be efficient. Application specific and application independent knowledge are required for learning systems. The knowledge intensive viewpoint (application independent) is that which characterises the third learning paradigm. Independent of differences in detail, this paradigm considers common structures and viewpoints as an initial orientation.

Whereas the 1950's were characterised by surmounting the initial learning paradigm of numerical–statistical learning systems without any domain specific knowledge, the second learning paradigm occupied researchers of the 1960's. This paradigm was learning with purely symbolic methods, but still essentially surviving without any knowledge component. Both failed in terms of breadth and depth of applicability.

The transition to knowledge intensive learning in artificial intelligence occurred at the same time as the transition to specific knowledge oriented paradigms in problem solving systems, such as knowledge based systems. Including knowledge in the paradigm removed the reason for the failure of the first two attempts, at a price of increased complexity.

6.1.3 Solution Strategies and Experiences

6.1.3.0 Introduction

There are just three possible solution strategies that can be used to reconcile the problems arising from knowledge based systems on one side, and learning systems on the other:

— the island strategy
— the global strategy
— the mixed strategy.

6.1.3.1 The "Island" Strategy

This is essentially a bottom-up strategy. The problems that exist and arise during development are considered individually and those that can be resolved are completed. This builds up small islands of isolated solutions. Then attempts are made to bridge these islands to form a growing domain until the whole problem is solved via a connected (even if not very cohesive) network of solutions. Finally, seemingly insoluble problems are re-visited, circumvented or optimised out of the model.

6.1.3.2 The "Global" Strategy
Starting at a distance from the problem, and at an abstract level, a top-down strategy is attempted to solve the problem. Initially a theoretical systematic framework is established. Then this is realised stepwise, thus finally arriving at a fully defined system. This strategy is commonly used in traditional large scale software developments of significant complexity.

6.1.3.3 The "Mixed" Approach
The previous approaches are used in a balanced and thoughtful manner to optimise the advantages of both methods to reach the goal. Getting the right balance is the art!

6.1.3.4 Experiences
With some exceptions [Michalski *et al.* 1983], artificial intelligence attempted to progress along the axis of the third systems paradigm (knowledge) using the insular strategy. Numerous isolated systems were realised, such as "Meta-Dendral" [Buchanan and Mitchell 1978], "Teiresias" [Davis 1982b] and "AM" [Lenat 1982]). Conversely it does not seem wise to adopt a purely global top-down approach either. At a theoretical level one would be confronted with problems of such enormity and complexity that the probability of success would be minimal; and at a practical level the goal would be missed.

Because of this, the mixed approach must be adopted. The strategies must be handled in such a manner that eventually a theoretical global concept can emerge, even while some autonomous parts are split off and handled and others are glossed over initially. The objective of reaching a practically useful knowledge based system must be the priority, however. This mixed bi-directional strategy gives practice a basic foundation and orientation. The mixed strategy supports the theory in that the practical component supplies invaluable insight into the problem solving for the extension of the theory.

6.1.3.5 TWAICE Strategy
The solution strategy adopted by the TWAICE developers was to build increasingly more powerful knowledge acquisition and manipulation tools to support the mixed strategy of section 6.1.3.3., and thus realise TWAICE and its family of application specific expert systems, while supporting an optimal level of top-down developments based on firm theoretical foundations.

6.2 THEORETICAL FRAME OF REFERENCE

6.2.1 Learning Concepts and Learning Theories

6.2.1.0 Introduction
The term automatic learning in general is understood to refer to changes of components and/or structure of an automatic system that persist. The

change is effected through the execution of a learning programme and the overall effect in the raising of the systems performance in terms of the performance or effectiveness. "Automatic" is of course meant to refer implicitly to "machines", in this case a computer. However, the concept developed below can refer generally to models of learning and teaching, and although "programme" is implied to be a computer program, a human teaching programme is equally applicable.

6.2.1.1 Automatic Learning and Knowledge Based Systems

The two definitions in section 6.2.1.0 combined are too abstract to be useful in practical work. Therefore a more concrete definition is required. This concept in the context of knowledge based systems lays down five criteria:

(1) the medium of the learning in automatic systems is knowledge based
(2) a change in the system consists of a change in its internal knowledge base
(3) a change in the knowledge base is persistent (i.e. not transient)
(4) the change of the knowledge base is brought about through the execution of a learning system, but not by tools for direct knowledge acquisition
(5) the change must be a raising of knowledge in the knowledge base so that the problem solving capabilities of the system are extended or optimised.

6.2.1.2 System Components and System Structure

Definition (2) in section 6.2.1.1 precludes changes in the system component or structure, and thus these are removed from the problem domain. This means that the learning system can only make limited changes in its environment, confined to the application domain. The external computer system (i.e. the hardware/software environment) cannot be altered in order to modify the program behaviour.

6.2.1.3 Learning and Direct Knowledge Acquisition

Definition (4) in section 6.2.1.1 defines the limits of learning relative to direct knowledge acquisition and in the form of tools supported (i.e. semi-automatic knowledge acquisition). In direct knowledge acquisition, the knowledge input given to the system via some acquisition process has the same information content as that which is eventually deposited into the knowledge base. The only difference may be a change in its representation from having undergone some equivalence transform. Effectively, the "system" has not learned at all; it has only acted as a categoriser and storer of the new knowledge.

By learning knowledge acquisition is meant that the knowledge input is of a lower quality than that eventually deposited in the knowledge base. Thus the system raises the quality of the knowledge by learning.

6.2.1.4 Learning Categories

Criterion (5) in section 6.2.1.1 defines that learning can occur in three different categories:

— extension
— improvement
— effectiveness

of the learning system's performance.

6.2.1.5 Learning Theories

Equally well developed learning theories are only available from the cognitive psychology domain. For an overview, see [Arnold *et al.* Vol. 2] [Herkner p. 24 *et seq.*, p. 84 *et seq.*]. Psychological learning theories are theories about human behaviour, and as such turn out to be unsuitable for studying knowledge acquisition and learning in knowledge based systems. In fact, they can contribute almost nothing to the techniques and methodology of automatic learning. Many psychologists hope that the study of artificial intelligence will eventually yield benefits for psychological learning models. These hopefuls are mainly advocates of the school of analogy between human and machine or automatic learning. However, even learning theories originating in artificial intelligence are not particularly applicable to knowledge based systems, but take a somewhat different view.

Therefore, for the development of the expert system shell TWAICE, an independent theoretical development was investigated.

6.2.2 Knowledge Acquisition and Knowledge Based Systems

6.2.2.0 Introduction

As already established, knowledge based systems are realisations of a specific knowledge oriented system paradigm. They contain two active components:

— a knowledge base
— an inference machine.

It is understood that the term "knowledge acquisition" refers to any extension to the knowledge base by a write access, independent of whether the write access is to a still empty knowledge base (the "initial knowledge acquisition") or whether it extends a real, non-empty, knowledge base ("additional knowledge acquisition"). From another viewpoint, the qualitative relationship between the information contained in input knowledge and the acquired internal knowledge requires two types of knowledge acquisition to be defined:

— direct knowledge acquisition
— learning knowledge acquisition.

6.2.2.1 Direct Knowledge Acquisition — a Definition

It is understood that direct knowledge acquisition refers to acquisition where the qualitative contents of input knowledge and internal knowledge are similar.

6.2.2.2 Learning Knowledge Acquisition—a Definition

It is understood that learning knowledge acquisition refers to acquisition where the qualitative content of the input knowledge is lower than that of the internal knowledge to which it is to be added.

6.2.2.3 Knowledge Acquisition and Learning

From the understanding of the above three sections for the relation between knowledge acquisition and learning, the following three categories can be defined:

- — pure knowledge acquisition without learning characteristics, called "direct knowledge acquisition"
- — learning knowledge acquisition or knowledge acquisition learning, so-called "indirect knowledge acquisition"
- — pure learning without knowledge acquisition characteristics.

6.2.3 Theoretical Base Concepts: Rule Based Systems

6.2.3.0 Introduction

The knowledge bases of realistically sized knowledge based systems are normally not homogeneous, but heterogeneous. Like any realistic application or problem domain, they contain a variety of different types of knowledge, such as:

- — taxonomy knowledge
- — rule knowledge
- — tabular knowledge
- — procedural knowledge.

A particularly important, if not the most important, type of knowledge for knowledge based systems, and especially for expert systems, turns out to be the second category above—rule knowledge. The practical difficulty associated with acquiring this rule knowledge is one of the major contributory factors to the bottleneck in the application of these systems to real problem solving.

Therefore the theory to be developed below will be based on the essential concept of the "rule based system". In the rest of this section the theoretical tools will be developed prior to the investigation of the individual learning categories in section 6.3 onwards.

6.2.3.1 Some Notational Remarks

6.2.3.1.0 Introduction

Prior to developing a number of fundamental definitions and theorems, a remark on notation is required. The development below relies on a great deal of logic and set theory. The formal and correct expounding of definitions, theorems and proofs can be difficult to follow in the often terse, yet precise, means of expression developed for these fields. In order to make the notation more readable, the notation developed for use here is less than formal, but hopefully more readable to a lay person in regard to the specialist fields of logic and set theory. Definitions that relate to the theory used appear in Appendix A, again developed with a less than strict formality and correctness for ease of comprehension.

6.2.3.1.1 Subscripts and Indices

Subscripts are defined by square brackets such as "[" and "]", but on the same line height as the term or item to be indexed. For example, the third element of the vector **x** is written "**x**[3], the *n*-th term "**x**[*n*]. Indices are single symbols and are either constants such as "6" or variables such as "*i*" or "*n*". They could also be groups of constants and variables separated by arithmetic symbols, for example:

$$(6 + (i*n)).$$

A descriptor that is qualified by *N* indexed variables, constants, or expressions has exactly *N* dimensions. For example, a[*i j k*] is a three dimensional quantity. The "#" symbol ("spoken" as "hash") is used to indicate anonymous variables.

6.2.3.1.2 Superscripts

Superscripts such as those used as power signs are written at the same level as the quantity identifier, but the power sign used is the symbol "^" ("caret" or "circumflex"). Therefore the square of 6 is written as "6^2".

6.2.3.1.3 Set Theory Symbols—Relations

The relation "is-a-subset-of" is written as "ss". The relation "is-an-element-of" is written as "el".

6.2.3.1.4 Set Theory Symbols—Operators

The various operators and their notation in this text are described in Fig. 6.1.

6.2.3.1.5 Other Definitions

Formal definitions are terminated here with the percent symbol "%". The operator "−" has a number of definitions in the table above. This is called operator overloading [Rogers 1985, Section 1], which is a feature most recently used in the programming language Ada. In this context, the triple

Operator	Symbol
All	(A . , . . .)
Existence	(E . , . . .)
Non-identical	=|=
Additive	+
Difference	−
Empty Set	{}
Power Set	ps
Cardinality	|.|
Conjunction	&
Disjunction	V
Implication	→
Equivalence	↔
Negation	−
Anonymous variable, not Index variables	$

Fig. 6.1—Notational key to the text.

overloading of the operator "−" has to be disambiguated by the context in which it appears. The double overloading of the "+" operator has to be resolved similarily.

6.2.3.1.6 Other Relevant Issues from General Logic Theory

Before a more or less formal theory of knowledge acquisition and learning is developed, it is useful to recapitulate some basic issues from logic theory.

Assume the set V is given, and it is finite. The set V may contain the following:

— individual variables
— individual constants
— predicate variables
— function variables
— function constants
— assertion variables
— assertion constants.

The "Herbrand Universe" (written as "HDom(V)") of the finite set V is the set of all variable free terms that may be formulated through the deployment of individual and function constants in V by means of nesting.

A literal is an atomic formula that may or may not contain variables which may be prefixed by a negation operator.

6.2.4 Rule Based Systems—Basic Definitions

6.2.4.0 Introduction

The remainder of section 6.1 attempts to introduce a number of basic definitions and theorems for rule based systems that are essential for developing a more or less formal foundation for learning and knowledge acquisition.

6.2.4.1 Definition D1: "Rule Based System"

A rule based system S is an ordered six-tuple:

S = (V, DB, PR, RI, P, L)

where:

V is a finite non-empty set of symbols for the formulation of DB and PR, the so called "symbol reservoir" or "alphabet".

DB is the set of all finite sets d[h] of variable-free literals l[h#] over the Herbrand Universe HDom(V) of V:

d[h] = {l[h1], ... , l[h*m*]}

where

m>=0
l[h#] is variable free (section 6.2.3.1.6).

Also, d[h] may be logically encapsulated as the conjunction of the literals l[h#] in d[h]. This is termed the "database state space".

PR is the finite set of rules r[g], such that

r[g] = ({l[g1], ... ,l[g*n*]} → {l[g0]})

where

n>=1
l[g#] contains variables
{l[g1], ... ,l[g*n*]} is the premise of r[g]
{l[g0]} is the conclusion of the rule r[g]

PR may be viewed as the logical conjunction of all the single rules r[g] contained in the system. This is the "rule base".

RI is the forward chaining rule interpreter which bases itself on, amongst others, extended Modus-ponens rules as inference rules. It also computes unifiers and forward chains rules. It also selects a literal set from the current database state d[h] and directs this to an applicable rule r[g], the so called "rule interpreter".

P is the set of all problem solving instances that could be submitted to S = (V, DB, PR, RI, P, L). The elements of P are cases "fa[*i*]". A case fa[*i*] is a context specific finite literal set, so that:

P ss DB.

P is termed the "problem domain" of S.

L is the set of all possible solution instances under S. The elements ke[j] of L are called consultation results, and form a context dependent finite literal set:

L ss DB
| P |>= | L | .
%

L is termed the solution domain.

Some more detailed explanations will now be given to the above definitions.

6.2.4.2 DB—the Database State Space

DB is functionally dependent on V, therefore DB is not necessarily a conceptual component of S. In theoretical computer science the definitions used are much stricter, especially for computing machines with dynamic read/write memories. Architectures where this type of memory is provided are mathematically included in those machines defined to permit only static mathematical concepts. Input and memory alphabets are distinguished, and the transition functions of the machine referring to changes in the mathematical state of the machine are extended to include the memory state changes.

In artificial intelligence, however, the impression is (even if this is not reflected mathematically as such) that the memory (the "global database") is a necessary component of the concept of a "rule based system" (see Waterman and Hayes-Roth [1978], p. 4). This impression is incorrect. In the case of rules, it is less logical to differentiate between different alphabets, or to apply mathematical model theory in order to define the machine state. Nevertheless, it is very useful to be able to know the exact memory state for the examination of rule application. On this basis, and in this context, it is plausible to include DB, the database state space, as a component of the definition D1, that of a rule based system.

6.2.4.3 RI—The Rule Interpreter

Whether RI, the rule interpreter, in S is a backwards or forwards rule interpreter is of little consequence. Both may be regarded as equivalent for these purposes. In practice, though, it emerges that the forward rule interpreter is somewhat simpler to comprehend. This type is therefore preferred and thus assumed in cases where RI is included in the discussions.

6.2.4.4 P—The Problem Domain

The individual problems, called cases, fa[*i*] el P, that the rule based system has to solve are supplied by the user in the relevant application domain. How the individual facts that constitute a case fa[*i*] are supplied (whether, for example, incrementally over one consultation, completely at the beginning of a consultation, or by some other means over more than one consultation) is not relevant for these considerations.

6.2.4.5 L—The Solution Domain

The possible solutions in a rule based system fall in a domain called the solution domain, or L. Individual components of this are consultation results ke[*j*], therefore ke[*j*] el L . It should be noted that these are not dependent on any of the other components of the rule based system S.

6.2.4.6 Problem Solving Instances

The problem solving space of S over P and L (i.e. the set of all possible combinations of cases and consultation results) is obtained as the Cartesian product:

$$P * L$$

However, the only combinations that are of interest are those that form the set of pairs from P * L that are made up from cases fa[*i*] and the case related consultation result ke[*i*]. This is the set of all correctly related combinations of cases and consultation results. These pairs,

$$(fa[i], ke[i] \text{ el } P * L)$$

are termed the "problem solving instances" of S.

In order to handle the set of problem solving instances of S mathematically, the concept of the solution function is introduced. The solution function represents a possibility to normalise the semantics of a rule based system.

6.2.4.7 Definition D2: Rule Based Systems: The Solution Function

If S is a rule based system (V,DB,PR,RI,P,L) assume it is with a set P of possible cases to be submitted to S, and with a set L of possible consultation results from S; and fa[*i*] el P is any case, and ke[*i*] el L the related correct result from fa[*i*] in S.

The solution function

$$f : P \rightarrow L \text{ of } S$$

delivers for every case fa[i] exactly its correct consultation result ke[i]. Symbolically:

$$f(fa[i]) \leftrightarrow ke[i]$$

It is also permitted to write as equivalent (based on the set theoretical meaning of functions) the following:

$$(fa[i],ke[i]) \text{ el } f$$

where f is a total solution function.

6.2.4.8 Computing the Solution Function f

It remains to indicate how f could be calculated. Computational processes on S are in essence deduction processes. Every deduction process on S is commenced with a given case fa[i] el P, and the attempt is made to progress to the associated result f(fa[i]) el L. In order to do this, deduction processes on S have to be formally defined.

6.2.4.9 Definition D3: Rule Based Systems: Deductive Processes

If S is a rule based system, and fa[i] any case from P of S, a deduction process dp over S is a series, thus:

$$\langle d[0],r[0],u[0]\rangle,$$
$$\langle d[1],r[1],u[1]\rangle,$$
$$\ldots,$$
$$\langle d[h],r[h],u[h]\rangle,$$
$$\ldots$$

This series represents a series of discrete process states, where the following hold:

(1) Every process state el dp is described by a triple of the structure

$$\langle d[h],r[h],u[h]\rangle, 0 =< h$$

the so-called state triple. Also, here:

d[h] el DB
r[h] el PR

and u[h] is the most general unifier of r[h] based on a selected literal set from d[h].

(2) The process state dp starts with

fa[*i*] = d[0] .

(3) The process terminates properly when the following is valid:

f(fa[*i*]) ss d[h] .

(4) For all d[h] and r[h], 0=<h the following are valid: (4.1) r[h] is a non-deterministic rule selected from PR:

r[h] <= nd_el_select(PR).

(4.2) The literal set {l[h1],l[h2],...,l[h*n*]} is a subset of a non-deterministic nature of the database state d[h]:

{l[h1],l[h2],...,l[hn]} <= nd_ss_select(d[h]) .

(4.3) u[h] is the most general unifier of {l[h1],...,l[hn]} and the premises prem(r[h]) of r[h]:

u[h] = mgu({l[h1],l[h2],...,l[h*n*]},prem(r[h]))

where "mgu" is the most general unifier, and it is only a partial function.

(4.4) The direct successor database state d[h+1] to d[h] is obtained through the adjunction of the conclusion (unified via u[h]) conc(r[h]) of r[h] to d[h] as follows:

d[h+1] = d[h] + {(conc(r[h])) u[h]}.

6.2.4.10 Recognise—Act Cycle

There is a regular application cycle definable that will achieve the following step:

from ⟨d[h],r[h],u[h]⟩, 0 =<h
to its immediate state successor
⟨d[h+1],r[h+1],u[h+1]⟩, 0 =<h
in dp in a computational step.

This cycle consist of five parts, which will be itemised below:

(1) The non-deterministic selection of

{l[h1],...,l[hn]} ss d[h].

(2) The non-deterministic selection of

r[h] el PR.

(3) Unification Step:
compute and apply u[h];
if successful, go to step (4);
if not successful, and more rules left, go to step (2);
if not successful, and no rules left, go to step (1);
if all r[h] and l[h*i*] exhausted and the computation and application of u[h] is still not successful, then trigger an abnormal termination of the process dp due to inability to unify.

(4) Deduction step:

adjunction of the unified conclusions of r[h] to d[h];
if d[h+1] = d[h] (not a genuine extension adjunction) and rules left, go to step (2);
if d[h+1] = d[h] (not a genuine extension adjunction) and no rules left, go to step (1);
if d[h+1] = d[h] (not a genuine extension adjunction) and possibilities under (1) and (2) are exhausted, then trigger an abnormal termination due to stagnation of the deduction process.

(5) Results step:

f(fa[*i*]) ss d[h+1]?
%

6.2.4.11 Computing the Solution Function—an Example

The definitions D1,D2 and D3 may be easier to understand in the light of an example. In order to keep the example clear, the aspects of predicate logic and unification are excluded, and the example focusses on the assertion aspects. Assertions are symbolised by small letters (i.e. "a").

Suppose S is (V,DB,PR,RI,P,L) where

```
V = {a,b,c,d,e}
DB = { {},
    {a},{b},{c},{d},{e}
    {a,b},{a,c},{a,d},{a,e},
        {b,c},{b,d},{b,e},
            {c,d},{c,e},
                {d,e},
    {a,b,c},{a,b,d},{a,b,e},{a,c,d},{a,c,e},{a,d,e},...
    {a,b,c,d},{a,b,c,e},...
    {a,b,c,d,e}
    }
```

$$
\begin{aligned}
PR &= \{r1,r2,r3\} \text{ with:}\\
&\quad r1 = (\{a\} \rightarrow \{c\})\\
&\quad r2 = (\{c\} \rightarrow \{d\})\\
&\quad r3 = (\{b,c\} \rightarrow \{e\})\\
P &= \{\{a,b\},\{b,c\}\\
L &= \{\{d,e\},\{e\}.
\end{aligned}
$$

and f of S is characterised by the following:

$$\{a,b\} \mapsto \{d,e\}\ ,\ \{b,c\} \mapsto \{e\}.$$

A properly terminating process on S is then described by the following state triple:

$$\langle \{a,b\},r1,\_\rangle,\langle \{a,b,c\},r3,\_\rangle,\langle \{a,b,c,d,e\},r2,\_\rangle,\langle \{a,b,c,d,e\},\_,\_\rangle.$$

Another possible properly terminating deduction process on S can be:

$$\langle \{b,c\},r3,\_\rangle,\langle \{b,c,e\},\_,\_\rangle$$

%

6.2.5 The Database State and Rules—their Logical Relationships

6.2.5.0 Introduction

The mechanisms introduced to date allow the postulation of three trivial theorems. These theorems handle the logical relationships between the database state and the rules in a rule based system.

The theorems are handled here from the point of view of learning aspects, where there are three integrity conditions that are of interest:

— consistency
— completeness
— correctness

under the definitions D4, D5 and D6 described below. These requirements can be expressed with the usual predicate logic forms superimposed on the theorems T1, T2 and T3, but it is also possible to introduce an explicit formal deduction relation between database states relative to the rules in S.

6.2.5.1 Theorem T1: Rule Based Systems: a Computational Step

In this first theorem, the functional properties of the rule interpreter RI are considered. For this, it is sufficient to regard RI as a function that is applied to the actual database state d[h] and with the selected rule r[h] as an argument.

Assume that ⟨d[h],r[h],u[h]⟩ is any state triple of a deduction process dp on a rule based system S.

Then the given database state d[h], and the selected rule r[h] (from RI in

S) logically imply the direct successor state d[h+1], where d[h+1] = RI(d[h],r[h]). Symbolically :

$$d[h] \;\&\; r[h] \rightarrow d[h+1] \quad 0=<h$$

where

$$d[h],d[h+1] \text{ el } DB$$
$$r[h] \text{ el } PR$$
$$d[h+1] = RI(d[h],r[h])$$
%

The proof for T1 may be shown based on the postulated properties of RI, the rule interpreter.

6.2.5.2 Theorem T2: Rule Based Systems: Directly Adjacent Database States

Assume d[h] is any database state under the deduction process dp, and that d[h+1] is the immediate successor state of the database relative to d[h].

Then d[h] and d[h+1] are equivalent under PR. Symbolically:

$$PR \rightarrow (d[h] \leftrightarrow d[h+1]),\ 0=<h$$
%

Whereas the proof of T1 is based on the properties of RI, T2 may be proved using simple assertional logic rules.

6.2.5.3 Theorem T3: Rule Based Systems: Initial State and Partial States of Successor States

Assume that d[0] is any initial state of the database DB of a rule based system under a deduction process dp. Assume d[h] is any successor state of d[0] under dp, and that d[z] is a partial sub-state of d[h].

Then d[0] implies d[z] under PR. Symbolically:

$$PR \rightarrow (D[0] \rightarrow d[z])$$

where

$$d[z] \text{ ss } d[h]$$
$$h=<0$$
%

T3 can be proven similarly to T2. T3 does not require as a precondition that d[0] is an element of the problem domain P, nor that d[z] be an element of the solution domain L of S. These preconditions assume a role in the integrity conditions for rule based systems that are discussed below.

6.2.6 Integrity of a Rule Based System

6.2.6.0 Introduction

In D1 the conceptual preconditions of a rule based system were defined. In the following sections, three conditions for integrity of a rule based system are sketched out. A fourth criterion is also briefly discussed. Integrity conditions are not basic conceptual criteria, but potentially desirable properties of a practical rule based system. The integrity conditions discussed are not globally applicable to a rule based system, but apply only to individual system components.

The conditions formulated here apply either to the rule base PR of a rule based system S, or to the rule interpreter RI of S.

6.2.6.1 Consistency

6.2.6.1.0 Introduction

The first integrity condition to be considered is that of "consistency". Consistency is a property of the rule based system S. In mathematics, based on formal logic and not semantic model theory, the concept of consistency is understood to be the non-deducability of a logical contradiction from a set of formulae. For comparison see Hilbert and Ackermann [1972], p. 98 *et seq*. This concept of consistency, though, is too abstract for investigating the problems of a rule based system and it's associated integrity constraint.

The problems arise from the fact that a rule base is in the last analysis a set of if–then constructs, i.e. a set of implication formulae. For example, consider the trivial rule based system S1 with the trivial rule base PR1 and the problem domain P1. Suppose PR1 contains two rules so that the premises are identical, but the conclusions contradict each other:

$$\mathrm{PR1} = \{(\{\mathrm{p}\} \rightarrow \{\mathrm{c}\}), (\{\mathrm{p}\} \rightarrow \{-\mathrm{c}\})\}$$

Then the assertion "−p" is deducible from PR1. This implies that the common premise to the two rules "p" is False, i.e. not satisfied. A contradiction is not derivable from PR1. Based on the strict mathematical concept, then, PR1 would be viewed as consistent. The derivation of a contradiction is only possible when the cases fa[*i*] el P1 are included in the formation of the current complete deduction base for a consistency check of PR1.

A contradiction may be deduced from PR1 in a given case fa[*i*] only when fa[*i*] and −p are mutually contradictory, in other words when the case fa[*i*] implies the premise p.

6.2.6.1.1 A Concept of Consistency

Because of the problems discussed above, a compromise has to be reached when defining consistency for practical purposes. A consistency definition based purely on the rule based system requirements is an essentially static concept. A definition based on the individual states of the current deduction process is a fully dynamic concept, based on individual case relevances.

Between these two extremes is a semi-dynamic concept for consistency: a case related but process abstracted definition, which will be defined formally below.

6.2.6.1.2 Definition D4: Integrity Conditions: Consistency

Assume S is a rule based system (V,DB,PR,RI,P,L) with the rule base PR. Assume fa[*i*] is any case suitable to be an initial database state for the deduction process dp in S. Finally, assume l[h#] is any literal in any successor state d[h] of fa[*i*] under dp.

Then PR is termed "consistent" ("Cons(PR)") when there are no l[h#] such that PR implies, for any case fa[*i*] el P, the conclusion l[h#] as well as its negation -l[h#]. Symbolically:

Cons(PR) ↔ (A fa[*i*],l[h#])−(fa[*i*] el P
& fa[*i*] & PR → l[h#] &−l[h#])
%

6.2.6.2 Completeness

6.2.6.2.0 Introduction

The second integrity condition to be introduced for a rule based system is that of completeness. The completeness refers to the solution power of a rule base PR in relation to the solution function f of a rule based system S. In this case, it is a concept of semantic completeness which must be differentiated from a syntactic concept in that, amongst other differences, the completeness is measured by a semantic target criterion.

Completeness as a concept cannot be just taken over from mathematics without regard to the context of a rule based system. Even mathematics has a number of semantic based completeness criteria, quite independent of the target criteria. For example, in meta-mathematics one understands the completeness concept of a calculus to be the situation:

> A logic calculus K is complete when the formula A follows logically from the formula set G, and A is derivable from the calculus K from G [Schneider 1983].

Predicate logic and assertion logic of the first order have a complete calculus. Higher order logics have no complete calculus, as shown by Gödel's Incompleteness Theorem [Hofstaedter 1979, 1985].

In relation to a rule based system, completeness is understood to be a relation between PR and f so that PR is at least sufficiently rich so that for any case fa[*i*] el P the associated solution f(fa[*i*]) can be deduced with help from PR.

6.2.6.2.1 Definition D5: Integrity Condition: Completeness

Assume S is a rule based system (V,DB,PR,RI,P,L) with a rule base PR, and that fa[*i*] is any valid case and f(fa[*i*]) the associated consultation result ke[*i*], and f the solution function of S.

Then PR is "complete" with relation to f ("Comp(PR,F)") when for every case fa[*i*] el P the solution f(fa[*i*]) is implied. Symbolically:

$$\text{Comp(PR,f)} \leftrightarrow (\text{A fa}[i])(\text{fa}[i] \text{ el P} \\ \& \text{ fa}[i] \text{ \& PR} \rightarrow \text{f(fa}[i]))$$
%

6.2.6.3 Consistency and Completeness and Göedel's Incompleteness Theorem

We have outlined above two desirable properties of a rule based system. These properties may be reformulated in the language of meta-mathematics as:

— Consistency:
that property that ensures that the set of theorems of the formal system should be exactly consistent (i.e. coincide) with the informal theory.
— Completeness:
that property that ensures that all true statements of a theory are somehow capable of being generated as theorems.

Applying Göedel's Incompletenss Theorem to the above suggests that the two goals are not able to be reached at the same time, for any sufficiently complex theory, which in this case is a significantly complex (i.e. realistic) application of a rule based system. These goals may be approached incrementally, though, using increasingly powerful formulae and theories to improve the approximation of reaching the two goals. The goals cannot be reached by formal methods alone [Hofstaedter 1985, p. 265].

6.2.6.4 Correctness

6.2.6.4.0 Introduction

The third and last significant integrity condition to be introduced is that of correctness. The correctness of a rule based system is in fact the correctness of a rule base PR relative to its solution function f. Correctness is a relation that is in a sense complementary to completeness, but completeness tackles the step from the formal concept to the semantic target criteria, while correctness is relevant to the step from the semantic to the formal concept.

6.2.6.4.1 Definition D6: Integrity Conditions: Correctness

Assume S is a rule based system (V,DB,PR,RI,P,L) with a rule base PR. Assume fa[*i*] el P is any case related to a deduction process dp over S as a database initial state. Assume further that d[z] is a partial state of a complete successor state of fa[*i*] under dp, and that f is the solution function of S.

PR is said to be correct with respect to f ("Corr(PR,f)") when for any case fa[*i*] el P the implied consultation result via PR, d[z] el L, is the result that corresponds exactly to that related to fa[*i*], i.e. that the application of PR to fa[*i*] yields the correct, corresponding result d[z] el P. Symbolically:

Corr(PR,f) ↔ (A fa[*i*],d[z])
((fa[*i*] el P & fa[*i*] & PR →
d[z] & d[z] el L) →
(d[z] ↔ f(fa[*i*])))
%

6.2.6.5 A Fourth Integrity Condition

There is a fourth desirable property for a rule based system to possess, but as it is of very limited consequence for the considerations here, it is only mentioned for "completeness". The rule interpreter RI should also possess integrity. An implementation of RI must possess a sufficiently rich set of tautological inference rules in order to make this requirement at all practicable.

6.2.7 Theorems Related to Integrity

6.2.7.0 Introduction

In the previous sections three properties for integrity have been defined, and a fourth mentioned. They relate to individual components of the rule based system in each case. From these definitions it is possible to formulate some interesting theorems, but whose full explanation is beyond the scope of this text. However, it is important to grasp the scope and implication of such theorems, so a more or less trivial example is developed. The theorem presented deals with the conditions needed to be satisfied in order for a case fa[*i*] to imply its consultation result ke[*i*] in a rule based system.

6.2.7.1 Theorem T4: Rule Based Systems: Cases and their Solutions

Assume S is a rule based system (V,DB,PR,RI,P,L) with a rule base PR, any valid case fa[*i*] el P, and f(fa[*i*]) el L is the related consultation result.

Then S must be complete, so that fa[*i*] and PR together imply f(fa[*i*]). Symbolically:

(A fa[*i*]) (Comp(PR,f)
& fa[*i*] el P & fa[*i*] & PR → f(fa[*i*]))
%

Theorem T4 can be proven by a simple transformation of the definition of the completeness concept D5, hence its almost trivial status.

6.2.8 Implementation

A PROLOG implemented rule based system based on the given definitions is relatively easy to realise, with the exception of directly implemented backward chaining of the rules. The rule base PR of S is loaded as a PROLOG program together with the case to be solved fa[*i*]. The solution f(fa[*i*]) is formulated as a PROLOG query. Therefore individual situations can be prototyped quite rapidly.

6.3 AUTOMATIC LEARNING

6.3.0 Introduction

The concept of automatic learning has already been discussed in terms of a number of criterion. The fifth criterion of this discussion required an extension or optimisation of the problem solving capability of the system. These criteria can be decomposed into three disjunctive sub-criteria:

(1) the quantitative extension of,
(2) the qualitative improvement of, and
(3) the complexity reducing, more effective

rule based system problem solving capability.

In this way, three orthogonal learning types are established, called "learning categories". In the following section, these learning types or categories are examined individually, and it will become apparent that there are major differences in the method and results of learning to be employed.

6.3.1 Learning Category 1: Extension of the Problem Solving Capability

6.3.1.1 Learning Goal and Learning Criteria

Assume S is a rule based system (V,DB,PR,RI,P,L), and S′ is also a rule based system (V′,DB′,PR′,RI′,P′,L′), and that RI = RI′ (i.e. so that S′ = (V′,DB′,PR′,RI′,P′,L′). The learning goal may then be defined in terms of the increment in the solution function f.

6.3.1.1 Definition D7: Learning Category 1: Learning Goal

The learning goal of learning in learning category 1 (extension) is, starting from a rule based system S with solution function f: P→ L′ to construct a rule based system S′ with the solution function f′: P′ → L, by "learning" so that f′ of S′ is genuinely more powerful than f of S.

Symbolically, in the sense of the relational meaning of functions as sets of ordered (argument,value) pairs, the definition D7 may be written as:

$$f \text{ ss } f' \ \& \ f =|= f'$$

or, equivalently, as:

$$|f| < |f'|$$

%

Therefore the essence of the learning goal in learning category 1 (extension) is to transform S with f into S′ with f′, where f′ is more powerful as a solution function. This also implies that the problem solving behaviour of S′, inasmuch as it effects only the component P, is not altered with respect to that of S. The new solution function f′ is identical to f if one confines one's consideration of P′ to that which refers to the original component P of S. A transformation from S to S′ is termed a learning step.

Based on these definitions, the only modification of the learning behaviour of S′ relative to the original learning behaviour of S consists of the extension of the solution function f′ relative to that of f, the solution function of S. After the learning step, the extended problem domain P′ of S′ has to be completely covered by f′, i.e. the extension of the problems solving capability has to be covered by the incremental extension of the solution function from f to f′.

The difference between f and f′ is now introduced, as:

$$\text{delta-f} = f' - f.$$

The learning goal of learning category 1 (extension) can now be reformulated by stating that delta-f must be non-empty, symbolically:

delta-f =|= {}.

A well-formulated learning goal could also be used to decide if learning had taken place. If the goal is reached, by implication, learning has taken place at some stage in some manner. On this basis, learning goals may be also termed as a learning criterion.

6.3.2 Learning Strategy

6.3.2.0 Introduction

Assume S is a rule based system (V,DB,PR,RI,P,L), and S′ is also a rule based system (V′,DB′,PR′,RI′,P′,L′), and that RI = RI′ (i.e. so that S′ = (V′,DB′,PR′,RI′,P′,L′), and that f: P → L is the solution function. The learning goal in this learning category consisted of extensions to f by delta-f, delta-P → L′; so that f′ : P′ → L′ is reached by a genuine learning extension.

Any method that achieves this extension is termed a learning strategy.

In order to extend f to f′, S has to be transformed to S′. In order to change S, at least one of the six components have to be modified. The components V, DB and RI are unsuitable. As P and L are dependent on f in terms of the domain of applicability, the same dependencies apply for P′, L′ and f′ and therefore the means of reaching the learning goal under definition D7. Therefore only the rule base PR is a possible component of S that is a candidate to accommodate a learning strategy.

If

delta-PR = PR′ − PR
%

the learning strategy consists, as a necessity, of taking PR and adding certain rules (the set delta-PR of rules) to create PR′ (rule based extension) so that f is extended to f′. From a practical point of view, the rule base is ideal for this, as it is composed entirely of single rules, and it is built up in a modular fashion.

Therefore it is crucial, for the learning step S to S′, which rules are chosen to be in the rule base extension sêt delta-PR. The making of this choice is not without problems, as the initial solution function f associated with the learning step S to S′ should not be utilised for this purpose.

However, the relationship between PR, delta-PR, PR′, f and f′ allows four interesting theorems to be developed (T5 to T8). These theorems, when applied to the problem, ease the selection of rules when attempting to form a suitable extension rule set delta-PR.

6.3.2.1 Theorem T5: Learning Category 1: Learning Step S to S′, under Conservation of Consistency

Assume S is a rule based system with the rule base PR, problem domain P and that S′ is a rule based system with rule base PR′, then:

PR′ = PR + delta-PR
P′ = P + delta-P

Furthermore, assume that dp is a deduction process of S′, fa[*i*] a case from P′ and r[g] a rule from PR′. Then if the rule base extension delta-PR is consistent, then the consistency of the rule base PR is conserved under the learning extension from S to S′. Symbolically:

```
Cons(PR) & Cons(delta-PR)
  & (A dp)(A r[g])(A fa[i])
    (dp = ⟨fa[i],$,$⟩, ... , ⟨$,r[g],$⟩, ...
      & 1=<g →
        (fa[i] el P → r[g] el R)
          & (fa[i] el delta-P →
            r[g] el delta-PR) )
              → Cons(PR′)
                %
```

T5 may be proved relatively easily, by inverting the theorem and using appropriate statements about the nature of the problem domain with which cases fa[*i*] are associated.

At first sight, T5 may not appear particularly plausible. To understand T5 though, recall that f, as well as delta-f and the corresponding computational pre-requisites for PR and delta-PR, are assumed to be disjunct. That means that the "old" rule base PR refers to the "old" problem domain P, even after the extension from S to S′. The new problem domain extension delta-P (to accomplish P to P′) is handled purely by rules in the "new" extension rule base delta-P. If one wished to use T5 in practice, then the non-trivial problem is to ensure that the conditions stipulated are in fact met.

6.3.2.2 Theorem T6: Learning Category 1: Learning Sep S to S′ with Conservation of Correctness

Assume S is a rule based system with the rule base PR and the solution function f, and similarily that S′ is a rule based system with a rule base PR′, and solution function f′. Assume that delta-PR is the difference between the respective rule bases, and delta-f the difference between the respective solution functions.

Then if delta-PR is a correct rule base extension relating to delta-f, the correctness of the rule base during the extension of S to S′ is conserved. Symbolically:

Corr(PR,f) & Corr(delta-PR,delta-f) → Corr(PR′,f′)
%

The proof of T6 is much more difficult than that of T5, and is too extensive to be recapitulated here.

6.3.2.3 Theorem T7: Learning Category 1: Learning Step S to S′ under Conservation of Completeness

Assume that S is a rule based system with rule base PR and solution function f, and similarly that S′ is a rule based system with rule base PR′, and solution function f′. Assume that delta-PR is the difference between the respective rule bases, and delta-f the differences between the respective solution functions.

Then if delta-PR is a complete rule base extension relating to delta-f, the completeness of the rule base during the extension of S to S′ is conserved. Symbolically:

Comp(PR,f) & Comp(delta-PR,delta-f) →
Comp(PR′,f′)
%

The proof of T7 is again more difficult than that of T5, and is too extensive to be recapitulated here, but it is similar in nature to the proof of theorem T6.

6.3.2.4 Theorem T8: Learning Category 1: Learning Step S to S′ under Conservation of Integrity

The theorems T5 to T7 may be combined to form one integrated theorem. Assume S and S′ are as defined in theorems T5, T6 and T7. Assume dp is a deduction process of S′, fa[*i*] a case of P′ and r[g] a rule from PR′.

Then the system's integrity is maintained in the extension learning step from S to S′, assuming that delta-PR has the properties of "integrity" relative to delta-f. Symbolically, this may be written as an adjunction of the three individual conditions thus :

Cons(PR) & Cons(delta-PR) &

```
Corr(PR,f) & Corr(delta-PR,delta-f)   &
Comp(PR,f) & Comp(delta-PR,delta-f) &
  (A dp)(A r[g])(A fa[i])
  (dp = ⟨fa[i],$,$⟩, ... , ⟨$,r[g],$⟩, ...
    & 1=<g →
    (fa[i] el P → r[g] el PR)
      & (fa[i] el delta-P →
        r[g] el delta-PR) )
  → Cons(PR′) & Corr(PR′,f′) & Comp(PR′,f′)
  %
```

6.3.2.5 Conditions for use of Theorem T8

With the background of T8, the conditions for an integrity conserving use of a learning strategy of learning category 1 (extension) during a rule based system extension are established. In brief,

— completeness
— correctness
— consistency

must be maintained. These conditions allow the formulation of a slightly weakened but practically useful set of conditions to be defined for implementation in a rule based system S. In order to transform an integral (i.e. one possessing integrity) rule based system S with solution function f into an equally integral rule based system S′ with solution function f′ by means of a genuine learning extension delta-f which extends f to f′, seven conditions can be listed which need to apply:

(1) Initially, at the commencement of the learning step S with f and PR, the following must apply:
  (1.1) PR must be consistent
  (1.2) PR must be correct relative to f
  (1.3) PR must be complete relative to f.

(2) It is required to obtain a delta-PR such that:
  (2.1) delta-PR must be consistent
  (2.2) delta-PR must be correct relative to delta-f
  (2.3) delta-PR must be complete relative to delta-f
  (2.4) delta-PR is responsible for the cases in delta-P in isolation, and PR remains covering that set of cases in P which it covered at the beginning of the learning step, at a time S.

These are the seven essential practical conditions that have to be fulfilled.

6.3.2.6 Theorem T9: Learning Category 1: Necessary Conditions for the Learning Goal "Extension of the Solution Function"

The last theorem is relatively trivial, but it does cover the relation between the learning goal of learning category 1 ("extension") on the one hand, and that of the problem domain and solution domain on the other hand (i.e. P, P′, L and L′ of S and S′ respectively).

Assume that S and S′ are rule base systems with solution functions f and f′ respectively, and P and P′ as problem domains with L and L′ as solution domains. Also:

delta-P = P′ - P
%

Then, in order for the goal of an extension learning step to be met, a genuine extension of P to P′ is required. Symbolically:

f ss f′ & f =|= f′ →
P ss P′ & P =|= P′ & L ss L′
%

Or, equivalently:

f ss f′ & f =|= f′ →
delta-P =|= {} & L ss L′
%

In words, the theorem states that the learning goal of learning category 1 is only reached when the problem domain of P in S is extended by at least one case fa[*i*], to reach P′. Note that the solution domain L′ of S′ can, theoretically, be identical to L of S, but would then have to be more powerful in its problem solving capability.

6.3.3 Learning Types.

6.3.3.0 Introduction

At the level immediately below the learning strategies, the individual learning tactics (the so-called learning tasks) are classified by numerous criteria. These overlap partially, extend each other, or can be mutually excluding or reinforcing. The classification is still highly problematical [Carbonell *et al.* 1983]. In this chapter, the classification is made in accordance with the style of the related learning input. As the existing categorisations were not satisfactory, this section attempts to reconstruct all possible learning types that could apply e.g. to section 6.2.2: where learning category 1 was defined as the extension of problem solving capabilities of a rule based system.

This reconstruction carries with it its (pragmatic) price. The reconstructed use of language in learning categories and learning types differs—as is in the nature of reconstructions—and these differences are not insignificant from the normal use of language. The following learning types presented below are listed in reducing order of information content of the learning input forms.

6.3.3.1 Learning by Instruction

6.3.3.1.1 A Definition

The term "learning by instruction" for the extension of the solution function f of a rule based system S is understood to be a particular type of automatic learning by S. This must work in such a way that S can, given a full specification of the finite or infinite solution function extension delta-f, generate the extension rule set delta-PR. The individual cases follow below.

6.3.3.1.2 Learning Input

Learning by instruction assumes as learning input (i.e. the learning source) that the function delta-f to be added to f of S is given in a full (descriptive) specification. If (fa[i],ke[i]) is any problem instance, delta-P, the definition domain and L′ the range domain of delta-f, then the following classes of input have to be specified:

(1) delta-P
(2) L′
(3) {(fa[*i*],ke[*i*]) | delta-f(fa[*i*]) ↔ ke[*i*]} where delta-f: delta-P → L′
(note that the above infact specify delta-f)

If delta-f is finite, then the specification of (3) can consist of the enumerated set of individual problem solution instances, even though it is a little less elegant. If one wishes to make the implementation as easy as possible, then the generation of the extension rules can be readily accomplished using the ordering of cases fa[*i*], given by the problem solving instances, as a basis for allocating the appropriate solutions. The finite property of delta-f is theoretically as unlikely as the practical possibility that it will occur. However, if delta-f cannot be enumerated in some way, then the unavoidable finite nature of the specification poses some problems. Then a finite form of specification that cannot be enumerated must be chosen.

6.3.3.1.3 Learning Output

Learning by instruction requires, as output, "learning objects" to generate the extension rule set delta-PR, with which the original rule base PR in S is to be extended through learning to S′. The set delta-PR is a computational prerequisite for delta-f. The extension rule set delta-PR is common to all learning types of learning category 1 (extension) as a minimum output (see sections 6.2.3.2.2 and 6.2.3.3.2).

6.3.3.1.4 Learning Tasks/Learning Methods

Generally, the automatic learning system of S has to perform certain assignments in order to accomplish a learning step. These learning assignments are characteristic of each learning type. They are called "learning tasks". A learning step by instruction consists of only one learning task. A full, descriptive functional specification of an operational prescription for the computation of, the specific function delta-f is the step which is to be accomplished.

This learning task is the "operationalisation" task.

The operationalisation task has substantial problems in common with those in automatic programming. Learning by instruction is additionally characterised by the fact that functional specifications and computational pre-requisites can be expressed in the same language—the tokens in V′ of S′ (where S′ = (V′,DB′,PR′,RI,P′,L′)). This is not the case in automatic programming where the transformation is from a descriptive to a somewhat different operational language. The learning task only uses one language.

6.3.3.1.5 Learning Agents/Learning Roles

Generally, learning types differentiate themselves by the number of carriers that are used in a complete learning step. These carriers are called learning agents. Also, there are characteristics of how the learning roles are distributed over the agents. These individual roles within a complete learning step, taken as a whole, represent a characteristic distribution of the learning task over the learning agents. Learning by instruction requires that two learning agents participate in each learning step:

— the (automatic) learner
— the (automatic) tutor.

The role of the learner is to "operationalise" the specification of delta-f supplied from the instruction by the tutor. The role of the tutor is to instruct the pupil (learner) fully as regards the requirements to correctly (and completely) specify delta-f.

6.3.3.1.6 Value for Knowledge Acquisition

Of the five essential phases of the knowledge acquisition process, learning by instruction affects mainly the implementation and test phases.

6.3.3.1.7 Validation Criteria

The output generated in a learning step must be subjected to validation criteria. Based on Theorem T8, the relevant validation criteria can be defined. T8 states that the output, the extension rule base delta-PR, must be:

(1) consistent
(2) correct relative to delta-f (the given input)
(3) complete relative to delta-f.

In short, delta-PR must have integrity.

6.3.3.1.8 Exactness, Another Validation Criterion?

Sometimes, in an application domain the rules are already available in a natural format. Examples of these are in:

— legal definitions
— physical laws
— engineering definitions.

In these cases it may be considered useful if, above the requirement for the integrity in the rule set to be learned, a fourth validation criterion could be introduced. This fourth criterion may be termed "exactness", being in a pragmatic sense the measure of similarity between a learned rule and a "natural" rule.

6.3.3.1.9 Learning Resources

Learning assumes that the learner, independent of the variable learning input, has at his permanent disposal more or less powerful means of learning called "learning resources". These must be sufficient to accomplish a learning step. Generally four types of learning resources are distinguished:

— application independent knowledge
— application dependent knowledge
— domain independent knowledge processors
— domain dependent knowledge processors.

Knowledge processors are necessary for the application of knowledge. The term "domain independent knowledge processors" means those that are capable of handling application independent knowledge as well as application dependent knowledge. The term "domain dependent knowledge processors" means those processors that can only process domain dependent knowledge, and therefore not knowledge from other domains. The differentiation drawn here between knowledge and knowledge processors is only a terminological distinction at the conceptual level. It should not imply that processor and knowledge should necessarily be separated in the strict systems architectural sense. Knowledge (procedural) can also reside inside the processor and thus appear hidden.

The four types of learning resources are not relevant to the same extent for all learning types; indeed, some are totally redundant under specific learning types. Conversely, the individual learning types differentiate themselves by the nature and quantity of the required learning resources.

6.3.3.1.10 Application Independent Knowledge

Learning by instruction requires that the pupil (i.e. learner) is conversant with:

— the generation of rules in general (so called general rule generators)
— the execution of rules
— the consistency of rule sets.

6.3.3.1.11 Application Dependent Knowledge
Learning by instruction requires that the pupil (i.e. learner) is conversant with:

— the language of formulation of the rules (i.e. V′ of S′)
— the ability to decide the completeness of the rule set.

Additionally, there are two ways in which the pupil can be helped in the "operationalisation" objective during learning by instruction. The first is a sufficiently rich and powerful formulation of a rule constructing language allowing use of standard rule constructs as often as possible. Secondly, the construction of an application dependent rule library is a very practical aid for operationalisation. Unfortunately, it is not possible to create a rule library as a learning resource in isolation; it has to be compatible with a broader and application independent management of the library, bearing in mind that further knowledge objects will be deposited into S′ during the learning process.

6.3.3.1.12 Domain Independent Knowledge Processors
Learning by instruction requires three sorts of knowledge processors:

— a rule generator
— a rule interpreter
— a rule validator.

The rule generator accesses the general rule generator and the rule language, as well as the relevant knowledge objects. The rule interpreter must have knowledge about the rule execution. The rule validator accesses that knowledge that is required for the validation criteria to be checked and tested, i.e.

— consistency
— correctness
— completeness
— (possibly) exactness.

6.3.3.1.13 Domain Dependent Knowledge Processors
These are not required for learning by instruction.

6.3.3.2 Learning by Example

6.3.3.2.0 Introduction
It is understood that the term "learning by example," for the purpose of extending the solution function f of a rule based system S, refers to automatic learning by S so that it generates, from the finite extension solution function delta-f, the extension rule base set delta-PR (subject to certain partial specification requirements of delta-f). The individual aspects are now considered in sequence.

6.3.3.2.1 Learning Input

In learning by example, it is required that a finite part of the function delta-f which is to be added to f of S during the learning step to S′ has to be defined. This must be in the form of a partial specification of a finite subset of delta-f, the so-called "extension examples".

For learning by example, it is sufficient to have learning input that is weakened in two senses relative to learning by instruction. In the first case, it is sufficient at the specification level to specify delta-f only partially, rather than make a complete specification as required under learning by instruction. Secondly, learning by example requires, at the level of delta-f, the definition of only a finite part of delta-f. Even infinite example sets have to be specified in a bounded manner. Learning from an infinite example set is similar to learning through a finite specification of an infinite extension function delta-f; which is essentially learning by instruction. Therefore this discussion confines itself to the finite case here.

Assume that there are n specific problem solving instances ("examples"), so then:

$$(\text{fa}[i],\text{ke}[i]),\ 1 <= i <= n)$$

Further, assume that delta-P is the definition domain and L the range domain of delta-f. As input for learning by example, the following classes of input have to be available:

(1) delta-P
(2) L′
(3) $\{(\text{fa}[i],\text{ke}[i]) \mid \text{delta-f}(\text{fa}[i]) \leftrightarrow \text{ke}[i]\ \&\ 1 <= i <= n)\}$
(4) $\{(\text{fa}[j],\text{ke}[j]) \mid -\text{delta-f}(\text{fa}[j]) \leftrightarrow \text{ke}[j]\ \&\ 1 <= j <= m)\}$

The set described under (3) above can be easily specified by an enumeration of $(\text{fa}[i],\text{ke}[i]), \ldots, (\text{fa}[n],\text{ke}[n])$ of the individual problem solving instances. The generated rule set delta-PR must be able functionally to cover this example set in a positive sense (i.e. so-called "positive examples").

It may be equally necessary or helpful for the generation in delta-PR in certain application domains to give certain additional examples which delta-PR must NOT cover under any circumstances.

These are called "negative examples". If this is so, then the category of input defined in (4) above is necessary. However, it is not clear that this type of learning by negative examples is at all useful as a learning input in typical rule based systems encountered to date.

In artificial intelligence there is a further differentiation between selected and non-selected examples [Carbonell *et al.* 1983], but this is not pursued here.

6.3.3.2.2 Learning Output

In learning by example, just as in the case of learning by instruction, the output that has to be generated is the extension rule set delta-PR, with which the rule set PR of S is extended in the learning step from S to S′.

6.3.3.2.3 Learning Tasks/Learning Methods
In the framework of learning steps and learning by example, two learning tasks are defined:

— operationalisation
— induction.

The first is required because learning by example has to produce operational rules from the descriptive problem solving instances. This is similar to the situation in learning by instruction.

Induction is necessary because, unlike in the situation of learning by instruction, starting with a finite subset of problem solving instances, and thus a finite part of delta-f, the extension rule set delta-PR must be generated. This must be done in such a way that delta-PR represents some sort of general computational pre-requisite for the whole function delta-f.

6.3.3.2.4 Learning Agents/Role Distribution
In learning by example, it is required that there are two learning agents called "teacher" or "tutor" and "pupil" or "learner", just as in learning by instruction.

The role of the learner in learning by example is to take the examples submitted by the tutor and to produce by induction a full specification of delta-f, and to "operationalise" this specification. The learner therefore has a dual role to play in this case—and correspondingly the role played by the tutor has to go some way towards that required for partial learning by instruction. Relative to learning by instruction, in learning by example the role of the learner is greater, and that of the tutor reduced. The responsibility for achieving the learning is moved to the learner, rather than residing in the tutor. This tendency away from the role played by the tutor continues throughout the remaining categories of learning types in learning category 1 (extension).

6.3.3.2.5 Value for Knowledge Acquisition
Of the five essential phases of the knowledge acquisition process, learning by example is relevant to the phases "formalisation", "implementation" and "test". Relative to learning by instruction, therefore, a further phase of knowledge acquisition is affected by learning by example, prior to those affected by learning by instruction.

6.3.3.2.6 Validation Criteria
The criteria relevant for validation of the learning by example rule set delta-PR are the same as those for learning by instruction (see section 6.3.3.1.7). In this case, however, there is no consideration for a fourth validation criterion, unlike that in section 6.3.3.1.8.

6.3.3.2.7 *Learning Resources*

The cumulative occurrence of learning tasks such as "operationalisation" and induction requireslearning by example to have other resources than those necessary for learning by instruction. There are four possible categories of learning resources that may apply. These are listed in the following four sections (6.3.3.2.8 to 6.3.3.2.11), related to those aspects of the current context.

6.3.3.2.8 *Application Independent Knowledge*

Learning by instruction requires that the pupil (i.e. learner) is conversant with:

— the generation of rules in general (so-called general rule generators)
— the execution of rules
— the consistency of rule sets.

In this, learning by example is identical to learning by instruction.

6.3.3.2.9 *Application Dependent Knowledge*

In learning by example, it is required that the pupil meets the following criteria:
— familiarity with the rule generation in certain application domains (i.e. specific rule generation instances)
— awareness of a model or theory of the application domain.

Learning by example additionally requires that the pupil (i.e. learner) is conversant with:

— the language of formulation of the rules (i.e. V′ of S′)
— the ability to decide the completeness of the rule set.

Additionally, there are two ways in which the pupil can be helped in the "operationalisation" objective during learning by example. The first is a sufficiently rich and powerful formulation of a rule constructing language allowing use of standard rule constructs as often as possible. Secondly, the construction of an application dependent rule library is a very practical aid for operationalisation. Unfortunately, it is not possible to create a rule library as a learning resource in isolation; it has to be compatible with a broader and application independent management of the library, bearing in mind that further knowledge objects will be deposited into S′ during the learning process. This latter set of requirements is therefore identical to learning by instruction.

6.3.3.2.10 *Domain Independent Knowledge Processors*

Learning by example requires three sorts of knowledge processors:

— a rule generator
— a rule interpreter
— a rule validator.

The rule generator accesses the general rule generator and the rule language, as well as the relevant knowledge objects. The rule interpreter must have knowledge about the rule execution. The rule validator accesses that knowledge which is required for the validation criteria to be checked and tested, i.e.

— consistency
— correctness
— completeness.

6.3.3.2.11 Domain Independent Knowledge Processors
Domain independent knowledge processors are not required under learning by example, again as for learning by instruction.

6.3.3.3 Learning by Observation
6.3.3.3.1 Learning by Observation — Definition
Under learning by observation in order to achieve the extension of the solution function f of a rule based system S to S′, it is understood that automatic learning by S is such that a finite set of real (is-state, shall-state) pairs be acquired by passive observation of the application domain. Through this observation, the extension rule set delta-PR is generated. The individual components are discussed below.

6.3.3.3.2 Learning Input
In learning by observation, it is required that the learner/pupil in the application domain observes a finite set of real, problem solving processes. These observations are analysed and an initial process state is identified, termed an is-state. A final process state associated with every initial process state is identified and termed a shall-state. Overall, this generates a finite ordered set of (is-state, shall-state) pairs of observations. From this, a formulation of an observation/measurement language for V and V′ in S and S′ respectively is possible.

If is[*i*] is any real is-state, and ss[*i*] the related real shall-state in the application domain, then learning by observation requires specification of the following classes of the language U:

$$\{(is[i],ss[i]) \mid 1 =< i =< n\}$$

The language U is an observation/measurement language to enable the direct representation of so-called "basic" statements of the real application domain.

In the terminology of scientific theory, the parallel could be drawn with consideration of the three-step concept in the natural sciences where

$$\text{Theory} = \text{Empirical Base} + \text{Correspondence} + \text{Pure Theory}.$$

In this case, U may seem be seen as an empirical base language, whereas V and V′ are purely theoretical languages in S and S′ respectively. U is more concrete, but less abstract than V or V′ would be in general.

In moving from learning by example to learning by observation, the demand on the requirement for the contents of the learning input has been further relaxed.

6.3.3.3.3 Learning Output

In learning by observation, three outputs have to be generated. These are:

(1) the extension of delta-P of the problem domain P of S to P′ of S′
(2) the solution domain L′ of S′ and, primarily:
(3) the extension rule set delta-PR.

Note that only the third output, regarding delta-PR, is common to the output already discussed for the other two learning types, learning by instruction (see section 6.3.3.1.3) and learning by example (see 6.3.3.2.2) of learning category 1 ("extension").

6.3.3.3.4 Learning Tasks and Methods

The learner/pupil has to accomplish three learning tasks at every learning step, being:

— operationalisation
— induction
— transformation.

In addition to the "learning by example" learning tasks of operationalisation and induction, the task of transformation is added as a third learning task. This is necessary, as the transformation is actually that of translating the U-represented observation set into a V′ specified example set. This transformation establishes correspondence between empirical basic statements in U and the corresponding literal constructs in V′.

The transformation is similar to the correspondence encountered in the three-phase theory of natural science mentioned above. This is usually with the aid of correspondence rules between the base and the pure theory components. The problems that arise in science theory and in learning in this context are closely related. Generally, one may summarise learning by observation to be the situation where an "old" theory in a given rule based system S in a selected application domain is replaced by a new theory S′, which is inclusive of the observations in the domain made during the S to S′ learning step.

6.3.3.3.5 Learning Agents/Role Distribution

Learning by observation requires, as opposed to learning by instruction or learning by example, only a learner and no longer any type of tutor. Instead of the tutor, there is only the anonymous systems environment, without taking any learning role in the learning process whatsoever. The learner/pupil has to carry out three learning roles in this scenario:

— operationalisation
— induction

— transformation.

The responsibility for the success of the learning process is completely concentrated in the learner for the "learning by observation" type of learning. There is no longer an apportioning of responsibilities as in learning by instruction and learning by example.

6.3.3.3.6 Value for Knowledge Acquisition

Of the five essential steps in the knowledge acquisition process, learning by observation affects the four phases:

— conceptualisation
— formalisation
— implementation
— testing.

Therefore, relative to learning by example, learning by observation affects one further phase which immediately precedes those affected by learning by example and learning by instruction.

6.3.3.3.7 Validation Criteria

The criteria for validation of the rule set delta-PR generated from the learning type "learning by observation" are the same as those for learning by instruction and learning by example (see sections 6.3.3.1.7 and 6.3.3.2.6).

6.3.3.3.8 Learning Resources

There are even more learning tasks in learning by observation than in the previously discussed learning types:

— operationalisation
— induction
— transformation.

Therefore, it is a consequence that more learning resources have to be made available for learning by observation than for the other types discussed so far. These are listed below individually (sections 6.3.3.3.9 to 6.3.3.3.12).

6.3.3.3.9 Application Independent Knowledge

In learning by observation, it is assumed that the learner is familar with the following:

— the general rule generation
— the rule execution
— the consistency of rule sets.

This resource requirement is identical to that for learning by instruction and learning by example.

6.3.3.3.10 Application Dependent Knowledge
There are some requirements for the learner under learning by observation. These are that he must be:

— conversant with the observation/measurement language U
— capable of evaluation of the observations
— able to achieve the transform from U to V′.

In addition to the above, the needs of the learner must also include the following:

— familiarity with the rule generation in certain application domains (i.e. specific rule generation instances)
— awareness of a model or theory of the application domain
— knowledge of the language of formulation of the rules (i.e. V′ of S′)
— the ability to decide the completeness of the rule set
— knowledge about the formulation of rule constructs.

Additionally, there are two ways in which the pupil can be helped in the "operationalisation" objective during learning by observation. The first is a sufficiently rich and powerful formulation of a rule constructing language allowing use of standard rule constructs as often as possible. Secondly, the construction of an application dependent rule library is a very practical aid for operationalisation. Unfortunately, it is not possible to create a rule library as a learning resource in isolation; it has to be compatible with a broader and application independent management of the library, bearing in mind that further knowledge objects will be deposited into S′ during the learning process.

6.3.3.3.10 Domain Independent Knowledge Processors
Just as for learning by instruction and learning by example, learning by observation requires the same three domain independent knowledge processors:

— a rule generator
— a rule interpreter
— a rule validator.

6.3.3.3.12 Domain Dependent Knowledge Processors
Unlike learning by instruction by example, learning by observation requires three different domain dependent knowledge processors, being:

— a receptor for observation of the selected application domain
— an observation evaluator for representation of the observations in the observation/measurement language U
— a transformer for language translation from U to V′.

The observation evaluator requires knowledge of the observation language U, as well as application independent knowledge about the evaluation of the observations in the application domain. The transformed needs to access the knowledge about the language transformation of U to V′. The receptor performs the work of observing in the application domain. Therefore it does not function as a knowledge processor in the strictest sense, but more like a scheduler/planner.

6.3.3.4 Learning by Experiment

6.3.3.4.0 Introduction

Under the term "learning by experiment," in order to extend the solution function delta-f of a rule based system S to S′ with solution function f′, automatic learning by S is necessary. In order to accomplish this learning, S must capture a finite set of real (is-state, shall-state) pairs through active experimentation in its application domain. From this set, the extension rule set delta-PR is generated.

6.3.3.4.1 Learning Input

In learning by experiment, it is assumed as input that the learner investigates a finite set of real problem solving processes in the application domain. The result of the experimentation with these processes, via the identification of the appropriate end state of a process as a shall-state with the relevant initial state is-state, gives rise to a finite ordered set of (is-state, shall-state) pairs ("experiments") in the observation/measurement language U.

Given that is[*i*] is any real is-state, and that ss[*i*] is the associated real shall-state in the application domain, then learning by experiment requires a specification of the scope of:

$$\{(\mathrm{is}[i],\mathrm{ss}[i]) \mid 1 =< i =< n\}$$

Therefore, learning by experiment is no different from learning by observation in its input requirements, but only in the nature of acquisition of the input. In moving to learning by experiment from learning by observation, the learning load placed on the learner is not increased (as in learning by observation it is already at a maximum in that there is no tutor role or task), but the learner's role in input knowledge acquisition is greater.

6.3.3.4.2 Learning Output

In view of the above similarities, it is reasonable to expect that the outputs are the same for learning by experiment as they are for learning by observation, and this is indeed the case.

6.3.3.4.3 Learning Tasks and Methods

Every learning step from S to S′ has to complete four major tasks, being:

— operationalisation
— induction
— transformation
— experimentation.

The first, operationalisation, occurs in learning by observation although the observations are passive. Induction and transformation tasks have also been covered in the relevant earlier sections—the requirements under learning by experiment are the same. The additional task, that of experimentation, is added in learning by experiment because the learner/pupil is responsible for the availability of his own input.

6.3.3.4.4 Learning Agents/Role Distribution
In learning by experiment, the learner/pupil has to assume all the four roles listed in section 6.3.3.4.3. Otherwise there are no variations between learning by experiment and learning by observation in the characteristics of learning agents and their role distribution.

6.3.3.4.5 Value for Knowledge Acquisition
Learning by experiment has the same value for the various phases than learning by observation (see section 6.3.3.3.6).

6.3.3.4.6 Validation Criteria
Learning by experiment has the same validation criteria as learning by observation (see section 6.3.3.3.7).

6.3.3.4.7 Learning Resources
Because of the great loading placed on the learner, in that all four learning tasks are allocated to him (see section 6.2.3.4.4), learning by experiment requires slightly different learning resources than learning by observation. There are also additional needs to cope with the new task "experimentation".

These resources are itemised in the next four sections.

6.3.3.4.8 Application Independent Knowledge
In learning by experiment, it is assumed that the learner is conversant with the following:

— the general rule generator
— rule execution
— the consistency of rule sets.

Note that all four learning types of learning category 1 ("extension") have the same application independent knowledge requirements.

6.3.3.4.9 Application Dependent Knowledge
The learner is expected to be informed about the following under learning by experiment:

— planning of experiments in the application domain
— strategy of experiments
— nature and form of the evaluation of the experiments.

As well as the above specific requirements, the other expectations include familiarity with:

— the observation/measurement language U
— the ability to achieve the transform from U to V′
— rule generation in certain application domains (i.e. specific rule generation instances)
— awareness of a model or theory of the application domain
— knowledge of the language of formulation of the rules (i.e. V′ of S′)
— the ability to decide the completeness of the rule set
— knowledge about the formulation of rule constructs.

However, it is possible to dispense with the knowledge about the evaluation of the observations, as this knowledge is more than covered by the requirements for knowledge about experiment planning and experiment evaluation. Additionally, there are two ways in which the pupil can be helped in the "operationalisation" objective during learning by observation. The first is a sufficiently rich and powerful formulation of a rule constructing language allowing use of standard rule constructs as often as possible. Secondly, the construction of an application dependent rule library is a very practical aid for operationalisation. Unfortunately, it is not possible to create a rule library as a learning resource in isolation; it has to be compatible with a broader and application independent management of the library, bearing in mind that further knowledge objects will be deposited into S′ durint the learner process.

6.3.3.4.10 Domain Independent Knowledge Processors

In learning by experiment, there are three processors needed, as already expounded in the other three learning types:

— a rule generator
— a rule interpreter
— a rule validator.

6.3.3.4.11 Domain Dependent Knowledge Processors

Domain dependent processors required for learning by experiment are:

— an actor/receptor for
  — execution of the experiments
  — collection/reception of the results of the completed experiments
— an experiment planner to plan the proposed experiments and strategies to complete the experiment set
— an experiment evaluator to enable a representation of the experimental results in the observation/measurement language U
— a transformer for the language translation of U to V′.

The actor executes the planning drawn up by the experiment planner. The receptor/collector takes the results of these experiments and makes them available to the experiment evaluator. In these cases, it is not a knowledge processor activity in the strictest sense, however. The experiment planner uses the knowledge about the planned experimentation in the application domain. The experiment evaluator requires the language U and the transformer of the knowledge of the language transformation of U to V′.

6.3.3.5 Learning Category 1 "Extension", Cost/Benefit Considerations

If all learning types of the "extension" category are considered on a cost/benefit basis, an interesting result is obtained. Moving from learning by instruction through to learning by exapmle, to learning by observation and lastly to learning by experiment, the initial content of the respective learning input is reduced at every step. The learning resources, though, as demanded from the learner, are increased at each step. If one grades learning by instruction as the lowest, and learning by experiment as the highest learning type, the results may be summarised thus:

— learning type level and learning input content are negatively correlated
— learning type level and requirements for learning resources are positively correlated

without making any value judgement as to the linearity or otherwise of any empirical relationship.

6.4 LEARNING CATEGORY 2: IMPROVEMENT OF PROBLEM SOLVING CAPABILITY

6.4.1 Learning Goal and Learning Criteria

6.4.1.0 Introduction

Assume that S= (V,DB,PR,RI,P,L) and S′= (V′,DB′,PR′,RI′,P′,L′) are two rule based systems with RI=RI′ and P=P′. Assume =q< is a two-dimensional relationship of L∗L′; Ke[*i*] el L is the appropriate consultation result in L, while Ke[*i*]′ el L′ is the appropriate consultation result in L′, though both are related to the generating case fa[*i*]. The relation =q< may be given the following informal interpretation:

> ke[*i*] =q< ke[*i*]′ ↔
> "the consultation result ke[*i*]′ is qualitatively at least as good (i.e. as precise, as complete, as expressive) as the consultation result ke[*i*]"

Symbolically, =q< represents a quality relationship between consultation results. As an initial formalisation of =q<, one could imagine:

> Ke[*i*] =q< ke[*i*]′ ↔
> | ke[*i*] =< ke[*i*]′ |
> v expressive-power (ke[*i*]) =< expressive-power (ke[*i*]′)

This formalisation is not pursued here, but =q< is introduced here as a basic, formally undefined, quality relationship. With the aid of =q< one may define as quality relationship =Q< for the solution function f of S.

6.4.1.1 Definition D8: Solution Function: a Quality Relationship

Assume $=q<$ is the quality relationship defined in section 6.4.1.0 above, and f: $P \rightarrow L$, and also $f':P' \rightarrow L'$. Further assume that f and f′ are the solution functions, of the rule based systems S and S′ respectively. Assume P is the common problem domain of S and S′, and L and L′ the solution domains of S and S′.

Then f and f′ are related by the relationship $=Q<$ if, for all cases P, the consultation result ke[*i*]′ under f′ is at least as "good" as that under f. This may be expressed symbolically:

$$f =Q< f' \leftrightarrow (A\ fa[i])\ (f(fa[i]) =q< f'\ (fa[i]))$$

where:

$$=Q<\ ss\ PM(P * L) * PM(P * L'),$$
$$f : P \rightarrow L$$
$$f' : P \rightarrow L'$$
%

6.4.1.2 Definition D9: Learning Category 2: Learning Goals

With the aid of the definition D7 of $=Q<$, the learning goals of learning category 2 ("capability improvement") can be defined.

The learning goal of learning category 2 learning is, given an initial rule based system S with the solution function f: $P \rightarrow L$, to construct a rule based system S′ with a solution function f′: $P \rightarrow L'$ such that f′ is genuinely qualitatively better than the original solution function f. Therefore a borderline case of the identity of f and f′ had to be excluded. Symbolically:

$$f =Q< f'\ \&\ f =|= f'$$
%

The learning goal therefore is to transform S with f into an S′ with an f′ that is "better" as a solution function. A learning step from S to S′ can also be seen as a step to improve S in the sense that S′ may be viewed as a qualitative optimisation of S′ relative to S. Therefore a learning step from S to S′ under learning category 2 is termed an "improvement learning step".

It is quite possible to pursue the learning goals of category 1 ("extension") and 2 ("improvement" or "capability") concurrently. The goals of each learning category are not in conflict with one another. However, for the purposes of clarity, the objectives were discussed and presented separately. Both goals are usually pursued in a rule based system.

6.4.2 Learning Strategy

6.4.2.0 Introduction

Assume S is a rule based system with (V,DB,PR,RI,P,L) and that f is the solution function with f: $P \rightarrow L$. In learning category 2 the learning goal is, as already mentioned, the "real" improvement of f to f′. In order to transform f to f′ with improved characteristics, the rule based system S has to be transformed into the rule based system S′ in some orderly process. This, on the other hand, can only be achieved by a transformation of the rule set PR in S to Pr′ in S′.

However, there is a significant difference from learning category 1 in that the latter required changes to PR by pure extension (i.e. a pure adjunction of the set delta-PR). There is no constraint under learning category 2 in modality to achieve the learning step. This means that the nature of the change to PR is unconstrained, so any valid set operation is theoretically legitimate. This difference has some unpleasant consequences for the treatment of learning steps of the "improvement" category. It can be shown, assuming the conservation of integrity in the individual learning steps, that although theoretically substraction and adjunction of rules are both equally valid operators/modalities, this exceeds the possible modifications permitted under other constraints.

Therefore it is shown that a new rule base PR′, which is a desired end state after the learning step, is not necessarily compatible with the state of the set PR prior to the commencement of the learning step. Especially, it is possible to show that during the improvement step at least one old rule has to be removed from the set PR. The rest set {PR − r[*i*]} after the substraction of rule r[*i*] has to have at least one new rule added to it to generate PR′ that meets other constraints.

6.4.2.1 Conservation of Integrity: Theorems T5 to T8

In learning category 1 (extension), the theorems T5 to T8 were developed to support and ease the conservation of integrity during learning. However, in learning of the "improvement" category, the theorems do not aid this. Because the theorem T8 is not valid, there is no weakened formulation variant that is usable.

6.4.2.2 Conservation of Integrity: Requirements

In order to transform a rule based system S with a solution function f with integrity to a rule based system S′ with a qualitatively better solution function f′, the following seven conditions must be met:

Given initially an S with f and PR so that:

(1) PR is consistent
(2) PR is correct relative to f
(3) PR is complete relative to f,

what is required is an S′ with f′ and PR′ such that:

(1) PR′ is consistent
(2) PR′ is correct relative to f′
(3) PR′ is complete relative to f′

and, most importantly:

(4) f′ is qualitatively better than f.

6.4.3 Learning Types

6.4.3.0 Introduction

In learning category 2, the qualitative improvement of problem solving capability, only three learning types are reconstructed:

— learning by instruction
— learning by example
— learning by experience.

6.4.3.1 Learning by Instruction

6.4.3.1.0 Introduction

The term "learning by instruction" relating to the qualitative improvement of the solution function f of a rule based system S is understood to mean automatic learning by S of a nature that enables it to generate the complete specification of the qualitatively better solution function f′ of the improved rule base PR′. The individual learning characteristics are now discussed in detail.

6.4.3.1.1 Learning Input

Learning by instruction assumes that the qualitatively better solution function f′ of S′ is available in the form of a complete specification. Therefore the following have to be supplied :

(1) L′
(2) {(fa[*i*],ke[*i*]′) | f′(fa[*i*]) ↔ ke[*i*]′
    where
    (A fa[*i*]) (f(fa[*i*]) &
    −(f(fa[*i*]) ↔ f′(fa[*i*])))
    and
    f : P → L
    f′: P → L′
    %

Alternatively, the above may be written more elegantly as:

f′

where

f =Q< f′ & f =|= f′
%

6.4.3.1.2 Learning Output

Learning by instruction has to generate the improved rule base PR′, and PR′ is a computational pre-requisite for f′. This is also required in all learning categories of learning type 1 ("extension").

6.4.3.1.3 Learning Tasks and Methods

Learning by instruction consists of precisely of the operationalisation task that has already occurred in the instructional type of learning in learning category 1.

6.4.3.1.4 Learning Agents and Role Distribution

With regard to the active learning agents and the distribution of the learning roles, there are no fundamental differences from the instructional learning of learning category 1. The only difference is the learning category 1 objective, being the pure extension of the rule base PR, which is not the same as that for learning category 2, whose sole objective is the qualitative improvement of PR.

6.4.3.1.5 Value for Knowledge Acquisition

Learning by instruction under learning category 2 has no direct value for knowledge acquisition, as far as all learning types of this category are concerned.

6.4.3.1.6 Validation Criteria

With regard to the validation criteria for PR′, the same principles apply as for learning category 1:

(1) PR′ must be consistent
(2) PR′ must be correct relative to f′.

The relative optimisation step from f to f′ is, in itself, no validation criterion.

6.4.3.1.7 Learning Resources

The instructional learning of this category requires the same resources as that of this learning type under learning category 1 (see earlier sections of this chapter).

6.4.3.2 Learning by Example

6.4.3.2.0 Introduction

It is understood that learning by example, for the purpose of a qualitative improvement in the solution function f of a rule based system S, refers to automatic learning by S so that it generates a specific partial specification of f′ which may generate the improved rule base PR′.

6.4.3.2.1 Learning Input

Learning by example assumes as input that a finite part of the solution function f′ of S′ which is qualitatively better than f of S is given in the form of a partial specification of a finite partial function of f′ (so-called improvement examples). Symbolically:

(1) L′
(2) $\{(\mathrm{fa}[i],\mathrm{ke}[i]') \mid \mathrm{f}'(\mathrm{fa}[i]) \leftrightarrow \mathrm{ke}[i]'$

& 1 =< i =<n}
where:
(A fa[i]) (f(fa[i]) =q< f′(fa[i]) &
-(f(fa[i]) ↔ f′(fa[i])))
with
f : P→L
f′: P→ L′

or, more concisely:

f′

where

f =Q< f′ & f =|= f′
%

The positive example set in (2) above may also be most readily specified by the enumeration of

(fa[1],ke[1]′), . . . ,(fa[n],ke[n]′)

of the individual improved problem solving instances. The rule base PR′ which is to be generated must at least cover the positive examples. For the eventuality of additional negative examples, the rationale is like that for learning by example under learning category 1.

6.4.3.2.2 Learning Output
Learning by example has to produce an improved PR, exactly like the other output requirements for other learning types and categories.

6.4.3.2.3 Learning Tasks and Methods
In the framework of learning steps to learn by example there are two learning tasks to be accomplished:

— operationalisation
— induction.

6.4.3.2.4 Learning Agents and Role Distribution
In learning by example, just as in learning by instruction, a pupil is required as well as a tutor. The role of the learner/pupil here is to induce a full specification of f′ from the available example set. The tutor's role is to instruct the learner to enable the learning step S to S′ to happen.

6.4.3.2.5 Value for Knowledge Acquisition
None.

6.4.3.2.6 Validation Criteria

The criteria that apply are :

(1) PR′ must be consistent
(2) PR′ must be correct relative to f′.

The relative optimisation step from f to f′ is, in itself, no validation criterion.

6.4.3.2.7 Learning Resources

Learning by example in learning category 2 requires the same learning resources as those specified in learning by example under learning category 1 (extension).

6.3.3.3 Learning by Experience

6.4.3.3.0 Introduction

Learning by experience in order to achieve a qualitative improvement of the solution function f of a rule based system S to obtain a new solution function f′ which is qualitatively better in S′ is defined to be automatic learning by S of a particular type. Either S has computed a finite set of problem solving instances (fa[*i*],ke[*i*] el f in real consultation processes, or it has been found (based on a measure supplied by the quality criterion =q<) that the problem solving instances are qualitatively unsatisfactory for improvement learning. With this experience, the appropriate set of qualitatively better problem solving instances (fa[*i*],ke[*i*]′) el f′ is computed; and so an improved f′ of S′ results which is used to generate a qualitatively better rule base PR′.

6.4.3.3.1 Learning Input

Learning by experience assumes as input that the learner/pupil has actually carried through a finite set of real consultation processes in the application domain. It is further assumed that the pupil has some sort of yardstick for the evaluation of the quality of the outcome of consultation results.

Assume (fa[*i*],ke[*i*]) is any problem solving instance from f in S, and that =q< is the above defined quality relationship [Carnap and Stegmueller 1958] between respective consultation results. Then learning by experience requires the following inputs:

(1) {(fa[*i*],ke[*i*]) | f(fa[*i*]) ↔
ke[*i*] & 1 =< *i* =< *n*}
(2) =q<.

6.4.3.3.2 Learning Output

Learning by experience generates two outputs:

(1) the solution domain L′ of S′
(2) the improved rule base PR′ of S′.

6.4.3.3.4 *Learning Tasks and Methods*

At every step of learning by experience, the pupil has to accomplish three learning tasks, namely

— operationalisation
— induction
— critique/optimisation.

The first two are familiar from previous sections. The new task is that of critique and optimisation. This consists of the learner/pupil having to examine the finite set of problem instances, and criticise it under certain quality criteria, and optimise it based on the relationship =q<. Based on the resulting set of optimised problem solving instances, the learner now uses induction to generate a full specification of the improved solution function f′, which is then operationalised to PR′ via by now established methods, in the improved rule base of S′.

6.4.3.3.4 *Learning Agents and Role Distribution*

Learning by experience only has the pupil/learner as an explicit learning agent. In place of the tutor, only the anonymous systems environment appears, without participating in any learning role. Experience learning is a type of autonomous learning, like the observation and experiment types in learning category 1.

6.4.3.3.5 *Value for Knowledge Acquisition*

None.

6.4.3.3.6 *Validation Criteria*

The criteria for learning by experience are the same as those for learning by instruction in learning category 2:

(1) PR′ must be consistent
(2) PR′ must be correct relative to f′.

The relative optimisation step from f to f′ is, in itself, no validation criterion.

6.4.3.3.7 *Learning Resources*

The learner requires for learning by experience the following specific learning resources in three categories (see sections 6.4.3.3.8 to 6.4.3.3.10). There are no learning resources needed for the area of domain dependent knowledge processors.

6.4.3.3.8 *Application Independent Knowledge*

Learning by experience assumes the following:

— the general rule generation
— the rule execution
— the consistency of rule sets.

6.4.3.3.9 Application Dependent Knowledge
Learning by experience assumes knowledge about the following topics:

— the quality of consultation results
— the specific generation of relatively optimised consultation results.

As well as the two categories of knowledge above, learning by experience also has requirements similar to those of learning by experiment in learning category 2, i.e. knowledge about

— specific rule generation in application domains
— a model or theory of the application domain
— the language for formulation of the rules
— the language for rule construction
— the completeness of rule sets.

Finally, a rule library would be useful.

6.4.3.3.10 Domain Independent Knowledge Processors
Learning by experience requires, like learning by instruction and learning by experiment in learning category 2, the following:

— a rule generator
— a rule interpreter
— a rule validator
— a consultation result "criticiser"
— a consultation optimiser.

The consultation criticiser assesses the quality of the results of the consultations which are the source for gathering experience. The quality assessment is made relative to the application dependent knowledge. The consultation optimiser requires knowledge about the relative value of results to assess the possible degree of optimisation of each result.

6.4.3.3.11 Domain Dependent Knowledge Processor
No learning resources are required in this category.

6.4.3.3.12 Cost Benefit Analysis
If the three learning types of learning category 2 ("improvement") are considered together from the viewpoint of cost/benefit analysis criteria, an important conclusion may be drawn that has significant parallels to those arising out of learning category 1 ("extension").

The assumed content of the respective learning input from learning by instruction to learning by experiment and finally to learning by experience is reduced. Conversely, the respective learning resources are increasing at each step. Within the learning category the level of learning and input content are inversely related, whereas the level of learning and learning resources are directly proportional.

6.5 LEARNING CATEGORY 2: IMPROVEMENT IN EFFECTIVENESS OF THE PROBLEM SOLVING CAPABILITY

6.5.1 Learning Goal and Learning Criteria

6.5.1.0 Introduction

Assume that S =(V,DB,PR,RI,P,L) and S′ = (V′,DB′, PR′,RI′,P′,L′) are two rule based systems with V = V′, DB = DB′,RI = RI′, P = P′ and L = L′. Therefore, S and S′ only differ in the rule bases PR and PR′, which are the computational pre-requisites for f of S and for f′ of S′ respectively. Further assume that tc and tc′ are the associated computational times; and sc and sc′ the associated computational space complexities of PR and PR′ respectively.

Therefore, c=(tc,sc) and c′ = (tc′,sc′) are the total computational complexities of PR and PR′ respectively. As this complexity measure is independent of the rule interpreters RI and RI′, this is also the complexity of S and S′ respectively. The total complexity of the rule base S is thus c, which is a measure of the computational capability of S. The total complexity c may be compared using strong partial ordering relation "<" or ".smaller than.". The relation "<" is a Pareto ordering. Symbolically:

```
c′ < c ↔ c=(tc,sc) & c′=(tc′,sc′) &
     ((tc′ < tc & sc′ =< sc ) v
       tc′ =< tc & sc′ < sc ))
       %
```

For the following discussions, the concepts of time and space complexity are defined as basic quantities which have to be accepted. Suitable definitions have to be able to take into account the following characteristics of rule based systems deduction processes:

— size of the given cases fa[*i*]
— size of the desired consultation results ke[*i*]
— size of the rule base
— size of the respective deduction step
— searching the rule base
— non-deterministic selection of rules per deduction step
— possible repetition of certain selections
— searching of the current actual DB
— unification of premises of selected rules and literal sets
— adjunction of the unified rule conclusions

— increasing size of the DB state per deduction step
— testing of the reached state for attainment of desired result.

Therefore completely appropriate and formally precise definitions of time and space complexity would be too extensive to develop here.

6.5.1.1 Definition D10: Learning Category 3: Learning Goal

The learning goal of learning category 3 is defined with the aid of the concept of total complexity as described by "c" in section 6.4.1.

Assume a rule based system S with a solution function f: $P \rightarrow L$ with total complexity c. Assume that there can exist S′ with a solution function f′: $P \rightarrow L'$ with total complexity c′. Note that by definition $P' = P$ and $L' = L$. S′ is the objective to be reached such that $c' < c$, with f remaining "invariant". Symbolically:

$$c' < c \;\&\; f = f'$$

%

The learning goal may also be interpreted as trying to transform S with f and c to a solution function semantically equivalent to that needed for the rule based system S′ with a reduced complexity c′ relative to c.

A learning step in learning category 3 could be seen as a complexity reducing step, or an optimisation step in terms of complexity. These types of learning are called "effectiveness" learning steps. Unlike the learning goals of the first two learning categories which can be pursued in parallel, this particular learning goal type cannot be pursued at the same time as extension and/or qualitative improvements.

The first two learning categories assume that f and f′ are non-identical, whereas the third category requires this identity to be maintained. Therefore, at any one time an automatic learning system may pursue either complexity reduction or the other learning types.

6.5.2 Learning Strategies

6.5.2.1 Definition

Assume S is a rule based system with (V,DB,PR,RI,P,L) with the solution function f: $P \rightarrow L$ and total complexity c. In learning category 3, the learning goal is to reduce the total complexity while maintaining f invariant. In order to achieve this, S has to be transformed to S′, which is in turn only possible via a transformation of the rule base PR to PR′. From a functional semantic viewpoint this transformation is an equivalence transform from PR to PR′. A procedural viewpoint is here invalid because of the objective of a complexity reduction delta-c prohibits it.

6.5.2.2 Transformation of PR to PR′

6.5.2.2.0 Introduction

As discussed above, the means of accomplishing the learning step from S to S′ is by the transformation of PR to PR′ with the solution function f invariant. Three possible means of achieving this transformation exist

— compilation
— macro substitution
— meta-rules.

Each type will now be discussed.

6.5.2.2.1 Compilation

The rule base PR is compiled into a set of trees. These can then be easily traversed for identical premises that appear in separate rules. These can be reduced to single instances, thus reducing overall complexity by reducing redundancy. However, compilation cannot be repeated in the chained learning steps, nor does it meet the requirements of the learning output. Therefore, compilation is not an appropriate learning strategy.

6.5.2.2.2 Macro Substitution

This process is the substitution of certain groups of rules in PR by one rule, a "macro" rule. This macro rule is functionally and semantically equivalent to the group of rules it replaces. However, in the procedural semantic context, it is more powerful because just one new rule has replaced more than one old rule. Macro substitution can be iteratively chained and is, relative to the rule based concept, a closed operation. It seems ideally suited for a learning step strategy in learning category 3.

6.5.2.2.3 Meta-rules

Separate from the rule base PR a second group of rules is maintained containing so called "meta-rules" that steer the selection and application of rules in PR. These rules in PR are therefore object rules. Selection and application of these object rules must occur in such a manner that the total complexity is reduced. The complexity is computed in terms of this selection and application. This is less than the total complexity obtained by the non-deterministic selection and application of the rules in PR. Selection implies a higher degree of learning than pure stochastic selection, therefore it has a lower complexity associated with it. However, the whole problem of rule learning has now been raised to the meta level, and, because of the overall demand to reduce complexity, to an accentuated degree. A complete treatment of this subject is well beyond the scope of this text.

6.5.2.3 Conditions for a Learning Step

In order to transform a rule based system S with solution function f and total complexity c into a rule based system S′ with an identical solution function f but a reduced complexity c′ by learning while maintaining the integrity requirements, the following conditions have to be met:

Assume that at the beginning of the learning step S with f and c and the rule base PR the following are valid assumptions:

(1) PR is consistent
(2) PR is correct relative to f
(3) PR is complete relative to f.

the learning step is achieved when an S′ rule based system is reached with f and c′ such that:

(1) $c' < c$
(2) PR′ is consistent
(3)PR′ is correct relative to f
(4) PR′ is complete relative to f.

6.5.3 Learning Types

Learning by instruction and experiment are possible learning types for the complexity reduction learning. A complete discussion, however, is beyond the scope of this text.

6.6 AUTOMATIC LEARNING

6.6.1 Conceptual Generalisation

6.6.1.1 System Performance and General Learning Step Concepts

The results obtained from examining the individual learning categories should now be reviewed for any generalities. Firstly, the components f (the solution function of S) and c (the computational complexity of S) are termed to be the general system performance characteristics of the rule based system S.

6.6.1.2 Definition D11: Performance Function

Assume that SR is the set of all rule based systems S; and R the set of real numbers. Assume that S and S′ are any two different rule based systems in the set SR. The performance function Pf can then be defined as Pf: SR → R of S′, i.e. Pf(S″) of S′ is exactly ordinally larger than Pf(S) of S when a learning step has taken place (of any of the three learning types discussed previously). Symbolically:

$$\mathrm{Pf(S)} < \mathrm{Pf(S')} \leftrightarrow$$
$$(\mathrm{f\ ss\ f'}\ \&\ \mathrm{f} =|= \mathrm{f'})\ \mathrm{v}$$

(f =Q< f′ & f =|= f′) v
(c′ < c & f = f′)
%

6.6.1.3 A Generalised Concept of One Learning Step

The generalised concept of a learning step can now be expressed concisely as a transformation from S el SR to S′ el SR when Pf(S) < Pf(S′).

6.6.1.4 Learning as Searching in the System Space

Assume that S is a rule based system (V,DB,PR,RI,P,L) before a learning step and S′ a rule based system with solution function f′ after a learning step from S, and where complexity is reduced from c to c′ during the learning step. As has been demonstrated for every learning type in every learning category, a common learning task is the operationalisation of PR′′and thus f′. However, this is not normally an algorithmic process—a termination is not guaranteed nor may it be assumed. The operationalisation can only be effected by generating a series of PR, and testing the generated version at each step to establish to what degree it meets the requirements of operationalisation of f′ in the result. Basically this is a generate and test procedure. In any real sized problems, though, this procedure cannot be initiated without thought for the computational consequences. The systems space SR must have some sort of structure. The requirement is that of continuity. The system space SR is continuous when a small change in PR, from PR*n*′ to PR*n*+1′, effects a similar small change in S*n*′ el SR to S*n*+1′ el SR.

6.6.1.5 Continuity and Similarity

Assume "∼" is a similarity relationship, without delving into the numerous problems that such a definition could give rise to. Further assume S1′ and S2′ are rule based systems in SR with rule base PR1′ and PR2′ and the respective solution functions f1′ and f2′ and total complexity c1′ and c2′. Then continuity of SR may be expressed as:

Cont(SR) ↔
(A PR1′,PR2′)(A S1′,S2′ el SR)
(PR1′ ∼ PR2′ → S1′ ∼ S2′)
%

The similarity between systems is measured by the similarity between the solution functions f and f′, and the total complexity c and c′ (or whatever generations are being compared). Symbolically:

(A S1′,S2′ el SR) (A f1′,f2′) (A c1′,c2′)
(S1′ ∼ S2′ ↔ f1′ ∼ f2′ v c1′ ∼ c2′)
%

The continuity postulate may now be written as:

$$
\begin{aligned}
&\mathrm{Cont(SR)} \leftrightarrow \\
&\quad (\mathrm{A\ PR1',PR2'})\ (\mathrm{A\ f1',f2'})\ (\mathrm{A\ c1',c2'}) \\
&\quad (\mathrm{PR1'} \sim \mathrm{PR2'} \rightarrow \mathrm{f1'} \sim \mathrm{f2'}\ \mathrm{v}\ \mathrm{c1'} \sim \mathrm{c2'}) \\
&\quad \%
\end{aligned}
$$

Therefore it seems plausible, based on the definition D11, that the system performances of two rule based systems are similar when the respective solution functions are similar, or when the total complexities of the two systems are similar, thus:

$$
\begin{aligned}
&(\mathrm{A\ S1',S2'\ el\ SR})\ (\mathrm{A\ f1',f2'})\ (\mathrm{A\ c1',c2'}) \leftrightarrow \\
&\quad (\mathrm{Pf(S1')} \sim \mathrm{Pf(s2')} \leftrightarrow \\
&\quad \mathrm{f1'} \sim \mathrm{f2'}\ \mathrm{v}\ \mathrm{c1'} \sim \mathrm{c2'}) \\
&\quad \%
\end{aligned}
$$

The continuity postulate can now be finally formulated as:

$$
\begin{aligned}
&\mathrm{Cont(SR)} \leftrightarrow \\
&\quad (\mathrm{A\ PR1',PR2'})\ (\mathrm{A\ S1',S2'\ el\ SR})(\mathrm{PR1'} \sim \mathrm{PR2'} \rightarrow \\
&\qquad \mathrm{Pf(S1')} \sim \mathrm{Pf(S2')}) \\
&\quad \%
\end{aligned}
$$

These definitions allow a sub-postulate to be formulated, thus:

$$(\mathrm{A\ S1',S2'\ el\ SR})\ (\mathrm{S1'} \sim \mathrm{S2'} \leftrightarrow \mathrm{Pf(S1')} \sim \mathrm{Pf(S2')})$$

This indicates that the performance function Pf: SR $\rightarrow$ R is negatively monotonic. This requirement, plus that of continuity, are very difficult to achieve in practice, however.

6.6.2 Practical Consequences

6.6.2.1 Direct and Learning Knowledge Acquisition

It has been established that in all learning categories, the reducing content of the learning input is matched by the increasing requirements for learning resources by the learner, especially the assumed knowledge (*a priori* knowledge) of the pupil/learner. Shortcomings in learning input are therefore compensated for only by prior knowledge about the problem by the learner.

Learning knowledge acquisition, as all learning types of learning category 1 ("extension"), does not represent a real alternative to direct knowledge acquisition, in the sense that it could actually replace direct knowledge acquisition. In learning with characteristics of knowledge acquisition, the problems associated with acquisition are shifted to the structure of the pupil, especially the acquisition of learning resources. The structure of the pupil also gives rise to a number of further problems that increase with the level of the learning type that the pupil tries to implement.

If a learner of learning category 1 ("extension") has already been built, though, and the initial investment made, then this model is generally pursued. Only the additional costs of implementing the learning input and preparing the knowledge to be acquired have to be met. These are generally far less than those of the direct knowledge acquisition methods.

Direct and learning knowledge acquisition are not mutually exclusive, but in practice they are complementary modalities of learning acquisition that can be equally useful and relevant. They are not alternatives.

6.6.2.2 Developments of an Architecture

6.6.2.2.0 Introduction

The results of the available investigations imply that learning rule based systems require an architecture for a practical implementation. Conceptual (i.e. macro-) architectures that may be considered include:

— autonomous subsystems
— co-systems
— integrated systems.

Each model may be most applicable under certain circumstances.

6.6.2.2.1 Autonomous Subsystems

In this situation, the rule based system and the learning system are treated as quite separate, autonomous systems, subsystems of an overall learning rule based system. As the learning requires frequent input from S, interfaces between S and the learning system have to will be well specified.

6.6.2.2.2 Co-systems

In this configuration, the rule based system S is the main system with the learning system configured as a co-system. It differs from an autonomous system architecture in that the main system shares some facilities with the learning system, such as the rule interpreter (a component) or knowledge about the consistency of a rule set (a resource).

6.6.2.2.3 Integrated Systems

A fully integrated system has the learning system embedded in the main rule based system S, and all possible shared resources or components are in fact shared, thus reducing redundancy to a minimum, if there is any at all.

6.6.2.3 Tools

6.6.2.3.0 Introduction

The results obtained make it self evident that some comprehensive tools are required if the learning step from S to S′ is to be facilitated within the existing constraints. There are mono-functional, quite specific knowledge acquisition tools, and so-called universal acquisition tools (these being multi-functional tools).

6.6.2.3.1 Specific Knowledge Acquisition Tools

Within the knowledge acquisition framework, the following classes of tools are differentiated:

— those specific for direct knowledge acquisition such as

  — rule editors
  — rule compiler
  — taxonomy editors,

— those specific for learning knowledge acquisition such as

  — rule generators
  — rule libraries
  — rule librarian,

— those which may be considered as general knowledge acquisition tools with a specific function such as

  — rule base consistency checkers
  — rule base correctness checkers
  — rule base completeness checkers.

6.6.2.3.2 Universal Knowledge Acquisition Tools

Within the framework of the tools discussed here, the following are usually differentiated:

— dynamic tracers
— explainers (static rule based)
— explainers (dynamic deductive process based)
— libraries of problem solving instances
— libraries of problem solving knowledge bases.

6.6.2.3.3 Development Strategy for Tools

Universal tools, specific tools and special tools all have a common function in learning knowledge acquisition, in that they support the goal of learning acquisition directly. The universal and specific tools will be needed anyway during the construction of the rule based system, but the special tool requirements generally only arise when the learning itself has to be completed. A sensible development strategy for tools would be initially to develop the broader support tools, i.e. universal tools. The experience gained here helps to build better general (but narrower in applicability) tools, and only at the last hurdle should special tools be attempted. For the special tools in learning acquisition, those tools supporting the lower learning types should be implemented first. This is realistic and practical.

This strategy takes into account the pragmatic requirements and what is feasible during such a system construction.

6.7 SUMMARY

In Chapter 6, the aspects of automatic learning and knowledge acquisition relevant to a typical rule based expert system shell like TWAICE are examined. The unsuitability of existing methodologies led to an independent approach being developed. Three basic learning categories are examined in detail:

— extension of
— improvement of
— more effective

problem solving capability. For each category, the learning goals and criteria are defined. A strategy for learning under each type is proposed, followed by an investigation of the possible learning types under each learning category.

For each learning category, the

— learning input
— learning output
— learning tasks
— learning methods
— learning agents
— learning role distribution
— relation to knowledge acquisition
— validity criteria
— learning resources

are discussed and practical, pragmatic solutions proposed.

Finally the learning categories are overviewed and some general lessons drawn together with their practical consequences. The tools needed to achieve the learning goals based on the different requirements of the learning types are also briefly reviewed.

7

Learning by Example

A. M. Tjoa, R. R. Wagner, K. Macho and L. Winkelbauer
Institute of Statistics, University of Vienna, Austria

7.0 INTRODUCTION

The nature of learning in computer system that are artificially intelligent may be categorised into three classes:

— learning by knowledge acquisition
— learning by examples
— learning by discovery.

Most of the systems implemented today implement only the first category of learning—because it is the easiest in that it involves highly specialised human skills, and minimal computer "intelligence". The other categories have rarely been implemented [Macho 1984, Oakey and Cawthorne 1981, Rissland and Soloway 1981, Sammut 1981, Selfridge 1981, Winston 1985] and when they have, it has been invariably on an already existing large knowledge base.

A system is described here that comes into the second category, learning by example, but it may not start with an existing knowledge base of examples, or about the specific environment in which the example occur. This system has the capability to construct general knowledge from examples in the learning domain, without any *a priori* knowledge about the examples, or the domain. The only assumption made is that of "willingness" to learn. In other words, at every stage every effort is made to abstract general knowledge from specific examples. The computer (the pupil) will be given a set of examples by the user (tutor) that consist of two components:

— Initial Expression
  A sequence of character strings that form a basis for the abstraction of certain key concepts
  e.g.
  Single in English: "book"
— Target Expression

A sequence of character strings that can be deduced from the initial expression form
e.g.
Plural in English: "books".

The objective of the system is that, from a set of initial expressions and target expressions (i.e. examples) it learns to build its own target expressions.

7.1 LEVELS OF KNOWLEDGE IN LEARNING SYSTEMS

In order for the requirement that learning can be only by example and without any fundamental background knowledge about the topic, the basic knowledge assumed by the learning system restricts itself to the following points:

— the ability to compare two strings, and determine if they are identical
— the length comparison of two strings
— the relative position comparison between two strings
— a blank on input is a phonetic break, and not part of the example itself
— memory for the past examples, and the knowledge gained from them.

These basic abilities (or knowledge about how to perform five simple functions that do not imply any specific domain knowledge) are used by the system to deduce concepts and rules about the domain in which the examples are based. The knowledge so gained is retained as "pupil knowledge", which consists of some or all of the following levels:

— memory
— meta-rules
— rules
— exceptions.

7.1.1 Memory

The individual examples are analysed extensively, based on the initial and target expressions, and groups are built up. The system searches for sets of examples that have similar changes in pattern between the initial and target formats. The initial expressions are then searched for similarities, which are graded on a scale of 0 to 100. When the memory capacity is exceeded, the individual examples are deleted in the order they were input. There has to be a memory level present at all times.

7.1.2 Meta-rules

Meta-rules are built up from the memory level. They attempt to establish general rules to build the correct target form from an initial expression form. This step is also a level of abstraction, as the meta-rules contain only structural patterns, but no actual exemplary content. The structured expressions in the memory level are examined sequentially to establish if, as a minimum, the same characters appear in the same positions. A summary of all similarities is stored in a pattern list, with exact pointers to the origin of the similarity.

The combination of modification (to arrive at the target form) and the structural pattern together form a meta-rule. Every meta-rule also has a status flag and a utility indicator. The utility indicator is split into a positive and a negative part. The negative portion is a count of the number of times the meta-rule was invoked and led, by its application, to an incorrectly designed target form. The positive part counts the successful uses. If the rule is currently used and efficient, then the status is "active"; when the use efficiency falls below a certain level, the status is set to "debased" (in the sense that a once applicable and efficient meta-rule has been superseded for some reason).

7.1.3 Rule Level

The rule level aims to improve the efficiency of the meta level. Active meta-rules are tested in pairs for identical changes to the target form, and the resulting patterns matched for similarity. When the matching exceeds a certain level, the two meta-rules are then used to create a new meta-rule that combines the knowledge of them into one. This new proposed rule is then compared with all available rules in order to determine if a rule with this pattern and these changes already exists. IF no such rule exists, then a new-one is built that is functionally a meta rule, but with a more abstract pattern.

The negative indicator is initialised to zero for such a new rule, and the positive indicator is set to the maximum of all the positive indicators in all the meta-rules used to build the new rule. The status of the new rule is, naturally, "active", and the status of all the meta-rules used to build it "debased", in order to prevent the same (outdated) meta-rules being used again. It is therefore possible to imagine that, given sufficient examples, the new rules will, in turn, be abstracted themselves and so on and so on. It has been known for the system to develop super-rules (above meta-rules) and hyper-rules (above super-rules), which to date are the highest form of rules encountered.

7.1.4 Exception Level

The exception level is a short term memory that is used in the first attempts to generate target expressions from the initial expressions automatically. It retains all examples that, after application of the rule and meta-rule level processes, resulted in false target expressions. Examples are stored as pairs. In the event of all attempts failing, the "teacher" (user) supplies some corrections to these exceptions so that the set of successful attempts is not empty, and thus no base for learning is provided. Should the number of exceptions exceed a certain number, but there is currently also a level of overall success in learning, then the older exceptions are deleted from the memory.

7.2 APPLICATION OF THE SYSTEM

So that the learning behaviour of the pupil (i.e. computer) could be studied, as well as the fundamental process of learning by example, some so-called "intelligence" metrics were defined. These were the following:

— memory capacity
— meta-rule capacity
— rule capacity
— exceptions capacity
— rule estimation
— forgetting
— forgetting factor
— meta-rule building rate
— rule, super-rule and hyper-rule building rate.

7.2.1 Memory Capacity

The range of permitted values for this metric is from 0 to 200. The smaller the value, the fewer examples can be memorised by the system at one time. This means in practice that examples are lost, and this reduces the value of the learning base in general. This parameter is quite crucial to the overall capability of the system.

7.2.2 Meta-rule Capacity

The range of permitted values for this metric is from 0 to 200. The smaller the value, the more restricted the general knowledge that can be applied at any one time in a mature system. A high value enables optimal learning to take place.

7.2.3 Rule Capacity

The range of permitted values for this metric is from 0 to 100. Smaller values suggest that the pupil cannot build general knowledge easily, or only in a restricted manner. Higher values indicate efficient knowledge representation and shorter response delays under questioning by the "teacher".

7.2.4 Exception Capacity

The range of permitted values for this metric is from 0 to 50. Smaller values suggest that the pupil cannot remember many examples that are declared exceptions after the first attempts to infer target expressions. Higher values indicate that this is not a problem.

7.2.5 Rule Estimation Percentage

The range of permitted values for this metric is from 0 to 100. Lower values restrict the pupil's ability to forget general rules. Higher values encourage the forgetting of general rules, and thus the general knowledge accumulated by a pupil will be limited by the amount they can retain.

7.2.6 Forgetting

The "forgetting" factor is a value >= unity. The higher the value, the longer the pupil retains the examples in memory. The more complex the domain, with more levels of abstract (meta-) knowledge, the more important it becomes to retain all the examples for the longest possible time.

7.2.7 Forgetting Factor

The numeric value of this factor is >= 5. The higher the value, the longer the pupil's ability to retain learned examples.

7.2.8 Meta-rule Building Rate

The rate of building meta-rules is expressed as a percentage. The higher the rate, the less likely that an extension or improvement in the general knowledge of the pupil is made.

7.2.9 Rule, Super-rule and Hyper-rule Building Rate

All three intelligence parameters have similar meanings at their respective levels of knowledge abstraction, and all are percentages. The higher the numeric value, the longer the delay will be for the first rules to appear at that level. The tutor can preset these parameters to threshold values, and thus define different pupils with different learning abilities, and study the effectiveness and problems associated with his teaching methodology.

7.3 IMPLEMENTATION AND RESULTS

The system as described in its basic form above was implemented on a PRIME 750 in IMK-Interlisp [Macho 1984, Winkelbauer 1984]. The following areas were tested, with variation of the different intelligence metric to define a pattern of pupils under different learning methods:

— future tense in German
— plurals in German
— Latin conjugation
— Latin declension
— French plurals
— past tense in French
— present tense in English
— future tense in English.

The results suggest this is a potentially powerful method for learning in naïve situations (i.e. where there is no peripheral knowledge of the learning environment beforehand).

7.4 AN EXAMPLE

The example chosen is that of learning how to generate the plural form in German. The expression forms are:

Initial Expression:	SINGULAR: DAS BAND
Target Expression:	PLURAL: DIE BAENDER

The teacher has defined the following intelligence parameters:

— memory capacity	150
— meta-rule capacity	100
— rule capacity	75
— exceptions capacity	40
— rule estimation	50
— forgetting	10
— forgetting factor	10
— meta-rule building rate	10
— rule, super-rule and hyper-rule building rates	5, 2 and 1.

After the learning phase was completed, the status of the pupil was the following, at the different levels:

Memory Level:	The pupil memorised 91 examples and decomposed them into 16 groups.
Meta-rule Level:	The pupil built 44 meta-rules, from which 16 were debased and discarded, and 28 in current use.
Rule Level:	From the previous level, the pupil had built 12 rules, from which 5 were discarded and 7 in current use.
Super-rule Level:	From the rules, 4 super-rules were assembled, of which 3 were in current use and one was discarded.
Hyper-rule Level:	One hyper rule was built and in use.
Exceptions Level:	Six examples were memorised where the pupil had produced incorrect answers.

Statistics on the learning phase are as follows:

— The teacher introduced 50 basic examples.
— The teacher set 70 questions, of which the system (pupil):

answered 48 correctly	(68.6%)
answered 6 incorrectly	(8.6%)
did not answer 16 times	(22.8%).

— of the 48 answers which were correct, the source of the correct answer is of course of interest, and the analysis is as follows:

30 times RULES supplied the correct answer	(62.5%)
14 times MEMORY obliged	(29.2%)
4 times EXCEPTIONS supplied the answer	(8.3%).

7.5 CONCLUSIONS

These intelligence parameters are very subtle means of controlling the learning process. Self-evident differences in learning only appear after significant changes in the parameters. In order that the correct sets of parameters be selected for different pupil types, a number of simulations have to be run to gather the necessary statistics. In some areas, like that of learning how to build plurals, fine tuning in the parameters produces virtually no changes in the learning patterns. Also, higher intelligence characteristics only become apparent in the longer term; in the short term there appears to be little difference between responses under different characteristics. Most importantly, a "clever" pupil learns better over longer periods, and adds to that knowledge as times goes on, whereas lower intelligence settings create a situation where a pupil stagnates at a certain knowledge level.

In real life, this suggests that there is no real substitute for EXPERIENCE. Pupils with little ability to retain invariably make poor long term learners, but may perform quite well in the short term or simple, clear-cut situation (i.e. not in exceptions)—the word INSTINCTIVE may come to mind in these cases.

8

LEGAS — Inductive Learning of Grammatical Structures

Roman M. Jansen-Winkeln
Universitaet des Saarlandes, Saarland, FRG

8.0 INTRODUCTION

Throughout recent years Inductive Learning has again become a focal point of artificial intelligence research. Both in theoretical considerations and in practical applications remarkable results have been achieved.

LEGAS (LEarning of GrAmmatical Structures) takes up essential developments in the field of concept and rule learning. It is implemented in PROLOG. LEGAS induces grammar rules from examples. Strings are used as training instances. The examples are continuous in that they are neither described by a fixed number of attributes [Habel and Rollinger 1984] nor by constructs of the desired target formalism [Emde 1984].

8.1 LEGAS

LEGAS combines mainly two typical learning tasks.
First, it maps training instances from a given formalism onto rules given in another formalism—in this case "character strings" onto "transduction grammar rules".
Secondly, it manipulates expressions of the target formalism, i.e.

— generalisation
— specialisation
— ordering

of transduction grammar rules.

If one wishes to solve the first part of the task—rule hypotheses being generated and verified with examples—we have to adjust the techniques of concept learning, for example "specific conjunctive generalisation", to the requirements of rule acquisition. Implementing "generate and test" cycles is assumed by the evaluation strategy of PROLOG to be the best possible way.

The second part of the task—transduction grammar rules are analysed and manipulated—takes into account methods which Alan Bundy [Bundy *et al.* 1985] and Robert Michalski [Michalski 1983] describe in their analytic comparison of rule- and concept-learning systems. These methods are modified for application in LEGAS.

The evaluation strategy for transduction grammar rules has to be especially considered when applying these rules.

LEGAS has a special data structure which, in the case of a sequential depth first strategy, shows the procedural path to the formal consistency of a rule set.

PROLOG supports this procedure because of its ability to make meta-rule inference, i.e. the ability to generate and manipulate clauses in the PROLOG database.

LEGAS has been used with great success for the acquisition of rules for the analysis of compound nouns, verb inflection and plural formation in German and for the addition of binary numbers. The learnable language class is the class of transducers [Hopcroft and Ullmann 1979], which, however, by using special heuristics can be extended to the class of recursively nested transducers. In order to demonstrate LEGAS in an understandable way, we have selected English noun-plural examples for this paper. More complex examples can be found in the literature [Jansen-Winkeln 1986].

The next section introduces definitions of the terms "consistent" and "complete" and a broad specification of the program algorithm is presented. The second half of this chapter gives a detailed description of the representation of examples and rules.

After this, a procedure is presented for generating rule hypotheses and classifying the power of the learnable grammatical structures. The following chapter describes how inconsistencies within a rule set can be located and removed by the analysis of "near misses". The last section deals with an attempt to find what the essential features are for the realisation of these systems by comparing this approach with similar approaches.

8.2 LEARNING ALGORITHM FOR TRANSDUCERS

8.2.0 Introduction

LEGAS, a rule acquisition system, induces rules from examples. The process of learning is determined by three factors: examples, rules and the rule interpreter. Some definitions are:

— Examples are pairs of character sequences consisting of an input and an output form. The examples manifest the effect of the rules to be learnt.
— Rules are functional interdependencies for the manipulation of strings. They can be shown explicitly and evaluated.
— Rule Interpretation determines the procedural evaluation of rules when applied to strings. The interpretation is responsible for strategies of selecting rules and solving conflicts between them. A rule interpreter will be described which selects rules on the basis of an underlying partial order.

Summarising these factors, it can be said that they describe the State of Learning Process (the SLP) and control the incremental acquisition of a rule set.

8.2.1 The Learning Process

State of Learning Processes contain, apart from rules necessary for grammars, information on the chronological development of grammatical structures and a justification of the rules induced. In this respect the class of complete and consistent SLP's are of major importance. A SLP is "complete" if there is a deriving rule for every training instance. It is "consistent" if the rules can be ordered according to the relation "more specific than". Within these SLP's chronological data consisting mainly of examples are in line with the derivation scheme.

By using SLP's, this inductive approach to learning may be described as direct transition from one complete and consistent SLP towards another SLP within the process state space.

The learning process starts with an empty example and an empty rule set. A modification in the SLP is caused by adding new examples. If required, the rule set or its order are changed or extended.

This approach reflects the incremental nature of learning. The gradually increasing set of examples is constantly confronted with a set of plausible explanations. In addition, with this approach a first global specification of the inductive learning program LEGAS can be achieved.

Completeness, consistency and action to be undertaken are related by Fig. 8.1.

Completeness	Consistency	Action
−	?	Generate new complete rules
+	?	Acquire no more new rules
+	−	Modify existing rules or order
+	+	Rule set complete and consistent

Legend:
+ condition satisfied
— condition not satisfied
? condition not examined

Fig. 8.1—Completeness, consistency and action.

According to the specification, rule acquisition can be subdivided into two phases:

(1) Generation of rules completing an incomplete SLP.
This phase is called "acquisition of complete rules".

(2) Modification of a rule set until the SLP is consistent.
This phase is called "generation of consistent Rules".

8.2.2 Some Definitions.

8.2.2.1 Definition 1: State of Learning Process

A State of Learning Process (an SLP) is described by the triple of the form SLP=(D,R,SEQ).

If A is an alphabet, then the following definitions apply:

Example Set D

D is the set of known training instances, and is realised by pairs of input and output forms. Symbolically

D ss A+ * A+
D={(a[*i*],z[*i*])
|1<=*i*,*j*<=*n*, and *i*<>j=>a[*i*]<>a[*j*]}

Rule Set R

The set of induced rules consists of partial functions on strings over the alphabet A. Symbolically

R ss PF(A+ * A+)
R={r[*j*]|1<=*j*<=*k*}

Ordered Relation SEQ

The sequence of rules and examples is described by the following triple:

SEQ ss R * R * A+

For all r1,r2 el R and (a,z) el D, the set SEQ is defined as

(r1,r2,a) el SEQ if
r1[a] and r2[a] have defined values
r1[a]=z1 and r2[a]=z2
(a,z1) el D
(a,z2) NOT el D.

"Completeness" and "Consistency" are required to assess State of Learning Processes.

8.2.2.2 Definition 2: Completeness

Let PZ=(D,R,SEQ) be an SLP. PZ is complete if the following holds:

(A a[*i*],z[*i*]) el D)=>
r[*j*] el R with r[*j*](a[*i*])=z[*i*]

8.2.2.3 Definition 3: Consistency

Let PZ=(D,R,SEQ) be an SLP. PZ is consistent if the following holds:

(A r1,r2 el R : (r1,r2,a[*i*]) el SEQ)=>
(r2,r1,a[*j*]) NOT el SEQ)

An input form a el A* can be mapped onto an output form with the help of the corresponding derivation rule. In doing so, the SLP selects the fitting "derivation rule" : r[*j*] el R.

8.2.2.4 Definition 4: Derivation Rule

Let PZ=(D,R,SEQ) be an SLP. Suppose a el A+ is an arbitrary input. Then

RC(a)={r[*j*] el R | r[*j*](a) has a defined value}

If RC(a) <> {} then the derivation rule r[*i*] for a will be found as follows:

r[*i*] el RC(a)

and

(A r[*j*] el RC(a) | {r[*i*] holds: B(r[*j*],r[*i*],x) el SEQ

8.2.2.5 Lemma 1 of Definition 1.

All examples are derivable in an SLP if and only if (iff) the SLP is complete and consistent. A formal proof of this lemma may be found in Jansen-Winkeln [1986].

8.2.3 Representation of the Learning Process

LEGAS is implemented in PROLOG. Thus, stylistic means typical of PROLOG are used for the representation of SLPs. The rule set as well as the examples at the beginning of the induction are represented in a grammar formalism called "transduction grammar" (TdG). The name was chosen since a transducer exists for each grammar—which may be recursively nested and augmented — that accepts and generates the same languages. The syntax of TdG production closely follows the notation of Definite Clause Grammars [Pereira and Warren 1980].

Production consists of the following:
— one non-terminal symbol provided with an unambiguous rule index
— left and right sides of the production.

Left-hand and right-hand sides of a production consist of sequences of terminal and non-terminal symbols. Order and kind of non-terminal symbols are identical on both the right and the left sides of the rule whereas terminal symbols may show differences. Terminal and non-terminal symbols are presented as defined in Definite Clause Grammars.

8.2.4 Some Examples

8.2.4.1 Mapping of a String onto Itself

str/1: []→[]
str/2: [A], str.→[A], str.

The first rule says that the empty string maps onto itself. In str/2 any terminal symbol at the beginning of an input form is matched by the variable A and, without being changed, placed at the beginning of the output form. The predicate "str" is applied recursively to the rest of the input form.

8.2.4.2 Replacement of "y" by "ies"

The replacement of the character "y" by the character string "ies" at the end of an arbitrary string is expressed by the rule

plural/i: str,[y]→str,[ies].

The rule plural/i fails if the input form does not end with a "y".

8.2.4.3 Applicability

TdG rules are, like many other PROLOG predicates, bi-directionally applicable. They can be used to map input forms onto output forms and vice versa, as well as to verify whether a given pair of input and output forms is derivable with a transduction grammar.

Each TdG rule in PROLOG is provided, in contrast with many typical unification grammars, with an unambiguous index i.

By adding such an index to a non-terminal, the non-deterministic rule selection of the PROLOG interpreter becomes invalid and the rule with the index i is applied.

The user can access the TdG rules via a window oriented interface. It can be used as a monitor when training instances are recorded and for the control of the rules induced, as in Fig. 8.2. Furthermore, this interface provides acccss to the internal representation of TdG rules in PROLOG, as in Fig. 8.3.

8.3 ACQUISITION OF COMPLETE RULES

8.3.0 Introduction

A complete TdG rule is formed in three steps:

- proceeding from the input forms of the pairs of examples, the rule is generated bottom-up
- from the domain, hypothetical ranges can then be generated
- the resulting rule hypothesis is verified top-down against the output forms of the example pairs.

If one of these steps fails alternative solutions are searched for in the preceding step by backtracking. The algorithm terminates as soon as a rule according to the above system can be found for an example set or backtracking is carried out beyond the first step. In the latter case the example set is divided and the procedure is repeated for each subset.

The basic idea for the generation of rule hypotheses is the search for shared significant substrings among all input and output forms. Following Michalski [1984], the act of generalisation is denoted by the operator "|<".

When inducing rules from examples, the following procedure is applied:

- significant substrings of the input forms are mapped onto significant substrings of the output forms.
- insignificant substrings remain unchanged during mapping.

```
Input Form                        LEGAS          Output Form

2:diplomarbeit                    <<??>>         diplom-arbeit
1:diplompruefung                  <<??>>         diplom-pruefung
   cmp/cmp1: [diplom],str →
        [diplom−],str

2:eingabe                         <<??>>         ein-gabe
1:einbaum                         <<??>>         ein-baum
   cmp/cmp2: [e i n],str→[e i n−],str

2:diplompruefungseindruck diplom-pruefung-ein-druck
        diplom-pruefungseindruck
1:diplomarbeitseinband diplom-arbeit-ein-band
        diplom-arbeitseinband

Rule Hypothesis
   cmp/cmp3: cmp/cmp1,[s],cmp/cmp2→
        cmp/cmp1,[-],cmp/cmp2

Learning Goal:                    Action:        TR:  TE:

Compound-analysis                 Analyse        2.   0.
```

Fig. 8.2—Example recording and rule tracing window.

```
cmp(_80,_81,_82,_83,cmp3):—
        cmp(_80,_91,_82,_92,cmp1),
        _91=s>>_93,
        _92<<-=_94,
        cmp(_93,_81,_94,_83,cmp2).

cmp(_80,_81,_82,_83,cmp2):—
        _80=e>>i>>n>>_93,
        _82<<e<<i<<n-=_94,
        str(_93,_81,_94,_83,_97).

cmp(_80,_81,_82,_83,cmp1):—
        _80=d>>i>>p>>l>>o>>m>>_93
        _82<<d<<i<<p<<l<<o<<m<<-=_94
        str(_93,_81,_94,_83,_97).
```

Fig. 8.3 — Internal representation of TdG rules.

An example is given below.

All training instances of an example set are:

D={(lady,ladies),(body,bodies),(copy,copies)}

and are translated into basic rules, each describing the mapping of exactly one training instance. The following generalisation may be carried out:

```
[lady]→[ladies]          [body]→[bodies]          [copy]→[copies]
      |<                       |<                        |<
   str,[dy]        ———→ str,[dies]
                    |<
                 str,[y] ——————————→ str,[ies]
```

8.3.1 Specific Conjunctive Generalisation

The rule hypothesis in the example described above was unambiguous. If, however, there is a rule for a set of training instances, then the induced rule hypothesis need not be the only one.

The set VS(d) ss TdG of all possible rule hypotheses for an example set D is called the "Version Space", and elements of VS(d) are called "Specific Conjunctive Generalisations (SCG's)".

The rules of a version space can be partially ordered using the relation "more specific than". Here the minimal and maximal elements are of major interest.

Definition 5: MaxSCG (Maximal Specific Conjunctive Generalisation):
: Rule r is a maximally specific conjunctive generalisation (a MaxSCG) if no additional terminal symbol can be integrated into any significant substring of r.

Definition 6: MinSCG (Minimum Specific Conjunctive Generalisation):
: Rule r is a minimally specific conjunctive generalisation (a MinSCG) if no terminal symbol in r can be replaced by the non terminal "str".

For the example set

D={(lady,ladies),(body,bodies)}

there are amongst others, the following rules in VS(d):

MaxSCG: str,[dy]→str,[dies]

MinSCG: str,[y]→str,[ies] .

8.3.2 Acquisition of SCG's

Due to the distinction between MinSCG and MaxSCG, the basic system for the acquisition of rules has to be extended. The induction algorithm as described is modified in such a way that the result is the MaxSCG of the version space of a given example set. The MinSCG corresponding to any MaxSCG can be generated by dropping terminal symbols.

The MaxSCG of an example set is accepted as a rule in the rule set of an SLP. This approach takes into account a "careful" learning strategy which tries to avoid over-generalisation at the point of rule formation. The transformations of terminal symbols to be found within a MinSCG allow a classification of rules according to various criteria. Rules with the same transformations, i.e. the same MinSCG, are potential candidates for a subsumption to one rule.

If a rule r is found whose MinSCG coheres with at least part of the MinSCG of a rule s then r is a potential candidate for recursive application as non-terminal in s. In doing this, use is made of the selective, index driven application of TdG rules. Fig. 8.2 shows an application of this feature during compound analysis. Storing the MinSCG and its transformations by inverted indices make it possible to optimise rules efficiently within one SLP, and to allow an increased independence from the induced rules of the presentation sequence of associated examples. Furthermore, rule sets already fully acquired for a learning objective X can be integrated into a new rule set for a learning objective Y. The advantage of this integration is that no additional consistency checks on rule set X need to be carried out.

8.4 GENERATION OF CONSISTENT RULES

In the second phase of rule acquisition all rules generated by the examples and their substrings are to be integrated into an existing rule base.

In the first phase rules were merely considered when needed in order to further generalise a rule to be acquired. When rules are inserted, however, all rules of an SLP and their ordering must be taken into account.

Rules are to be inserted into the rule set in such a way that all examples can be derived correctly according to our broad specification. For this, according to Lemma 1, the SLP must be consistent.

One inherent feature of rule sets is that several rules may be applied to certain input forms. The set of all applicable rules for any input form "a" is called the "conflict set of a". This is why every interpreter uses conflict solving strategies to select the rule to be applied to a conflict set.

In order to integrate a rule consistently into a rule set, it has to be inserted in such a way that when the respective SLP is used to derive training instances there are either no rule conflicts or rule conflicts are limited to the case where the correct rule is selected.

If a learning system is to fulfil this task, information is required on how the interpreter works when discovering and solving conflicts. The way realised in LEGAS will be presented in the next section.

8.4.1 Inconsistent SLP's

The selection and application of the rules of a TdG correspond to a large extent to the selecting and processing strategy of standard PROLOG interpreters. The reason for this is that TdG rules, in a similar way to DCG rules, for example, can be transformed directly into PROLOG clauses. Thus the sequential order of TdG rules is of direct relevance.

Regarding our learning system LEGAS, the relation SEQ is part of the SLP so that information on the order of rules to be found in the PROLOG database can be evaluated. The elements of this relation contain information on which rules r[*i*] are part of the conflict set of an input form "a" and which of the rules are to be applied to "a".

By using SEQ, two different causes of inconsistencies of the SLP can be stated:

— control fault
  The order of the TdG rules (determined by SEQ) and of the corresponding PROLOG clauses in the PROLOG database do not coincide
— factual fault
  For two rules r[*i*] and r[*j*], contradictory information in the relation SEQ can be found stating that both r[*i*] is more specific than r[*j*], as well as that r[*j*] is more specific than r[*i*].

8.4.2 Insertion of Rules into the Rule Set

In the first step the newly acquired rules are added to the existing rule set. The PROLOG clauses belonging to the new rules are inserted arbitrarily into the PROLOG database. Normally, however, they are placed at the beginning of the database. In order to find out whether or not the extended rule set is still consistent, all training instances are processed and checked as to whether the rule used for derivation produces the correct results. If all examples were derived correctly, the rule set is complete and consistent according to Lemma 1. If not, the relation SEQ is established for the conflict set of all incorrectly derived examples. If, for example, the examples belonging to rule r[*i*] are derived incorrectly by rule r[*j*] then all the elements (r[*i*],r[*j*],e) and (r[*j*],r[*i*],e) of the relation SEQ are analysed.

The input forms can be split into two subsets:

NM(r[*i*])={(a,z) | (r[*j*],r[*i*],a) el SEQ and (a,z) el D}
NM(r[*j*])={(a,z) | (r[*i*],r[*j*],a) el SEQ and (a,z) el D}
where NM="Near Miss".

The abbreviation NM ("near miss") was introduced by Winston [1975] and designates those negative training instances for a concept which are very similar to the positive training instances. In contrast to Winston's system "ARCH", LEGAS does not predetermine near misses explicitly. LEGAS analyses positive training instances of one rule in order to determine whether or not they are suitable as near misses for other rules.

By carrying out case studies of the relation between near misses we can state causes for inconsistencies of a rule:

NM(r[*j*])=|={}
NM(r[*i*])={}

In this case r[*i*] can be applied to examples belonging to rule r[*j*]. On the other hand input forms of examples to r[*j*] cannot be processed by r[*i*]. Consequently, r[*j*] is more specific than r[*i*] and the sequence of these rules must be reversed in the PROLOG database

NM(r[*i*])=|={}
NM(r[*j*])=|={}

In this case r[*i*] can be applied to part of the examples belonging to r[*j*] and vice versa. The rules r[*i*] and/or r[*j*] have to be specialised, i.e. their domains have to be constrained.

Specialisation is done by

- calculating discriminating substrings within example sets
- searching predefined domain specific descriptors such as "vowel" or "consonant"
- proposing the acquisition of new domain specific descriptors
- splitting up a rule which is too general into more specific rules.

8.4.3 An Example

The incremental creation of a rule set for the English language plural could be done in the following way.

From an initial example set

D[1]={(lady,ladies),(copy,copies)}

the complete rule set, already introduced earlier

plural/1: str,[y]→str,[ies]

is induced and accepted as the first rule in the rule set R.

Suppose the example set is extended by

D[2]={(dog,dogs),(cat,cats)}.

This results in a new rule to be inserted consistently which is again placed at the beginning of the rule set thus:

plural/2: str,[]→str,[s]
plural/1: str,[y]→str,[ies] .

This sequence leads to inconsistencies of the SLP since, due to the sequential evaluation strategy, all input forms of the examples of the rule "plural/1" are processed by the rule "plural/2".

Therefore, two sets of near misses are created:

NM(plural/2)={(lady,ladies),(copy,copies)}
NM(plural/1)={}.

Consequently, the transformations of the TdG rules have to be reversed in the PROLOG database, leading to the following:

plural/1: str,[y]→str,[ies]
plural/2: str,[]→str,[s].

Another extension of the example set by training instances could be:

D[3]={(day,days)}.

This does not require the generation of a new rule, since plural/2 derives this training instance correctly. In spite of this, the new SLP becomes inconsistent, because plural/1 is applicable to "day", i.e.

(plural/1,plural/2,day) all SEQ.

A renewed exchange of rules would be to no avail. Since plural/1 is more specific than plural/2, plural/1 is constrained by a predefined domain specific descriptor, e.g. "consonant":

plural/1: str,consonant,[y]→str, consonant, [ies].

If the descriptor "consonant" is neither known nor can be acquired, plural/1 is split into the following:

plural/3: str,[dy]→str,[dies]
plural/4: str,[py]→str,[pies].

8.5 SUMMARY

8.5.1 LEGAS in Comparison with Other Systems

As far as its structure is concerned, LEGAS is in some respects similar to other inductive rule acquisition systems. If, for example, LEGAS is compared with the program for the acquisition of pronunciation rules by Oakey and Cawthorn [1981] or with SERA [Bollinger 1984], a system for learning recursive algorithms, then in all systems a first phase can be found for the generalisation of rules with the help of examples, a second for the improvement of rules and a third for specialisation, if this phase is required, as summarised in Fig. 8.4.

The target formalism of each of these programs (e.g. TdG rules in LEGAS) depends on the domain being learnt and describes its mappings in a domain specific way. Their representation may be interpreted directly [Oakey and Cawthorn] or, for efficient evaluation, may be translated into different formalisms (as in LEGAS and SERA).

Differences are reflected in the formalism of the obtainable learning results. For example, in both LEGAS and SERA upper limits of the learnable language classes are stated (regular expressions or primitive functions). Additionally, LEGAS provides a formal definition of the criterion necessary for consistency. Fig. 8.5 provides an overview of the issues relating to methods and data structures.

8.5.2 Implementation and Technical Data

LEGAS was implemented in the form of a PROLOG program. The program was developed at the University of the Saarland Department of Computer Science with the support of Nixdorf Computer AG, Paderborn.

Phase	LEGAS	System SERA	Oakey and Cawthorn
1st	Collection of training instances	Phase of evaluation	—
2nd	Acquisition of complete rules	Setup phase	Rule generation
3rd	Subsumption of rules	Integration module	Generalisation
4th	Generation of consistent rules	Correction Phase	Rule Stabilization

Fig. 8.4 — Flow of Control in LEGAS, SERA and the system developed by Oakey and Cawthorn [1981].

Issue for Comparison	LEGAS	SERA	Oakey and Cawthorn
Positive training instances support	yes	yes	no
Numerical Assessment	no	no	yes
Rule representation	TdG rules	Horn clauses	Domain specific
Rule Evaluation	Horn clauses	Lambda expres sions	Special interpretation
Language class	Regular expres sions	Primitive recursive functions	—
Criterion for consistency	All examples reproducible	—	All examples reproducible

Fig. 8.5 — Analytic comparison of LEGAS for methods and data structures.

LEGAS consists of about 150 predicates, and contains about 4000 lines of code and comments. It is implemented on a DEC Vax 11/780 in interpreted C-PROLOG Version 1.5.

Learning the most essential rules for the English plural, as well as some exceptions, requires about 90 seconds of CPU time and 0.5Mb of main memory.

The ideas presented here will be further developed within the framework of the German Special Collaborative Program on Artificial Intelligence and Knowledge Based Systems (referenced as SFB 314) of the German Science Foundation (DFG). They will be integrated into the knowledge acquisition tool which supports the establishment of a knowledge based, natural language front end "XTRA" ("Expert Translator") for interfacing various expert systems.

9

Outline of a Confirmation Theory in PROLOG

Helmer Gust
Universitaet Osnabrueck, FRG

9.0 INTRODUCTION

In order to model domains of knowledge for Expert Systems, classical logic is often inadequate. This is mainly because in such a classical approach uncertain knowledge and inconsistency cannot be represented. PROLOG has a further complication: the "negation by failure" defined negation that is frequently not adequate to represent the real situation. However, it is relatively easy to implement other logic systems in PROLOG, though there is usually a heavy price to pay in efficiency overheads. This chapter proposes an extension to PROLOG that removes this difficulty.

9.1 A PROLOG EXTENSION

The simple extension proposed can be easily implemented inside an interpreter, or can be compiled separately through a small front end preprocessor. It does offer a partial solution to the above problem by

— the introduction of a new logical negation operator "–"
— interpretation of a PROLOG proof as confirmation for an assertion.

It is not excluded that a confirmation exists for the negation of this assertion.

9.2 NEGATION BY FAILURE

"Negation by failure", in the following "NOT", is not a logical negation. Rather, it is taken to be a failure of an assertion. This results in a four-value logic [Belnap 1977] as illustrated in Fig. 9.1.

The four possible "truth" values (in this connection perhaps the term "confirmed" value may be more appropriate) for an assertion P are:

(1) (NOT P) and (NOT –P)

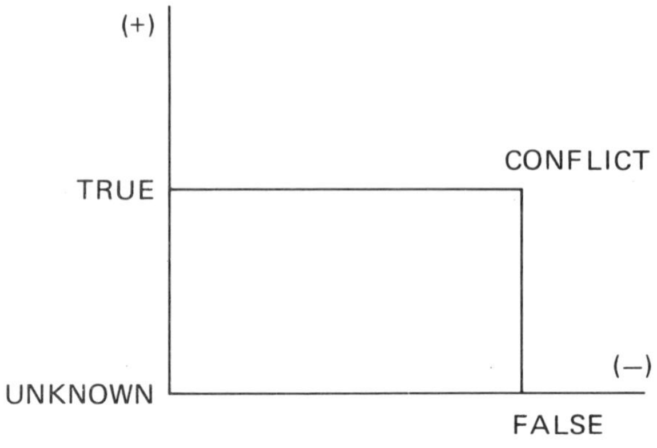

Fig. 9.1—Schematic representation of a four-value logic.

Neither P nor –P is confirmed.
This is the situation that occurs when nothing is known about the assertion P, and therefore no confirmation is possible.

(2) P and (NOT –P)
P is confirmed, but not –P.
This is the case where the truth of P may be asserted and confirmed, but not necessarily the negation, that the truth of P implies the falseness of the negation of P.

(3) (NOT P) and –P
–P is confirmed, but P is not.
The truth of the assertion –P is established, in the sense that –P is the falsehood of P.

(4) (4) P and –P
P and –P are both confirmed.
This case is the situation of "Inconsistency". Inconsistency is related to classical binary valued logic. This case, however, does not represent a situation of conflicting axiom systems in the sense of the four-value logic. "NOT" as used here corresponds to the use of "OUT" in Doyle [1979]. From this reference, it can be seen that it is possible to develop strategies for the structural transformation of knowledge whenever inconsistencies appear to arise.

9.3 RESOLUTION OF INCONSISTENCIES

The resolution of dealing with inconsistencies is an extension of classical two-valued logic, as applied to expert systems. It is possible to modify the proof algorithm of PROLOG so that no logical problems arise, even without structurally transforming the knowledge. The strategy consists of avoiding premises for which conflicting confirmations are available. In the following algorithm, a LISP-like syntax is used, with:

":" instead of "." as list constructor
"*" to indicate variables

(see Gust and Gust [1984]). The proof algorithm now reads thus:

```
(SOLVE () ).
(SOLVE (*GOAL :*GOALS)) ←
        (SOLVE–GOAL *GOAL)
        (NOT SOLVE–GOAL (← :*GOAL))
        (SOLVE *GOALS).

(SOLVE–GOAL *GOAL) ←
        (AXIOM *GOAL ← :*GOALS)
        (SOLVE *GOALS).
```

As an addition to an interpreter, alternatively a small pre-processor can be used in a compiled PROLOG implementation:

```
(TRANSFORM–CLAUSE (*HEAD :*GOALS) (*NHEAD
   :*NGOALS)) ←
        (TRANSFORM–HEAD *HEAD *NHEAD)
        (TRANSFORM–GOALS *GOALS *NGOALS).

(TRANSFORM–HEAD (– *P :*ARGS) (*P – :*ARGS)) ←
        (TRANSFORM-HEAD (*P :*ARGS) (*P + :*ARGS)).
(TRANSFORM–GOALS (*GOAL :*GOALS) (*GOAL+ *GOAL–
   :*NGOALS)) ←
        (TRANSFORM–GOAL *GOAL *GOAL+ *GOAL–)
        (TRANSFORM–GOALS *GOALS *NGOALS).

(TRANSFORM–GOAL (– – *P :*ARGS) *GOAL+ *GOAL– ) ←
        (TRANSFORM–GOAL (*P : *ARGS) *GOAL+
           *GOAL–).

(TRANSFORM–GOAL (– *P :*ARGS) (*P – :*ARGS ) (NOT *P +
:*ARGS)) ←/.
(TRANSFORM–GOAL (*P :*ARGS) (*P + :*ARGS ) (NOT *P –
   :*ARGS)).
```

Problems may arise when expressions containing free variables at evaluation time are embedded in NOT expressions [Clark 1978]. Therefore it is preferred to delay the testing of confirmations as far down the execution sequence as possible. There are limits to this in classical PROLOG systems. There are some extended PROLOG systems that allow the evaluation of premises to be made conditional on the instantiation of certain variables; see Carneghem [1982] and Gust [1984].

Considerations on evaluation in a two-dimensional evaluation space instead of four discrete values are to be found in Rollinger [1984]. Such a system is considerably more complex. Another reason for introducing a second negation operator in PROLOG is to be found in Reyle [1984]. "–P" is interpreted there as "FALSE <– P", with an associated extension of the proof algorithm to premises of the form:

B ← A1 & A2 . . . An).

9.4 RELATION TO DEFAULT LOGIC

The above is closely related to the problem of default logic as explored in Reiter [1980], as rules may be of the form:

P ← (NOT –P).

This implies the fact that P is true as long as there is not a confirmation for –P available.

10

PUNIFY—An Associative Processor for Unification

W. Dilger, O. Mayer and J. Mueller
University of Kaiserslautern, FRG

10.0 INTRODUCTION

This chapter deals with the associative processor PUNIFY that is designed for unification in first order predicate logic. It was developed on the basis of the unification algorithm published by Martelli and Montanari [1982]. This algorithm, called UNIFY, will be summarised here, and then the main components of PUNIFY will be described. A more detailed version is available [Dilger *et al.* 1984], and the details of associative processors in general can be found in [Fu & Ichikawa, 1982], Kohonen [1977] and [Dilger *et al.* 1983], amongst others.

10.1 THE ALGORITHM UNIFY

In the algorithm UNIFY, each variable in the terms to be unified is assigned a "box", with a name identical to the name of the variable, and as contents the terms that arise, in the course of unification, as substitutes for the variables.

A box for variable x[*i*] is imaginable as a rectangle divided into two unequal portions, the smaller portion containing the label, and the larger part the contents during unification. If a variable x[*j*] is substituted for x[*i*], then x[*j*] is not added to the contents portion, but to the label of the box x[*i*]. In this way several "boxes" are merged into fewer where the label then consists of multiple name tags. Full unification occurs when all the terms can be unified to just one "box".

The algorithm begins with a special "input box" which contains the terms to be unified. As long as a box contains more than one term, attempts must continue to identify the terms with one another so that differing sub-terms may be resubstituted by variables, and that the replaced sub-terms are placed into the appropriate boxes that are labelled with the respective variables. As soon as the situation is reached where each box in use contains one and only one term, then UNIFY stops. The most common unifier can be read off from the labels and contents.

For example, the two terms below are to be unified:

T1 = f(x[1],g(x[2],x[3]),x[2],b)
T2 = f(g(h(a,x[5]),x[2]),x[1],h(a,x[4]),x[4]).

The terms contain five variables; x[1], . . . , x[5], so five boxes plus a special input box (labelled "x") may be imagined (Fig. 10.1). Initially, the input box
0

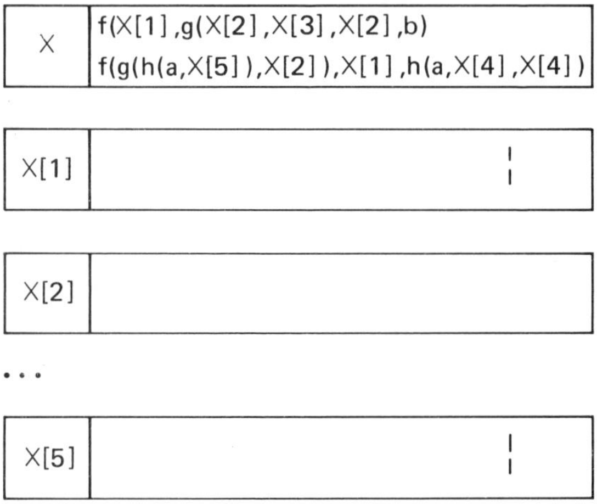

0Fig. 10.1—Status of the "boxes" at the outset in UNIFY (labels in place, but no content).

contains only the two terms T1 and T2, the rest of the boxes being empty apart from the label.

As the input box contains two terms, the conditions for ending UNIFY have not yet been reached. As both terms begin with the same function symbol ("f"), it is permitted to substitute the sub-terms by variables so that both terms become identical. The replaced terms are then allocated to boxes labelled with those variables that they are replaced by. Therefore in the example, the terms g(h(a,x[5]),x[2]) and g(x[2],x[3]) are allocated to the box labelled x[1]. The term h(a,x[4]) goes to box x[2], and the term b (a constant) to x[4]. The unified term remain in box "x". Fig. 10.2 shows the situation after this step.

Now the box x[1] contains two terms and these are processed rather like the "x" box was in the first step. Now in box x[1], the first terms are h(a,x[5]) and x[2], and as x[2] and x[3] are also the second term in each expression, so boxes x[2] and x[3] can be merged, as in Fig. 10.3.

Now only the box x[2],x[3] has more than one term in it. It is processed on the same basis as the previous two steps, which results in boxes x[4] and x[5] being merged, as shown in Fig. 10.4.

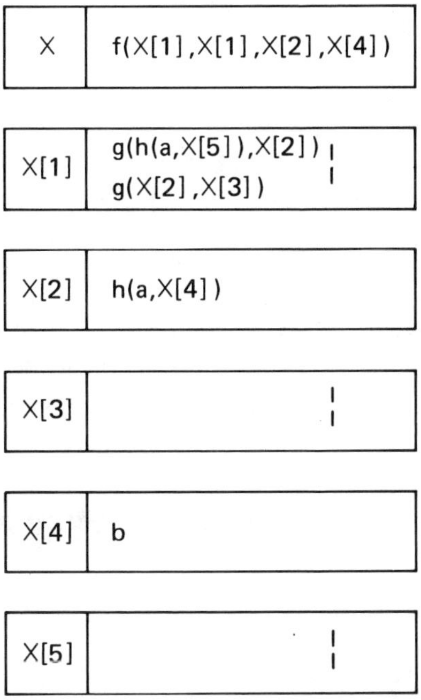

Fig. 10.2—Status of the "boxes" after one step of UNIFY.

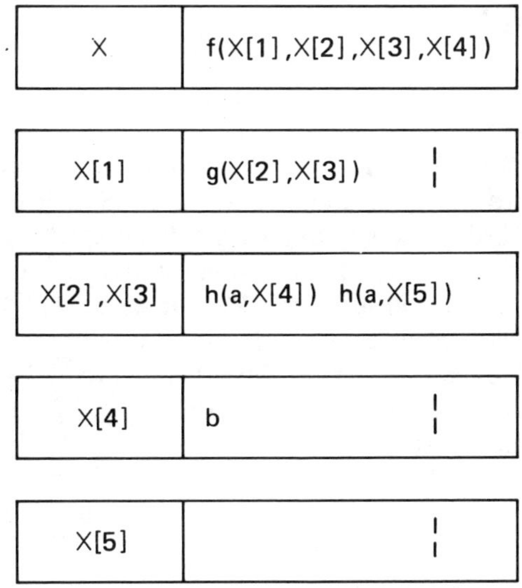

Fig. 10.3—Status of the "boxes" after two steps of UNIFY.

Now the criterion of only one term per box has been met, and the unifier can be extracted thus:

{x[1]/g(x[2],x[3]),
x[2]/h(a,x[4]),
x[4]/b,
x[5]/b}

There are two types of conflict that can arise in unification: a clash and circular references. A clash occurs when one box contains at least two terms that commence with different function identifiers. A circular reference occurs when, amongst the boxes still to be processed in an iteration, the variables of the label do not occur in labels or in the terms in the boxes.

10.2 THE ASSOCIATIVE PROCESSOR PUNIFY

10.2.0 Introduction

Fig. 10.5 shows the block diagram structure of the associative processor PUNIFY.

There are two associative memories: AS I acts as the input "box" to UNIFY, and as a temporary memory for intermediate values, while AS II assumes the roles of the "boxes" x[1],x[2]...x[*n*] in sequence. This is possible as each box is only handled once in isolation. AS I is implemented as a one-dimensional array, and AS II a two-dimensional array of cells. It is assumed that there are only ever two initial terms in the input box.

10.2.1 An Example

The example reflects the example of the earlier section 10.1 of this chapter. Only the relevant active parts of AS I and AS II are shown at any time. The entry terms are written into AS I at the start

In the first step, it has to be decided for which box AS II will act first—so a label has to be determined, and then AS II loaded with the appropriate values. In order to complete the first full step and fill AS II, a set of variables that only occur in cells that are unmarked (i.e. not marked with a "+" sign in Fig. 10.6) is determined. Only the variable x[1] falls into that category—all the other variables occur in one row at least that is marked, so the set is also {x[1]} in this case, and thus the first label to be loaded into AS II is x[1].

All terms that occur in AS I parallel to x[1] are entered in AS II, deleted in AS I, and AS I reordered (Fig. 10.7). Now AS II contains two terms. In order to unify these, the full rows of AS II are marked and processing is confined to these rows. Rows with identical function symbols are deleted and output to form the input to the box x[1].

Then the variables in the marked rows are assembled. From these the label for the next step is built up (contents of box x[1]). There are two sets in contention in this case, {x[2]} on the second row of AS II, and the set {x[2],x[3]} on the fifth row.

X	f(X[1],X[2],X[3],X[4])
X[1]	g(X[2],X[3])
X[2],X[3]	h(a,X[4])
X[4],X[5]	b

Fig. 10.4—Status at the conclusion of UNIFY.

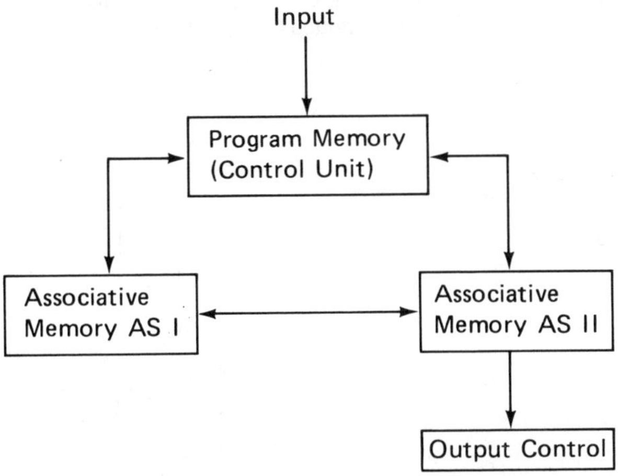

Fig. 10.5—Diagrammatic structure of the associative processing PUNIFY.

The next label is always selected from the highest order superset in these cases, as in Fig. 10.8.

Now AS II is reordered. Variables in marked rows, as far as they do not occur in labels, as well as the parallel terms in AS I are entered in AS II, using AS I as intermediate storage. This step is not required in the example. All x[2] and x[3] in AS I and AS II are entered into AS II, and AS I reordered, as in Fig. 10.9.

AS I

#f	#f	.
X[1]	g .	.
.	h	+
.	a	+
.	X[5]	+
.	X[2]	+
g	X[1]	.
X[2]	.	+
X[3]	.	+
X[2]	h	.
.	a	+
.	X[4]	+
b	X[4]	.

Fig. 10.6—Initial state of AS I (at this stage, AS II is empty as it is not known which box it is supposed to function as). Note: Identical function symbols can be deleted (i.e. #f), empty places are dotted ("."), and cells with only one symbol are marked "+".

AS I

X[2]	h	.
.	a	+
.	X[4]	+
b	X[4]	.

AS II

g	g	.
h	X[2]	.
a	.	.
X[5]	.	.
X[2]	X[3]	.

Fig. 10.7—AS I (upper) and AS II (below) after the completion of the first step.

AS I

X[2]	h	.
.	a	+
.	X[4]	+
b	X[4]	.

#g	#g	+
h	X[2]	+
a	.	.
X[5]	.	.
X[2]	X[3]	+

OUTPUT g(X[2],X[3])
NEXT LABEL: X[2],X[3]

AS II

Fig. 10.8—AS I (upper) and AS II (lower) after the second step.

The subsequent steps follow the same algorithmic pattern, and finally both AS I and AS II are empty. The unification process stops at that point.

Clashes and cyclical problems are monitored at all stages. Clashes are prevented by checking entries in the respective rows in the AS I and AS II arrays. Cycles are prevented by monitoring the marked rows of AS I and the unmarked rows of AS II. If variables occur there that also occur in the label portions, then cyclical referencing would occur sooner or later in the algorithm.

10.3 IMPROVED EFFICIENCY USING PUNIFY

The algorithm UNIFY is linear in computational resources. Based on the number of variables *n*, *n* steps are needed to achieve unification. One step of course consists of several sub-steps, as well as checking for clashes and possible circular references. As *n* is rarely very large, it is the additional sub-steps at each iteration that exert considerable influence on the run time performance of the system. In many cases it will be possible to introduce a measure of parallelism into the unification. PUNIFY exhibits these characteristics.

A less than linear model is theoretically not possible, but parallelism could influence the side checks' efficiency significantly. Parallelism is usable when, at the stage of identifying a candidate for a label for the next step, a number of disjoint variable sets occur. This can be handled in parallel as AS II can be partitioned, only having to pay some overhead for synchronisation of access to AS I.

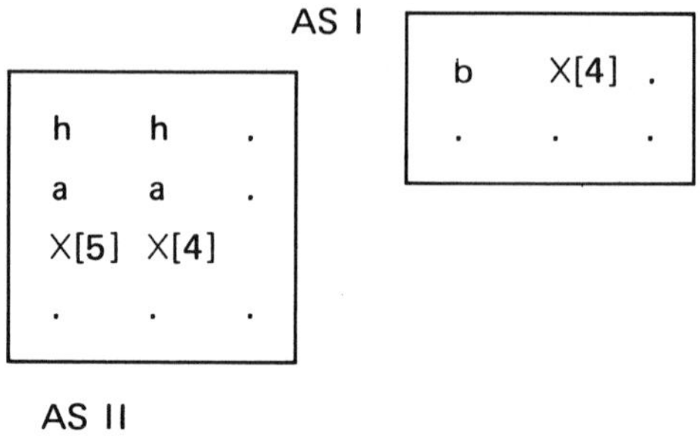

Fig. 10.9—AS II (left) and AS I (right) after the second step.

Appendix A

A Definition of Some Terms in Logic and Artificial Intelligence

These definitions are intended to be easily understood by the reader, and are not necessarily formally complete or precise.

Abstract syntax
The abstract syntax of a language defines the set of objects which are in the language, in contrast to the strings of concrete syntax.

Algorithm
A description of steps on how to reach another state from an initial state.

Alvey Programme
The UK government initiative in Information Technology to counter the Japanese Fifth Generation project, started in 1984 and due to finish in 1988.

Antecedent
The antecedent is the left-hand side (pre-condition) of an implication.

Application
An application is a small subset of a problem domain for which a system is constructed. For example, a fault diagnoser for M68000 micro-processors is an application within the domain of computer fault diagnosis.

Artificial Intelligence (AI)
That area of computer science that involves inferential thinking and problem solving.

Associativity
An operator "op" is associative if the following holds:

$$a \text{ op } (b \text{ op } c) = (a \text{ op } b) \text{ op } c$$

Attribute
A property of an object

Backtracking
A search procedure that makes guesses at various points during problem solving and returns to a previous point to make another choice, when a guess did not lead to an acceptable result.

Backward chaining
A control procedure that attempts to achieve goals by developing a chain of deductions leading back from the final goal to only a minimum of questions. It is essentially backward reasoning to see if known facts fit a given situation.

Bag
A bag is an unordered collection of values where values can occur more than once and those occurrences can be counted.

Certainty factors
Numerical weightings, first used in the expert system MYCIN to quantify the strength of a belief.

Commutativity
An operator "op" is commutative if the following holds:

a op b = b op a.

Completeness
An axiomatisation is complete with respect to a model if all statements which are true in that model can be proved from the axioms using the models' rules of inference.

Concatenation
Concatenation is the operator which creates a sequence from the elements of its two operands

Conclusion
In a rule, the conclusion is the logical expression on the right-hand side of an implication. For example, in "if a then b", b is the conclusion.

Concrete syntax
The concrete syntax of a language defines exactly the set of strings which form sentences of the language.

Conjugation
A collection of terms whose principal operator is "and".

Consequent
The consequent is the right hand side of an implication.

Contradiction

A contradiction is a logical expression if there are no contexts in which it may be evaluated to "true", e.g. A and NOT A.

Criticiser
The part of a learning system that evaluates proposed rules or concepts and accredits them with some score.

Database
A data collection of a number of records of a similar nature, describing the state of objects.

DARPA—Defense Advanced Research Project Agency
The main US funding organisation in advanced computer technology, sponsored by the US Department of Defense.

Data reification
Abstract objects are reified to chosen representations in the early stages of systems design.

Declarative languages
A language that allows the data structure to be used in solving a query to be described, rather than how the solution is to be located, as in procedural languages.

Default value
In the absence of indications to the contrary, usually from external sources, this is the value given to a variable in the system.

Demon
A demon is a self-contained action triggered by some external event.

Depth-first search
A search strategy that pursues one branch of a tree to exhaustion, and then backtracks in the absence of a success.

Derived rule
Results proved with general propositional variables can be used as inference rules in proofs; such inference rules are derived from basic axiomatisation.

Description language
A non-procedural language used to describe objects and their properties.

Disjoint
Disjoint sets are sets that have no common elements. For example, the sets {0,1} and {red,green} are disjoint.

Disjunctive

A disjunctive is a logical expression whose principal operator is "or".

Domain (AI)
A domain is a specialist area, such as medicine or geology. It is a wide category.

Domain (Logic)
A domain is the set of values to which a model can be applied.

Equivalence relation
Equivalence relations are those which are reflexive, symmetric and transitive.

Equivalent
Two expressions are equivalent if the same output is generated for all possible values of their variable input.

ESPRIT—European Strategic Programme for Research and Development in Information Technology
A 1300 million dollar programme for collaborative pre-competitive research and development in Information Technology, administered by the Commission of the European Communities from Brussels.

Expert Systems (ES)
A computer system that achieves a high degree of performance in task areas that, for human beings, require training and education, and which is able to explain its conclusions at any time. Expert Systems are a subset of knowledge based systems.

Formal language
A formal language is a language that consists of a precise syntax and uniquely interpretable semantics.

Formal logic
The science of formally correct reasoning which began with the Greek philosophers and was further developed by Boole. A subset was recently implemented as a computer language by Colmerauer and Kowalski [Campbell, J. C. 1984].

Formal proof
A formal proof is one where all steps are mechanical and the proof can therefore theoretically be checked by a computational device.

Forward chaining
Moving from the data to the goals, and thus the opposite way of proceeding to backward chaining.

Frame
A frame is a data structure describing an object or an event, with slots filled with data called attributes.

Free variables
Free variables are those variables in an expression not bound by, for example, a quantifier.

Functions
A function is a mapping between two sets of values.

Functional decomposition
Starting with a high level description, this is the process of dividing this into lower order sets of tasks or functions.

Functional specifications
Functional specifications defines the intended input/output behaviour of a system.

Fuzzy logic
Initiated by L. Zadeh [Zadeh 1985], fuzzy logic is the generalisation of formal Boolean logic to deal with differing degrees of belief in a proposition.

Generalisation
When the scope or range of a concept is extended, it is said to be generalised.

Heuristics
An incomplete method of problem solving for which no deterministic solution strategies are known. Mainly "rules of thumb" based on individual experience and traditional ways are employed. They are especially useful in diffuse and difficult problem areas, with incomplete knowledge.

Horn clause
A predicate logic clause type with more than one condition, but just one conclusion.

Hyper-rule
The highest level of rule that is normally encountered. It is generally applicable to the widest category of data in a domain.

Icon
A visual, graphic representation of a word or concept. For example, a red cross is a symbol for first aid in different contexts in Christian nations.

ICOT—Institute for New Generation Computer Technology
This is the Japanese organisation that leads research and development of

new information technology, the so-called "Fifth Generation" computer systems project, for example.

Implication
An implication is a logical expression whose principal operator is ("left-hand side" implies "right-hand side").

Induction step
In an induction proof, an induction step shows that the required expression inherits some property from the previous function.

Inference rules
Inference rules consist of a number of premises and a conclusion.

Intersection
The intersection of two sets is the set of common elements. For example, the intersection of {1,2,3} and {3,4,5} is {3}.

Induction
Obtaining a general truth from a number of individual examples. It is a widely used learning method, e.g. Quinlan's ID3 algorithm [Quinlan 1982].

Inference machine
An implementation of an inference mechanism.

Inference mechanism
An algorithm that draws conclusions from a knowledge base of facts and rules.

Knowledge acquisition
This is the process of eliciting, formalising, representing and testing knowledge for use in an expert system or knowledge based system.

Knowledge base
A knowledge set (mainly expert knowledge) formally represented and stored in computer usable form.

Knowledge based systems
Computer based systems are systems which incorporate factual and inferential data as well as uncertain, heuristic and subjective data.

Knowledge domain
A limited area of knowledge, such as modular construction of machines or computer failure diagnosis.

Knowledge engineering
This is an area of AI which is concerned with acquisition, representation and

application of knowledge not only in its factual parts, but also inexact, heuristic and individual knowledge. The aim of this activity is to represent knowledge and inference procedures to interpret this knowledge in computer usable form.

Knowledge representation
The formalism used to represent the knowledge for the system. There can be several within one system.

Learning
The process of acquiring more or better rules to process knowledge, and improve performance. Relies on some feedback mechanism usually.

Lisp
An AI programming language in use since the mid 1950's useful for the implementation of list structures and other symbolic representations, but not very useful for logic systems.

Meta-rule
A meta-rule is any rule about the use of another rule.

Model theory
Model theory for a calculus associates formulae with a set of mathematical objects.

Modus Ponens
Modus Ponens is an inference rule type which from "E1 implies E2" justifies E2 by the existence of E1.

Monotonicity
Monotonicity is a property of a function that preserves some ordering.

Monotonic functions
See Monotonicity.

Negation
Negation is a logical expression whose operator is "not".

Non-deterministic operator
A non-deterministic operator is one whose specification permits more than one result.

Object oriented paradigm
A style of programming based on objects which pass messages amongst themselves in order to communicate.

Parsing

The process whereby some information is analysed into its component parts, for example, natural language input.

Partial functions.
Partial functions are those which are not defined for all values in the domain (logic).

Partition of a set
A partition of a set S is a set of disjoint subsets of S whose union is S.

Power set
The power set of a set S is the set of all subsets of S.

Predicate
A predicate is a truth value expression with free variables.

Predicate calculus
Application of the rules of inference to predicates give rise to predicate calculus.

Production rules
Frequently used for a knowledge representation which formalises knowledge as a set of rules consisting of IF- and THEN-parts. If the IF part of a rule is applicable, then the THEN-part may be concluded or the problem solving activity triggered may be executed. These rules can be chained backwards or forwards.

PROLOG
PROgramming in LOGic, a computer language based on formal logic, often used in the implementation of expert and knowledge based systems.

Proof theory
A proof theory for a calculus provides a way of deducing formulae from instantiations of axioms via the use of inference rules.

Range
The range of a function is a specified set which contains the results of all function applications.

Recursive definition
A recursive definition is a definition which contains the name of what is defined within the definition to arbitrary levels of nesting. The classical example is the factorial function $F(n)=n*F(n-1)$.

Script
An organised collection of facts and experiences, on which some other communication process is often based.

Search space
The area in which solutions could lie, which therefore has to be searched.

Semantics
The study of meaning of language.

Semantic gap
The bridge between low level hardware capability, and high level language facilities. Bridged by compilers usually.

Semantic net
A frequently used form of knowledge representation which formalises knowledge as a network of relations between objects.

Set
A set is an unordered collection of distinct objects, unlike a "bag", which may contain replicates.

Signature
The signature of a function is its domain (logic) and range.

Slot
A slot is a field in a frame.

Specialisation
The opposite of generalisation.

Subset
A subset is an unordered collection of objects whose common property is that they are all elements of some larger set.

Syntax
The structure of language, such as grammar rules.

Tautology
A tautology evaluates to .TRUE. for any values of its constituent propositions, e.g. A or NOT A.

Taxonomy
Hierarchical structure of expert terminology in a domain, often represented by a tree.

Turing Test
The Turing Test for "AI" is that a computer program behaves intelligently when a person interacting with it cannot tell whether it is a machine or a human at the other end of a line of communication. This rather stresses the

anthropomorphic nature of human concepts of intelligence. Turing [1936–37, 1963] has one approach, whereas another definition may be equally useful: an intelligent machine is one that learns [Simon 1983].

Unification
Filling in of program variables at run time by pattern matching.

Union of sets
A union of two sets is a set that contains all the elements of both the original sets. For example, the union of $\{1,2,3\}$ and $\{3,4,5\}$ is $\{1,2,3,4,5\}$.

Well-founded relation
A well-founded relation is one in which there are no infinite descending chains.

Appendix B

Biographical Information on the (senior) Authors and Editors

Principal Editor:
Stuart E. Savory, Ph.D., B.Sc.(Hons)
Stuart Savory was born in Edinburgh and studied Physics at the City University in London, where he graduated in 1966 with honours. He joined Nixdorf Computer AG in 1975, and has been an assistant to the Board of Directors since 1981. He gained his Ph.D. in 1984 at the Southwestern University, in Arizona, USA. He leads the Expert Systems group at Nixdorf. In 1984 he was chairman of the AI OECD conference. He has over 50 publications in the fields of Computer Science and AI.

Other Contributors:
Lothar Fohmann, Dr. jur.
Dr Fohmann was born in 1947 in Karlsruhe, and completed the state examinations in Law in 1972 and 1975. He was awarded his doctorate in Heidelberg in 1977, and took up a research fellowship in Informatics at the London School of Economics the year after. His publications are to be found in Law, Mathematics and Informatics. He is now no longer with Nixdorf. Any queries on his chapter should therefore be sent to the editor.

Bernhard Mescheder, Dip. Math.
Born in 1953 in Paderborn, Bernhard Mescheder graduated in mathematics at the University of Bielefeld in 1979, after which he joined Nixdorf. He joined the Expert Systems team in 1983, and has publications in the field of mathematics to his name.

Uwe Noelke, Dip. Ing.
Uwe Noelke was born in Bad Rothenfelde in 1953, and obtained his Diploma in Telecommunications at the Technical High School in Bielefeld. After joining Nixdorf in 1980, he joined the Expert Systems team in 1983. His publications are in the AI field. He is currently on the Nixdorf AI salesforce.

Hannelore Roesner, Ph.D.
Born in 1949 in Burg/Fehmarn, Hannelore Roesnor graduated in Philology at the University of Goettingen in 1974. There she obtained her Ph.D. in

Psychology and Linguistics in 1981. In 1982 she became an Assistant Professor at the University of Braunschweig and in 1984 joined the Expert Systems team at Nixdorf. Now she is researching into expert systems and databases for Nixdorf in Munich. She is the author of many articles on the analysis and construction of educational material.

Mike Rogers, Ph.D., B.Sc.(Jt Hons), F.I.M.A., F.C.S.
Dr Rogers was born in Detmold/Lippe in 1950, and graduated with double honours in Chemistry and Applied Mathematics at University College Cardiff. In 1978 he was awarded his Ph.D. in Mathematical Modelling at Aston University. He joined the ESPRIT group at the Commission of the European Communities in 1981 and was responsible for the co-ordination of the Advanced Information Processing programme until mid-1986. After that date he assumed responsibilities for Information Dissemination for all of ESPRIT, as well as for the Commission's Ada Programme.

Jon Young,D. Sc.
Dr Young is the ICL Fellow in Logic Programming at St Cross College, Oxford. He is applying logic programming to communications tasks such as teaching, discourse analysis and dialogue modelling. He acts as consultant to several research projects in the area of knowledge based systems.

Appendix C

An Extract of European Publicity Funded Projects in the Area of Expert Systems

C.1 ACKNOWLEDGEMENTS

This information is an extract of an ECHO (European Community Host Organisation) database in Luxembourg sponsored by the Commission of the European Communities, DG XIII. It contains information on publicly funded Information Technology Projects and is being continuously updated and expanded.

The projects listed below are those that concern the area of Expert Systems only.

To become a user of this service, please write to M. Carpentier, Director General, DG XIII, Commission of the European Communities, 200 Rue de la Loi, B1049 Brussels, Belgium, quoting the nature of the database: PROJECT COLLECTIONS.

The projects listed cover ESPRIT and the UK's Alvey programme only at this stage. Any further details on new IT projects are requested in order to maximise the usefulness of this database.

C.2 EXPLANATIONS OF STRUCTURE

The printout is structured with identifiers ending in a colon followed by the data field to which the descriptor refers, thus:

TI: Title of the project.
PR: Funding Programme and Contract Reference, e.g. ESPRIT 25/A.
AR: Areas of research, by a small number of key phrases.
OS: Organisational short name, sometimes an acronym is faster!
OU: Organisational unit, name of the university department, holding company subsidiary or possibly site. or possibly site name.
ON: Organisation managing contract, e.g. Widget Plc.

OA: Company's mail address, where work is focussed.
CY: Country of location of the main contractor.
CP: Contact Point, from whom more information is obtainable by request.
TN: National telephone number. If dialling from another country, prefix with the appropriate country code. If dialling from within the country, usually add only a zero.
AB: This section contains a short abstract of the project. It tries to give a short overview of the flavour of the project without delving into too much detail.
PS: Project start date and duration (not always available).
DS: Date of last update of information from the project.

C.3 ESPRIT PROJECTS

C.3.1 ESPRIT Advanced Information Processing (AIP) Projects

TI: Message Passing Architectures and Description Systems
PR: ESPRIT 440
AR: advanced information processing; message passing architectures; AIP; computer architectures; expert systems development
ON: Delphi SpA
OA: 11 Via della Vetraia, I-55049 Viareggio
CY: IT
CP: Professor Giuseppe Attardi
TN: 584-39 51 61
AB: The project will build three levels of tools for the development of expert systems:
(1) message passing languages;
(2) description languages for knowledge representation;
(3) reasoning and strategy programming.
The project will develop techniques for implementing message passing languages that will exploit new highly parallel architectures. The techniques will cover issues of run-time support like allocation, migration, garbage-collection and persistency of actors. A description system will be developed to support the basic mechanisms of knowledge representation: conceptual hierarchies, inheritance, attributions. To perform reasoning on the description system, rather than providing a fixed strategy, primitives and constructs will be developed that will allow to programme deductive strategies tailored to specific applications. Strategy execution will be performed concurrently by a large number of actors each exploring a small portion of the knowledge base.
PS: 1985

TI: Design of Techniques and Tools to Aid in the Analysis and Design of Knowledge Based Systems

PR: ESPRIT 012, ESPRIT 304
AR: advanced information processing; AIP; IKBS; expert systems development
ON: Standard Telecommunication & Cables
OU: STC Technology Division—IDEC
OA: Six Hills House, London Road, GB-Stevenage, Herts, SG1 1YB
CY: GB
CP: Mr S. Hayward
TN: 438-72 61 61
AB: This was a pilot project that investigated the types of tools and design techniques necessary for the analysis, design, implementation and testing of Knowledge Based Systems. The purpose was to specify the techniques which will aid in the building expert system. In particular valuable work was done, and a good insight was made into analysing the process of Knowledge Acquisition. The findings of the project were used as a basis for the proposal of project P1098, also in ESPRIT.
PS: 1983
DS: 860825

TI: A Methodology for the Development of KBS
PR: ESPRIT 1098
AR: advanced information processing; AIP; IKBS; expert systems development
ON: Standard Telecommunication & Cables
OU: STC Technology Division—IDEC
OA: Six Hills House, London Road, GB-Stevenage SG1 1YB
CY: GB
CP: Mr S. Hayward
TN: 438-72 61 61 ext. 8333
AB: The prime purpose of this project is to assist the transfer of Knowledge Based Systems technology into commercial use by providing methodological guidance for the development process. It is believed that Knowledge Based Systems development can be treated as a particular case of software engineering and that the same requirements must be placed on the development of Knowledge Based Systems as on other types of software. In short KBS must be produced to specification and to acceptable standards by a controllable process.
DS: 860825
PS: 1985

TI: Graphics and Knowledge Based Dialogue for Dynamic Systems
PR: ESPRIT 857
AR: advanced information processing; knowledge engineering; industrial monitoring; man–machine interfaces; AIP
ON: CRI A/S

OA: 1A Vesterbrogade, DK-1620 Copenhagen V
CY: DK
CP: Mr O. Holst
TN: 1-13 11 66
AB: This project will develop improved user/system interfaces for dynamic large-scale industrial control systems by the design of intelligent graphics and knowledge base dialogue systems. Three co-operating knowledge processing expert systems will be built, that will give the operator of a supervision and control (S&C) system intelligent support in diagnosing and recovering from faults, and will provide an intelligent graphic interface. A further aim of the project is to assemble different KBS Demonstrators for use in "hard-tech" industrial environments and to identify appropriate metrication aspects and methods. The project will develop expertise by building a set of dialogue design and specification tools for use in solving problems identified during a survey of users of S&C systems. These tools will then be used and tested throughout the project, to build these systems. The project attempts to identify metrics which are of significance, and methods for their assessment.
PS: 1986
DS: 860825

TI: Knowledge Representation and Inference Techniques in Industrial Control
PR: ESPRIT 387
AR: advanced information processing; AIP; knowledge engineering; knowledge processing; expert systems; industrial monitoring
ON: Krupp Atlas Elektronik GmbH
OA: 235 Sebaldsbruecker Heerstrasse, Postfach 44 85 45, D-2800 Bremen 44
CY: DE
CP: Dipl. Ing. D. Eberitzsch
TN: 421-457 24 65
AB: The aim of the project is to design and implement an Expert System to assist maintenance, fault diagnosis, optimisation of data flows, and control in an industrial process-control environment of very high complexity. Therefore the Expert Control System must take the time-dependency into account, and capturing of input data must be accomplished automatically and intelligently. To overcome complexity barriers in such devices, a machine learning capability is included. Advances over existing Control Systems lie in making process-control more secure by assisting the operator in his decisions and by reducing the drop-out rate of the controlling devices.
PS: 1984
DS: 860825

TI: Expert System Builder — ESB
PR: ESPRIT 096
AR: advanced information processing; AIP; knowledge engineering; knowledge processing; expert systems
ON: Plessey Electronic System
OA: Grange Road, Christchurch, GB-Dorset BH23 4JE
CY: GB
CP: Mr Ian Gray
TN: 202-48 63 44
AB: The aim of the project is to provide a system enabling expert systems to be developed and tested by personnel inexperienced in artificial intelligence. A ring structured model has been identified for the system to allow progressive development and extension of the facilities within the individual layers, with the inner rings being completely independent of the domain. The test system provides the tool set for the upper layers, with the capability for later extensions. A particular domain has been chosen, that of diagnosis of electronic systems, because of its increasing demand in equipment and manufacturing, and labour intensiveness of the methods presently employed. Implementation of the tools on symbolic processors has commenced. Portability of the eventual software and the independence from domain specific characteristics are the main design factors. The first demonstrations ran successfully in September 1984, and the first virtually complete system was demonstrated at the 1986 ESPRIT Technical Week in Brussels.
PS: 1983
DS: 860825

TI: Communication Failure in Dialogue: Techniques for Detection and Repair
PR: ESPRIT 527
AR: advanced information processing; AIP; knowledge engineering; natural language processing; information retrieval
ON: Educational Research Centre
OA: St Patrick's College, Drumcondra, IRL-Dublin 9
CY: IRL
CP: Dr. Ronan Reilly
TN: 1-37 37 89
AB: The aim of this project is the development of a robust and portable natural-language interface to a relational database system. The initial stages of the project involve the study of human dialogues in a simulated database-query environment, including recovery from various types of communication failure. From an analysis of these dialogues a formal model of the dialogue process will be developed. The formal model will serve as a basis for a computer implementation of an English and Italian natural-language front-

end to a student's records database. An important element of the implementation will be the use of non-verbal systems (e.g. graphics, pointing, icons) in roles analogous to the non-verbal components of human dialogues. The robust dialogue component of the project has potential applications outside the database domain. Elements of it can be used in the development of a front-end to expert systems or for information retrieval in an office environment.

PS: 1985
DS: 860825

C.3.2 ESPRIT Microelectronics Projects

TI: Automatic Design Validation of Integrated Circuits Using E-Beam
PR: ESPRIT 271
AR: advanced microelectronics; MEL; electron beam techniques; circuits design validation
OS: CSELT
ON: CSELT
OA: 274 Via Reiss Romoli, I-10148 Torino
CY: IT
CP: Dr Marco Cocito
TN: 11-216 94 89
AB: The project seeks to develop a methodology for the automatic design errors diagnosis of VLSI devices based on the observability facility given by an electron beam system, connection to the CAD environment, pattern recognition to automatically position the E-beam, global methodology, possibly based on expert systems to define the diagnostic strategy, new hardware circuitry to enhance the EBT performance. The areas of
— computer control of the electron beam system,
— interfacing to CAD software,
— identification of circuit elements,
— methodology for design error diagnosis,
— test pattern generation for electron beam debugging,
— design for electron beam testability, and
— electron beam equipment development,
will be addressed in order to achieve these objectives.
PS: 1984
DS: 860825

TI: Advanced Integrated Circuit Design Aids (AIDA)
PR: ESPRIT 888
AR: advanced microelectronics; MEL; computer aided design; CAD; expert systems
ON: Siemens A.G.

OU: ZTI
OA: 6 Otto Hahn Ring, D-8000 Muenchen 83
CY: DE
CP: Dr K. Merten
TN: 89-63 64 88 25
AB: AIDA intends to explore the application of modern programming techniques and knowledge base engineering to CAD tool development. It will constitute a design assistant that proposes solutions rather than record and validate the designer's ideas. This allows the designer to apply his creativity where it is most efficient leading to improved design quality. Research and development work will be done, applying modern programming techniques (e.g. those developed for expert systems) to VLSI-CAD tools. The potential contribution of these techniques is twofold:
(1) the basic techniques may be used to make new tools much more efficient than classical ones;
(2) the basic integrated circuit design knowledge may be recorded into the machine, and used by "expert" modules under the control of a system designer.
The AIDA project intends to explore these two domains, to develop experimental tools using these techniques, and to experiment on real industrial cases to demonstrate the benefit they could give.
PS: 1986
DS: 860825

C.3.3 ESPRIT Office Systems Projects

TI: Investigation into the Effective Use of Speech at the Human–Machine Interface.
PR: ESPRIT 449
AR: office systems; OS; speech recognition; simulation; MMI
OS: BMT
ON: A British Maritime Technology
OU: Wallsend Research Station
OA: GB-Wallsend, Tyne and Wear NE28 6UY
CY: GB
CP: Mr P. Kelway
TN: 632-62 52 42
AB: This project is to identify the requirements for effective device interfaces in a wide range of professional, commercial and industrial application areas, with difficult operating environments and busy hands/busy eyes conditions. The major objective of this project is to examine the effectiveness of the use of speech as the man-machine interface for computer systems. It is intended that the operator of a system shall be able to control operations and interrogate the computer system principally by voice, freeing the

hands for use of other equipment. The computer would respond via image and voice media. It is proposed that the project will be composed of six major research areas. The work will be aimed at a range of application though special importance will be attached to the CAD/CAM/CAE environment. Hardware and software available contemporaneously with the study period will be used. The six major areas are:

(1) state of the art study of voice recognition and simulation techniques and equipment (VRS);
(2) study of current areas of practical application;
(3) communication aspects;
(4) application to database management;
(5) application to expert systems;
(6) sociology aspects.

PS: 1986
DS: 860825

C.3.4 ESPRIT Computer Integrated Manufacturing Projects

TI: Knowledge and Decision Support for Material Handling Systems
PR: ESPRIT 293
AR: computer integrated manufacture; CIM; AI; expert systems; computer aided design; CAD
OS: CGP
ON: CGP
OA: 98 rue d'Ambert, B.p. 1825, F-45008 Orléans Cedex
CY: FR
CP: Mr G. Minouflet
TN: 1-468-73-11-4
AB: The project is investigating the applicability of expert systems for decision support and will develop a knowledge base for modelling material handling systems. The objectives are to analyse and define the knowledge necessary to achieve valid assessments for system designs and of system operation. The knowledge will be implemented to decision support systems and would be used by engineers planning a material handling system.
PS: 1984
DS: 860825

TI: A Systems Technology for Optimising the Tradeoffs between Plant Availability, Product Quality and Safety
PR: ESPRIT 504
AR: computer integrated manufacture; CIM; plant availability; quality control; plant optimisation
ON: Stewart Hughes Ltd

OA: Chilworth Manor, GB-Southampton S09 1XB
CY: GB
CP: Mr D. Bonfield
TN: 703-76 02 22
AB: The subject of this project is the development of a systems technology for automating the management of discrete parts manufacturing plants based on maximising their availability, product quality and safety. A high percentage of the proposed R&D effort relates to the on-line processing of plant machinery health, tool performance, product quality and safety data. The enabling technologies include signal processing, expert systems, system modelling, action planning, sensor network, and computer system design. During the first year preliminary results have been obtained from two specially built small demonstrator systems. On one system, based on a numerically controlled milling machine, real-time process parameter monitoring has been carried out. On the other system, a plant simulator, the use of real-time software tools for automated action planning and scheduling, using knowledge based computing concepts, is being demonstrated.
PS: 1985
DS: 860825

TI: Integrated Information Processing for Design, Planning and Control of Assembly
PR: ESPRIT 384
AR: computer integrated manufacture; CIM; automated assembly
OS: GEC
ON: General Electric Company plc
OU: Dept. GEC Research Laboratories
OA: West Hanningfield Road, Great Baddow, GB-Chelmsford CM2 8HN, Essex
CY: GB
CP: Mr I.L. Powell
TN: 245-733 31 ext. 3231
AB: This project is aimed at demonstrating the principle of an integrated process for design, planning and control of small batch assemblies. The emphasis of the project is on defining and automatically assembling the product, rather than on the manufacture of the piece parts. The project also aims to demonstrate the concept an integrated system for the complete assembly process including design planning, scheduling and control aspects, considering all interdependencies and feedbacks from related assembly objects and processes. Current work has focussed on expert systems and simulation tools with attention to the existing systems for design, planning and scheduling an important precursor to the demonstrators in these areas.

PS: 1985
DS: 860825

C.4 ALVEY PROJECTS

C.4.1 Alvey IKBS Projects

TI: EMEX
PR: ALVEY IKBS 102
AR: intelligent knowledge based systems; IKBS; economics; expert systems
ON: Expert Systems International
OA: 9 West Way, GB-Oxford OX2 0JB
CY: GB
CP: Alex Goodall
TN: 865-24 22 06
AB: The primary aim of the project is to prmote awareness amongst the Club members of the protential of expert systems technology. This is done in the context of an application that is of mutual interest to the members. This application is an expert system to assist in the task of building econometric models. The system will be aimed at market specialists who have a good knowledge of a market but do not have the skills to build a mathematical model of that market. At the time of writing there was still opportunity for a few interested companies to join the Club.
PS: Start date: 25 November 1985, duration: 18-24 months
DS: 860729

TI: Water Industry Expert Systems Club
PR: ALVEY IKBS 060
AR: intelligent knowledge based systems; IKBS; natural resources management; expert systems
ON: University of Surrey
OU: Computing Unit
OA: University of Surrey, GB-Guildford GU2 5XH
CY: GB
CP: Dr K. Ahmad
TN: 483-57 12 81 ext. 3203
AB: A number of public and private sector organisations in the water industry, a software house, two universities, one polytechnic and the Her Majesty's Department of the Environment have formed a club to demonstrate the application and relevance of expert systems methodologies tools and techniques to the water industry. The project, which will run until the end of 1987, has the following aims:

(1) To increase the awareness of the potential of expert systems technology in the water industry.

(2) To build two expert systems for the industry,
— one for water distribution network control, and
— the other for sewerage rehabilitation planning.
These topics cover a major part of the activities within the industry.
(3) To make members more familiar with both technical and managerial aspects of the development of expert systems.

PS: Start date: 1 November 1985, duration: 24 months
DS: 860729

TI: TRACE Club
PR: ALVEY IKBS 059
AR: intelligent knowledge based systems; IKBS; services industries; transportation; expert systems
ON: Software Sciences Ltd
OA: London & Manchester House, Park Street, GB-Macclesfield SK11 6SR
CY: GB
CP: G. Williams
TN: 625-292 41
AB: Gain an understanding of the benefits offered by applying expert systems technology to problems in the transport and travel industries. A microcomputer based system, written in Prolog 2, is under development which will assist enquiry clerks in route selection and retail travel sales staff in selection of packaged holidays. Key characteristics are excellent MMI, rapid internal processing and capability to interface with electronic data bases e.g. Holiday Reservations Systems.
PS: Start date: 1 November 1986, duration: 18 months
DS: 860729

TI: ARIES Insurance Community Club
PR: ALVEY IKBS 057
AR: intelligent knowledge based systems; IKBS; insurance industry; expert systems
ON: Colonial Mutual Insurance Company Ltd.
CY: GB
CP: Anthony Butler
TN: 1-248 98 61
AB: The Club aims to give members useful experience in developing expert systems for the insurance industry. The final goal is that members should be able to decide if such systems are relevant techniques to use, including software and hardware, and should also have a good appreciation of the difficulties a successful implementation is likely to face.
PS: Start date: 1 September 1985, duration: 18 months
DS: 860729

TI: ALFEX—Alvey Finance Expert Systems Club
PR: ALVEY IKBS 050
AR: intelligent knowledge based systems; IKBS; finance; expert systems
ON: Helix Software Consultants Ltd
OA: 11 Ludgate Circus, GB-London EC4M 7LQ
CY: GB
CP: Mr John Berkin
TN: 1-248 17 34
AB: The ALFEX Club was formed in April 1985 with the objective of increasing awareness of expert systems techniques, uses and advantages in the financial community. This objective was to be achieved by undertaking a project to develop an industry specific company health adviser which would provide: assessment of company health, diagnosis of company health problems, and limited advice regarding financial and non-financial solutions to problems. The project comprises four phases:
(1) evaluation of commercially available expert system shells:
(2) investigation of non-shell implementation approaches;
(3) development of a market assessor;
(4) development of a full company health adviser.
PS: Start date: 1 April 1985, duration: 18 months
DS: 860729

TI: The Application of Expert Systems to Quantity Surveying Techniques
PR: ALVEY IKBS 035
AR: intelligent knowledge based systems; IKBS; public administration; expert systems
ON: The Royal Institute of Chartered Surveyors
OA: 12 Great George Street, Parliament Square, GB-London SW1P 3AD
CY: GB
CP: Mr Alex Trimmer
TN: 1-222 70 00
AB: To promote the development and use of expert systems in the quantity surveying profession by exploring areas of possible application and preparing appropriate computer software.
PS: Start date: 1 January 1986, duration: 18 months
DS: 860729

TI: 2-D Gel Electrophoresis Expert System
PR: ALVEY IKBS 104
AR: intelligent knowledge based systems; IKBS; analysis techniques; gel science; expert systems

ON: Unilever Research Colworth
OU: Unilever Research Laboratory
OA: Colworth House, Sharnbrook, GB-Bedford MK44 1LO
CY: GB
CP: Dr D.G. Rowlands
TN: 234-78 17 81
AB: To develop a software package based on a blackboard handler for analysing the "spots" on 2-D Gel Electrophoresis slides. Based upon this software package, to develop a prototype engineered instrument for slide analysis.
PS: Start date: 1 April 1986, duration: 12 months
DS: 860729

TI: A Knowledge Elicitation Methodology for Research Associations
PR: ALVEY IKBS 098
AR: intelligent knowledge based systems; IKBS; knowledge elicitation techniques
OS: BHRA
ON: BHRA
OU: The Fluid Engineering Centre
OA: Cranfield, GB-Bedford MK43 OAJ
CY: GB
CP: Mr W. L. McDowell
TN: 234-75 04 22
AB: To develop and make available to the independent Research Laboratories and Research Associations in the United Kingdom, the information necessary to specify and design knowledge bases, to improve the effectiveness of transferring expert knowledge to industry by Research Associations and to provide the capability of designing specific expert systems for their client companies.
PS: Start date: late 1986, duration: 36 months
DS: 860729

TI: An Advanced Graphical Tracing and Debugging Environment for Prolog
PR: ALVEY IKBS 081
AR: intelligent knowledge based systems; IKBS; programming support environments; PROLOG
ON: Expert Systems International
OA: 9 West Way, GB-Oxford OX2 OJB
CY: GB
CP: Mr Tony Dodd
TN: 865-24 22 06
AB: The aim of this project is to provide a collection of Prolog-specific tools for monitoring program execution. The tools are meant to take full advantage of modern display technology, and to merge

smoothly with other ongoing "environment" projects within the Alvey Logic Programming Initiative. Highlights of the envisaged system are as follows:
(1) it will be Prolog-specific, and based on the concept of browsing through a graphical display of the goal tree;
(2) it will be based on an investigation of the needs of expert Prolog users;
(3) it will provide a user environment whose tools, aids and debugging facilities are at least comparable in power to those found in modern Lisp system;
(4) the environment will be integrated with a popular version of Prolog (an Edinburgh-compatible dialect) running on a high-performance graphics workstation.

PS: Start date: 20 December 1985, duration: 36 months
DS: 860729

TI: PARALFEX
PR: ALVEY IKBS 077
AR: intelligent knowledge based systems; IKBS; finance; expert systems
ON: Rutherford Appleton Laboratory
OA: Chilton, Didcot, GB-Oxon OX11 OQX
CY: GB
CP: Dr Gordon Ringland
TN: 235-219 00 ext. 5557
AB: The project has two main objectives:
(1) to develop methods of making expert systems more easily modifiable, extensible and transformable (e.g. from an advisor for experts to a tutor for novices);
(2) to identify new problem solving strategies in, for example, the financial sector, and embody them in expert systems.

PS: Start date: 1 November 1985, duration: 24 months
DS: 860729

TI: Natural Language Interface for Expert Systems
PR: ALVEY IKBS 075
AR: intelligent knowledge based systems; IKBS; natural language processing; medicine; expert systems
ON: Imperial Cancer Research Fund
OU: Biomedical Computing Unit
OA: P.O. Box 123, Lincoln's Inn Fields, GB-London WC2A 3PX
CY: GB
CP: Dr David P. Frost
TN: 1-242 02 00 ext. 5478
AB: The overall aim of the project is to explore the design of natural language interfaces for expert systems with reference to medical applications. This entails the development of working prototypes

which evolve continuously through cycles of refinement and evaluation. An intermediate goal is therefore the development of a set of tools for exploring different architectures. In order to limit the scope of the project, state-of-the-art techniques from natural language processing and expert systems are used where appropriate. The research focuses on the problems of integrating these two components. Since most work in applied natural language processing has concentrated on interfaces to relational databases, some of the concepts and techniques from this area are employed. In particular, the concept of an expert system query language is explored.

PS: Start date: 1 January 1985, duration: 36 months
DS: 860729

TI: A Formal Evaluation of Knowledge Elicitation Techniques for Expert System
PR: ALVEY IKBS 062
AR: intelligent knowledge based systems; IKBS; knowledge elicitation techniques; expert systems
ON: University of Nottingham
OU: Department of Psychology
OA: GB-Nottingham NG7 2RD
CY: GB
CP: Dr A.M. Burton
TN: 602-50 61 01 ext. 3191/3265
AB: The economic and accurate elicitation of expert knowledge is a substantial problem in Expert System construction. This project will test the efficacy of various knowledge elicitation techniques both within and between domains. This will involve multi-expert factorial experiments (domains crossed with techniques).
PS: Start date: 1 April 1986, duration: 36 months
DS: 860729

TI: Real-Time Expert Systems in Process Control
PR: ALVEY IKBS 054
AR: intelligent knowledge based systems; IKBS; process control; expert systems
ON: Heriot-Watt University
OU: Dept. Electrical & Electronic Engineering
OA: 31-35 Grassmarket, GB-Edinburgh EH1 2HT
CY: GB
CP: Dr Roy Leitch
TN: 031-225 84 32
AB: To develop knowledge representation formalisms and inferencing methods suitable for real-time feedback control applications; to provide academic support for the Alvey Community Club, in real-time expert systems (RESCU).

PS: Start date: 1 November 1984, duration: 36 months
DS: 860729

TI: Implementation and Application of PARLOG
PR: ALVEY IKBS 043
AR: intelligent knowledge based systems; IKBS; PARLOG
ON: Imperial College
OU: Department of Computing
OA: 180 Queen's Gate, GB-London SW7 2BZ
CY: GB
CP: Keith Clark
TN: 1-589 51 11 ext, 5089
AB: To further develop and investigate the implementation of the concurrent logic programming language PARLOG and to explore its application to:
(1) systems programming;
(2) rapid specification and prototyping of concurrent systems;
(3) distributed knowledge bases and expert systems.
PS: Start date: 1 April 1985, duration: 36 months
DS: 860729

TI: An Intelligent Maintenance System for Telecommunication Networks
PR: ALVEY IKBS 042
AR: expert systems; intelligent knowledge based systems; IKBS; telecommunications
OS: BTRL
ON: British Telecom Research Labs.
OA: Martlesham Heath, Ipswich, GB-Suffolk
CY: GB
CP: G. J. Garwood
TN: 473-64 48 93
AB: To undertake a pilot research programme to explore certain Artificial Intelligence techniques (including knowledge representation methods, inference mechanisms and the treatment of uncertainty), and to identify those with the potential to enable an Intelligent Maintenance System (IMS) to be developed, at a later date. The IMS is to be capable of performing the Operation and Maintenance function pertaining to a Telecommunication Network. The results of the research programme are to be applied to a sub-part of the telecommunication network to evaluate their feasibility and to indicate how an IMS could be developed.
PS: Project completed.
DS: 860729

TI: An Expert System for the Design of Spatial Arrangements
PR: ALVEY IKBS 039

AR: intelligent knowledge based systems; IKBS; knowledge engineering; expert systems
ON: University of Strathclyde
OU: CAD Centre
OA: 131 Rottenrow, Glasgow G4 ONG, Scotland
CY: GB
CP: Dr K.J. MacCallum
TN: 41-552 44 00 ext. 3134
AB: The main objective of the project is to advance expert systems technology by developing knowledge representations suited to spatial arrangements. A new system which extends existing work on numerical modelling will be built by using the representations. Key features of the new system will be

(1) the ability to handle approximate geometries,
(2) the integration of the spatial representations with the numerical representations allowing extensive inference of performance measures from arrangements,
(3) the incorporation of expertise specific to an application domain which will allow the rapid generation and evaluation of arrangement concepts.

For the purpose of this project, ship arrangements will be chosen as the domain of expertise. However, critical examination of the application and its relationships to other similar design problems will allow generalisations to be made.
PS: Start date: 1 June 1985, duration: 36 months
DS: 860729

TI: An Investigation of Knowledge Acquisition Techniques
PR: ALVEY IKBS 036
AR: intelligent knowlege based systems; IKBS; knowlege engineering; knowledge acquisition; expert systems
ON: Helix Expert Systems Ltd
OA: 11 Ludgate Circus, UK-London EC4M 7LQ
CY: GB
CP: Ulvi Sami
TN: 1-248 17 34
AB: The major topics of the project include:

(1) Evaluate alternative knowledge acquisition techniques for structured selection problems.
(2) Develop a manual methodology based on the best techniques.
(3) Produce a working expert system to advise on government grants available to businesses.

PS: Project completed in 1986.
DS: 860729

TI: A Flexible Toolkit for Expert Systems
PR: ALVEY IKBS 031

AR: intelligent knowledge based systems; IKBS; development support environment; expert systems
ON: GEC Research
OU: Marconi Research Centre
OA: West Hanningfield Road, Gt Baddow, UK-Chelmsford, Essex CM2
CY: GB
CP: E. A. Pacello
TN: 245-73331 ext. 3254
AB: Tools for building expert systems have not had the success that might have been expected. Shells have been found too restrictive for both knowledge representation and control, whereas high level languages are too demanding on the knowledge engineer. This project is to provide an interactive expert system development environment and toolkit combining flexibility with ease of use. The knowledge engineer will have available knowledge base editing, logic selection user language definition and other tools. He will be able to provide the user with facilities for volunteering information, explanation and knowledge base browsing. A particular application to fault finding in software has been specified for toolkit evaluation but a prototype toolkit will be used for other tests during the project. The toolkit is being written in Common Lisp with SUN Poplog as a target environment.
PS: Start date: 1 January 1985, duration: 36 months
DS: 860729

TI: Read and Write Japanese Without Knowing It
PR: ALVEY IKBS 022
AR: intelligent knowledge based systems; IKBS; language processing; Japanese language; expert systems
OS: ICL
ON: ICL
OA: 322 Euston Road, UK-London NW1 3BD
CY: GB
CP: Graham Hook
TN: 1-387 70 30
AB: To develop a software package with a double-expert core including a dynamic English/Japanese dictionary, with modules to enable technologists speaking only English to

(1) understand Japanese texts their own fields;
(2) produce simultaneously English and Japanese versions of documentation in their own fields;
(3) teach themselves to translate Japanese texts in their own fields.

The J-E component is a computerisation of J Jelinek's integrated "Grammar Dictionaries", using Multiple-path Predictive Analysis. The E-J component is an analysis/transfer/generation model,

using Lexical-Functional Grammar (LFG), but with an interactive expert front-end to disambiguate the source text.
PS: Start date: 1 October 1984, duration: 36 months
DS: 860729

TI: Business Applications of Expert Systems—An Investigation
PR: ALVEY IKBS 058
AR: intelligent knowledge based systems; IKBS; service industries; demonstrations
ON: Telecomputing plc
OA: 244 Barns Road, UK-Oxford OX4 3RW
CY: GB
CP: Stephen Lunn
TN: 865-77 77 55
AB: The objectives of the project include:
(1) To investigate how aspects of IKBS technology can be used to extend the scope of automation in commercial activities, allowing systems to encompass both the business knowledge of commercial experts, and the technical knowledge of data processing practitioners.
(2) To demonstrate the applicability of IKBS techniques to the progressive automation of administration, by integrating an intelligent system with COBOL/4GL transaction processing systems and conventional data stores.
PS: Project under negotiation.
DS: 860729

TI: Knowledge Based Systems in Hydrology
PR: ALVEY IKBS 018
AR: intelligent knowledge based systems; IKBS; natural resources management
ON: University of Surrey
OU: Computing Unit
OA: UK-Guildford GU2 5XH
CY: GB
CP: Dr K. Ahmad
TN: 483-57 12 81 ext. 3203
AB: To investigate, develop and refine methodologies and tools for building expert systems which will provide advice and consultation for engineers dealing with complex real-world situations, for example, civil engineers and hydrologists involved in the management of water resources. These engineers first require ready access to data, which are often uncertain and difficult to acquire, and simulation models, which are not very easy to use; then they need subsequently to combine the simulation results with engineering (and economic) judgement to obtain the best possible results. We believe that such a system requires:

(1) logic programming technique to implement the judgemental knowledge rule-base and inference programs,
(2) techniques for building intelligent front-ends to interface the expert system with simulation models and subsequently with databases, and
(3) fuzzy logic and approximate reasoning techniques.

PS: Start date: 1 May 1984, duration: 16 months
DS: 860729

C.4.2 Alvey Software Engineering Projects

TI: The Development of IKBS Software Tools
PR: ALVEY SE 057
AR: software engineering; IKBS software tools
ON: BIS Applied Systems Ltd
OA: Ringway House, 45 Bull Street, UK-Birmingham B4 6AF
CY: GB
CP: Mr D. G. Hannaford
TN: 21-236 16 87
AB: This project aims to produce a set of IKBS based tools which can be used in the system design stage of a commercial data processing development. It is proposed that the BIS Structured Design Methodology is used as a basis for this work. The IKBS based tools will have two modes of operation—a designer mode and an adviser mode. To enable the adviser mode of operation to be user friendly, a front end query evaluation component should be developed which can be used with each expert system. The expert systems produced could become part of a wider framework of development support tools by subsequent insertion into an IPSE.
PS: Start date: September 1985, duration: 36 months
DS: 860729

C.4.3 Alvey Man–Machine Interface Projects

TI: The Human–Expert System Interface
PR: ALVEY MMI/HI 098
AR: man–machine interfaces; human interface; expert systems; MMI
ON: University College London
OU: Ergonomics Unit
OA: 26 Bedford Way, UK-London WC1H 0AP
CY: GB
CP: Dr Dan Diaper
TN: 1-636 21 87
AB: The work of the project includes:
(1) To develop a methodology for the design of future systems that are not yet realisable.

(2) To use this methodology to investigate the desirable properties that intelligent interfaces to expert systems should possess.

PS: Start date: 1 February 1985, duration: 2 years +
DS: 860729

TI: Human–Search Procedures and the Use of Expert Systems: an Exploratory Proposal
PR: ALVEY MMI/HI 027
AR: man–machine interfaces; human interface; expert systems
ON: University of Oxford
OU: Department of Experimental Psychology
OA: South Parks Road, UK-Oxford OX1 3UD
CY: GB
CP: Dr Donald E. Broadbent
TN: 865-512251 ext. 552
AB: This project looked at possible sources of difficulty in human acceptance of machine suggestions in problem solving. The work involved two major aspects. The first was a review of the problems and successes of people using expert systems in the UK. Numerous companies and research groups were visited. The second was a series of laboratory experiments which investigated whether users become excessively dependent on a specific form of machine assistance. Subjects used a small-scale advice system to solve a problem (determining the source of pollution in a river) and were subsequently required to solve similar problems without assistance, or with a different form of machine assistance. Note: Both parts of the project have now been completed and written reports are available.
DS: 860729

C.4.4 Alvey Large Scale Demonstrators

TI: The Department of Health and Social Security (DHSS) large Demonstrator
PR: ALVEY LD 001
AR: expert systems; decision support systems; public administration; law
OS: ICL
ON: ICL
OA: Arndale House, Arndale Centre, Manchester M4 3AR
CY: GB
CP: C. Portman
TN: 61 833 9111 ext. 2385
AB: The project aims to provide decision support systems to assist in a variety of tasks arising in large, legislation based organisations. These include:

(1) The application and maintenance of large volumes of legislative conditions.
(2) Application of conditions which require interpretation including the identification of relevant case law.
(3) The provision of advice to potential claimants both on their eligibility for benefits and how to make a claim.
(4) The formulation of changes in policy and the exploration of their possible effects.

PS: Start date: 2 April 1984, duration: 60 months
DS: 860729

TI: Mobile Information Systems
PR: ALVEY LD 002
AR: radio links; image transmission; data transmission; expert systems; IKBS
ON: Racal Research Ltd
OA: Worton Drive, Worton Grange Industrial Estate, Reading, Berkshire
CY: GB
CP: Dr J. Walker
TN: 734-868601
AB: To bring the benefits of information technology to the mobile user. The project contains 5 linked sub-projects:
(1) The Advanced Cellular Voice/Data Demonstrator (ACVDD) will develop a cellular radio hand-portable unit for voice and data transmission.
(2) the Mobile Electronic Office (MEO) will develop data networks and terminals operating over Private Mobile Radio and cellular radio.
(3) LOCATOR tracks vehicles overtly/covertly, and terminals data/image to them.
(4) The Traffic Information Collator Natural Language Undertanding IKBS (TIC) analyses traffic incident reports and prepares a message for broadcasting.
(5) The Fault Diagnosis IKBS (FD IKBS) will advise SEB control engineers during fault conditions on the electricity supply network.

PS: Start date: 1 September 1984, duration: 60 months
DS: 860729

Appendix D

Addresses of Some Organisations Mentioned in the Text

Alvey Directorate
Millbank Tower
Millbank
London SW1P 4QU
UK
Tel +44.1.211.00.99

Cambridge University
Computing Laboratory
Corn Exchange Street
Cambridge CB2 3QG
UK
Tel. +44.223.334.600

ESPRIT
DG XIII—A25
Information Dissemination
Commission of the European Communities (CEC)
200 Rue de la Loi
B1049 Brussels
Belgium
Tel +32.2.235.16.03

Fraunhofer Institute
IITB (Karlsruhe)
D-7500 Karlsruhe
FRG

Kaiserslautern University
Fachbereich Informatik
D-6750 Kaiserslautern
FRG

Linz University

Institute for Informatics
A-4040 Linz
Austria

Nixdorf Computer AG
PM Experten Systeme
Fuerstenallee 6–9
D–4790 Paderborn
FRG
Tel +49.5251.151840

Nixdorf Computer AG
Head Office and R&D
Pontanus Strasse 55
D-4790 Paderborn
FRG
Tel +49.52.51.14.6480

Osnabrueck University
Institut fuer Mathematik
D–4500 Osnabrueck
FRG

Queen Mary College
University of London
Mile End Road
London E1 4NS
UK
Tel +44.1.980.48.11

Saarland University
Fachbereich Informatik
Number IV
D–6600 Saarbruecken
FRG

Vienna University
Institute for Statistics
Liebiggasse 4
A–1010 Wien
Austria

Appendix E

Bibliography and Literature References

Addis, T. R. (1980)
Towards an "expert" diagnostic system, *ICL Tech. J.* May.
Addis, T. R. & Hartley, R. T. (1979)
A fault finding aid using content addressable file store, ICL Research & Advanced Development Centre, Tech. Report 79/3, Stevenage, UK.
Aikins, J. S. (1983)
Prototype knowledge for expert systems, *Artificial Intelligence* **20**.
Alexander, T. (1984)
Why computers can't outthink the experts, *Fortune Magazine*, 20 August, 99–108.
Arnold, W., Eysenck, H. J. & Meili, R. (1980)
Lexikon der Psychologie, Vol. 2, Herder Verlag, Freiburg, FRG.
Barber, G. (1984)
Trends in Artificial Intelligence Research and Applications, OECD Report, ICCP (84).
Barr, A. & Feigenbaum, E. A. (1981)
The Handbook of Artificial Intelligence, Vols 1/2, Kaufmann, Los Altos, USA.
Barrow, G. (1984)
Trends in Artificial Intelligence Research and Applications, OECD Paper, ICCP (84).
Barrow, G. & Tenenbaum, (1983)
Tutorial session on computational vision, IJCAI 83, Karlsruhe, FRG
Bartles, B. & Roehr, H.
The English Companion's Modern Grammar, Diesterweg Verlag, Frankfurt am Main, FRG.
Bauer, F. L. & Woessner, H. (1981)
Algorithmische Sprache un Programmentwicklung, Springer.
Belnap, M. (1977)
A useful four valued logic, in J. M. Dunn & G. Epstein, *Modern Uses of Multiple Value Logic*, Dordrecht.
Bernold, T. & Albers, G. (1985) Eds.
Artificial Intelligence: towards practical applications, North Holland, Amsterdam. ISBN 0444 87719 3.

Bibel, W. (1980)
Intellekt statt Kuenstliche Intelligenz, *Rundbrief der FGKI in der Gesellschaft fuer Informatik* **22**; 15–16.
Bibel, W. & Siekmann, J. H. (1982)
Informatik Fachberichte 59: Kuenstliche Intelligenz, Springer Verlag.
Billmers, M. A. & Swartwout, M. W. (1984)
Artificial Intelligence — SPEAR: Computer system failure analysis tool, *Proc. ECAI–84*, Pisa, Italy, pp. 65–73.
Biorci, M. (1986)
Address to the Industrial Liaison Panel of ECAI–84, Pisa, September 1984, In T. Bernold (ed.), *Knowledge Engineering and Expert Systems,* North Holland, Appendices.
Bobrow, D. G. & Collins, A. M. (1975)
Representation and Understanding: Studies in Cognitive Science, Academic Press.
Bolkaert, W., Kamm, J., Leibrandt, U. & Schnupp, P. (1984)
Sprachen der Vierte Generation, *Computer Magazin*, March, pp. 48–59.
Bollinger, T. (1984)
SERA—Ein System zum Erlernen rekursiver Algorithmen, Master's thesis, University of Bonn.
Bonissone, P. P.
DELTA—Diesel Electric Locomotives Troubleshooting Aid and CATS—Computer Assisted Troublshooting System. *The Knowledge Based Systems Program*, General Electric, Corporate Research & Development, 1 River Road Building 37–567, Schenectady, NY 12345, USA.
Brachman, R. & Levesque, H. (1983)
Ten collected papers on knowledge representation, in Tutorial on Artificial Intelligence, IJCAI 83, Karlsruhe, FRG.
Bramer, M. (1982)
A survey and critical review of expert systems research, in D. Michie (ed.), *Introductory Readings in Expert Systems*, Gordon and Breach, New York, pp. 3–32.
Breuker, W. & Wielinga, J. (1984)
Interpretation of verbal data for knowledge acquisition, *Proc. ECAI.*
Brighty, A. (1984)
Mit Artificial Intelligence lernen Computer selbstaending denken, *Computerwoche*, 13 April, pp. 20–21.
Brown, J. (1983)
Collected papers on knowledge representation, in Tutorial on Artificial Intelligence, IJCAI 83, Karlsruhe, FRG.
Buchanan, B. G. & Mitchell, T. M. (1978)
Model directed learning of production rules, in D. A. Waterman & F. Hayes-Roth (eds), *Pattern Directed Interference Systems*, Academic Press, pp. 297–312.
Buchanan, B. G. & Shortliffe, E. (1984)
Rule Based Expert Systems, Addison Wesley.

Buchanan, B. G. *et al.* (1984)
Construction of an expert system, in B. G. Buchanan & E. Shortliffe, *Rule Based Expert Systems*, Addison Wesley.
Buday, R. (1986)
Carnegie: schooled in expert systems, *Information Week*, No. 63, 28 April, pp. 35–37
Bundy, A. Silver, B. & Plummer, D. (1985)
An analytic comparison of some rule based learning programs, *Artificial Intelligence 27*, 137–181.
Burks, A. W. (1978)
Programming and Structure Changes in Parallel Computers, Report of the Michigan Ann Arbor University, Department of Computer Science, MSC78–26016, Ann Arbor, Michigan 48109, USA.
Businessweek (1984)
Artificial Intelligence machines burst out of the laboratory, *Businessweek*, 1 October, p. 75.
Campbell, J. C. (1984)
Implementations of PROLOG, Ellis Horwood, Chichester, UK.
Carbonell, J. G., Michalski, R. S. & Mitchell, T. M. (1983)
Machine Learning—An Artificial Intelligence Approach, Tioga Publishing, Palo Alto, California, USA.
Carnap, R. (1968)
Symbolische Logik, 3rd Edition, Springer.
Carnap, R. & Stegmueller, W. (1958)
Induktive Logik und Wahrscheinlichkeit, Springer.
Carneghem, M. (1982)
PROLOG II—Manual d'Utilisation. Groupe Intelligence Artificielle, ERA CNRS 363, Faculté des Sciences de Luminy Case 901, 70 Route Léon Lachamp, F–13288 Marseille Cedex 9, France.
Clancey, W. J. & Letsinger, (1984)
NEOMYCIN, in Clancey, W. J. & Shortliffe, E. H. Readings in Medical Artificial Intelligence. Addison-Wesley, Reading 1984, pp. 361–381.
Clark, K. L. (1978)
Negation as failure, in H. Gallaire, *Logic and Databases*, Plenum, New York.
Clark, K. L. & McCabe, F. G. (1980)
PROLOG: A Language for Implementing Expert Systems, Imperial College, London SW7, November.
Clocksin, W. F. & Mellish, C. S. (1981)
Programming in PROLOG, Springer Verlag.
Cohen, P. H. & Feigenbaum, E. A. (1982)
The Handbook of Artificial Intelligence, Vol. 3, Kaufmann, Los Altos, USA.
Coy, W., Mahr, B. and Makovsky, J. (eds) (1984)
Computerkultur, Kursbuch 75, Rotbuch Verlag.
Daiser, W. (1984)

Kuenstliche Intelligenz Forschung und ihre Epistomologischen Grundlagen, Peter Lang, Frankfurt am Main, FRG, Vol. 125.
Davis, R. (1982a)
Expert systems: Where are we? And where do we go from here? *The Artificial Intelligence Magazine*, Spring, pp. 3–22.
Davis, R. (1982b)
Teiresias: Applications of meta level knowledge, in R. Davis & D. B. Lenat (eds), *Knowledge Based Systems in Artificial Intelligence*, McGraw-Hill International.
Davis, R. & Lenat, D. B. (eds) (1982)
Knowledge Based Systems in Artificial Intelligence, McGraw-Hill International.
Davis, R. *et al.* (1982)
Diagnosis based on description of structure and function, *Proc. Nat. Conf. on Artificial Intelligence–82*, Pittsburgh, Pennsylvania, pp. 137–142.
Delaney, J. H. & Stiegler, M. (1984)
The light in the looking glass, *Analog* **CIV**, No. 9, September.
Devendran, T. (1984)
Kuenstliche Intelligenz: der Computer als Fachberater, *Bild der Wissenschaft* **12**, 112–116.
Dietterich, T. G. & Michalski, R. S. (1983)
A comparative review of selected methods for learning from examples, in J. G. Carbonell, R. S. Michalski & T. M. Mitchell, *Machine learning—An Artificial Intelligence Approach*, Tioga Publishing, Palo Alto, California, USA.
Dilger, W., Mayer, O. and Mueller, J. (1983)
Associative Processors. Internal Report 85/83, Fach Bereich Informatik, Universitaet Kaiserslautern, FRG, September.
Dilger, W., Mayer, O. and Mueller, J. (1984)
An associative processor for unification, *J. VLSI and Computer Systems*.
Doyle, J. (1977)
A truth maintenance system, *Artificial Intelligence* **12**.
Emde, W. (1984)
Inkrementelles Lernen mit Heuristischen generierten Modellen, KIT Report 22, TU Berlin.
Erdle-Haehner, R. & Klein, H.-W. (1971)
Etudes Français B **2**, Kett Verlag, Stuttgart, FRG.
Feigenbaum, E. (1979)
Themes and case studies of knowledge engineering, in D. Michie (ed.), *Expert Systems in the Microelectronic Age*, Edinburgh University Press, pp. 3–25.
Feigenbaum, E. & Feldman, J. (eds) (1963)
Computers and Thought, McGraw-Hill, New York.
Feigenbaum, E. & McCorduck, P. (1983, 1984)
The Fifth Generation, Addison Wesley.
Forsyth, R. (1984)

A database that learns, *Proc. Int. Symp. on Machine Learning*, The Knowledge Based Systems Centre, Polytechnic of the South Bank, London.

Forsyth, R. & Rada, R. (1986)
Machine Learning—Applications in Expert Systems and Information Retrieval, Ellis Horwood, Chichester, UK.

Fox, M. (1983)
Constraint Directed Search: a case study of job shop scheduling, Technical Report CMU–RI–TR–83–22, Carnegie Mellon University, Pittsburgh, Pennsylvania, USA.

Fox, M., Lowenfeld, S. & Kleinosky, P. (1983)
Techniques for sensor based diagnosis, *Proc. IJCAI–83*, Karlsruhe, FRG.

Fox, M. & Smith, S. (1984)
ISIS: a KBS for factory scheduling, *Int. J. Expert Systems* **1** (1).

Fox, M., Wright, J. & Adams, D. (1985)
Experience with SRL, Technical Report CMU–RI–TR–85–10, Carnegie Mellon University, Pittsburgh, Pennsylvania, USA.

Fu, K. S. & Ichikawa, T. (1982)
Special Computer Architectures for Pattern Processing, CRC Press, Boca Raton, Florida, USA.

Genesereth, M. G. (1982)
Diagnosis using hierarchical design models, *Proc. Nat. Conf. on Artificial Intelligence 1982*, Pittsburgh, Pennsylvania, USA, pp. 278–283.

Green, B. F. *et al.* (1963)
BASEBALL: an automatic question answerer, in E. Feigenbaum and J. Feldman (eds), *Computers and Thought*, McGraw-Hill, New York, pp. 207–216.

Grover, T. C. (1983)
A pragmatic knowledge acquisition methodology, in *Proc. IJCAI–83,* Vol. 1, Karlsruhe, FRG.

Guntram, U. (1984)
Kuenstliche Intelligenz — Die Fuenfte Generation, *Chip* **11**, 24 October, *et seq*.

Gust, H. (1984)
Constrained Variables: an extension to PROLOG. Internal paper, Osnabrueck University, FRG.

Gust, H. & Gust, B. (1984)
Einfuehrung in das PROLOG system MLOG. Internal Paper, Osnabrueck University, FRG.

Habel, C. & Rollinger, C.-R. (1984)
Lernen und Wissensakquisition, in C. Habel (ed.), *Kuenstliche Intelligenz Fruehjahrsschule Dassel/Solling*, Springer Verlag.

Hart, P. (1984)
Artificial Intelligence in transition, *The Artificial Intelligence Magazine* (3), Autumn.

Hart, P., Duda, J. & Einaudi, R. (1978)

A Computer Based Consultations System for Mineral Exploration, SRI Technical Report.

Hartley, R. T. (1982)
CRIB: Rule based configurer of computer systems, *Artificial Intelligence* **19**, 39–88.

Hartley, R. T. (1984)
CRIB: Computer fault-finding through knowledge engineering, *IEEE Computer Magazine*, March, pp. 76–83.

Haupt, H. & Mohnhaupt, M. (1984)
Kuenstliche Intelligenz: die Avant Garde Etabliert sich, *Computer Magazin*, October, pp. 20–36.

Hayes-Roth, F. (1984)
The knowledge based expert system: a tutorial, *Computer Magazine*, September.

Hayes-Roth, F., Waterman, D. A. & Lenat, D. B. (1983)
Building Expert Systems, Addison Wesley.

Hendrix, G. G. *et al.* (1978)
Developing a natural language interface to complex data, *ACM Trans. DBMS* **3**, pp. 105–147.

Herkner, W. (1981)
Einfuehrung in die Sozialpsychologie, 2nd Edition, Hans Hueber Verlag, Bern, Switzerland.

Hertz, D. B. (1983)
Artificial intelligence and the business manager, *Computerworld*, 24 October, section "In depth", p. 18 *et seq*.

Hilbert, D. & Ackermann, W. (1972)
Grundzuege der Theoretischen Logik, 6th Edition, Springer, Berlin.

Hodges, A. (1985)
Alan Turing, The Enigma of Intelligence, Burnett Books.

Hofstaedter, D. R. (1979)
Godel, Escher, Bach, an Eternal Golden Braid, Basic Books Inc.

Hofstaedter, D. R. (1985)
Metamagical Themas: Questing for the Essence of Mind and Pattern, Viking Publishers.

Hopcroft, J. E. & Ullmann, J. D. (1979)
Introduction to Automata Theory and Computation, Addison Wesley.

Humby, E. (1973)
Programs from Decision Tables, Macdonald.

Irving, T. (1986)
Fast PROLOG, published by *Systems International*, December.

Jansen-Winkeln, R. M. (1986)
LEGAS—Ein System zum induktiven Lernen grammatikalischer Strukturen. Memorandum of the University of the Saarland, D-6600 Saarbruecken, FRG.

Jones, C. B. & Bjorner, D. (1984)
Systematic Software Development using VDM, Prentice Hall.

Kempf, K. (1983)

Tutorial Session on Artificial Intelligence Applications in Robotics, IJCAI 83, Karlsruhe, FRG.

Kirsch, W. (1977)
Einfuehrung in die Theorie der Entscheidungsprozesse, 2nd Edition, Gabler Verlag, Wiesbaden, FRG.

Kohonen, T. (1977)
Associative Memory—A System Theoretical Approach, Springer Verlag, Berlin.

Kosy, D. & Dhar, V. (1983)
Knowledge-Based System support for Long Range Planning, Technical Report, CMU, Pittsburgh, Pennyslvania, USA.

Kosy, D. & Wise, B. (1984)
Self explanatory financial planning models, *Proc. AAAI.*

Kowalski, R. (1979)
Algorithm = Logic + Control, *Comm. ACM* **22** (7).

Langley, P. & Carbonell, J. G. (1984)
Approaches to machine Learning, Report CMU–CS 84–108, Carnegie Mellon University, USA.

Laubsch, H. (1983)
Lisp Maschinen, *Computer Magazin*, No. 7/8, pp. 50–53.

Lavington, S. (1980)
Early British Computers, Manchester University Press.

Leifer, J. (1983)
Expertensystems nicht nur fuer Japaner, *QECD/Online* **5**, 67 *et seq.*

Lenat, D. B. (1982)
AM: Discovery in mathematics as heuristics search, in R. Davis & D. B. Lenat (eds), *Knowledge Based Systems in Artificial Intelligence*, McGraw-Hill International.

Lindsay, R. K. (1963)
A program for parsing sentences and making inferences about kinship relationships, in Hoggatt and Baldeston, *Symposium on Simulation Models*, Cincinnati South West Publishing, pp. 111–138.

Luft, H. (1986)
Transcript of a Keynote Speech. IT Forum, 3rd ESPRIT Conference, Brussels, 1 October, 1986, DG–XIII ESPRIT, CEC, B1049 Brussels.

Macho, K. (1984)
Simulation of Human Learning, Technical Report, Department of Informatics, University of Vienna.

Marchand, H., Mohnhaupt, M. & Spoerl, J. (1984)
Kuenstliche Intelligenz—Revolution in der Programmierung, *Computermagazin*, October, pp. 46–54.

Marr, D. (1978)
Representing visual information, *Phil. trans. Roy. Soc. Lond.* Series B 275:483–524.

Martelli, A. & Montanari, U. (1982)
An efficient unification algorithm, *ACM Trans. Programming Languages and Systems* **4**, 258–282.

McDermott, J. (1984)
R1 re-visited: 4 years in the trenches, *The Artificial Intelligence Magazine*, Fall, pp. 21–32.
Mertens, P. & Allgeyer, K. (1983)
Kuenstliche Intelligenz in der Betriebswirtschaft, *Z. Betriebswirtschaft* **7**, 686–709.
Michalski, R. S. *et al.* (1983)
Machine Learning—an Artificial Intelligence Approach, Tiogas Publishing, Palo Alto, California, USA.
Michalski, R. S. (1983)
A theory and methodology of inductive learning, in R. S. Michalski *et al.* (eds), *Machine Learning—an Artificial Intelligence Approach*, Tioga Publishing, Palo Alto, California, pp. 83–134.
Michie, D. (1982)
Introductory Readings in Expert Systems, Gordon and Breach, New York.
Minsky, M. (1975)
A framework for representing knowledge, in P. H. Winston (ed.), *The Psychology of Computer Vision*, McGraw-Hill, New York.
Minsky, M. (ed.) (1968 and 1982)
Semantic Information Processing, MIT Press.
Mitchell, T. & Schwenzer, L. (1978)
Applications of Artificial Intelligence for chemical inference XXV: a computer program for automated empirical 13C NMR rule formation, *Organic Magnetic Resonance* **8**, 378.
Moerler, G. (1984)
Expertensysteme—nur ein neues Modewort? *Computerwoche* 31 August, 8.
Nado, R., Bock, C. & Fikes, R. (1985)
An Assertion and Retrieval Interface for a Frame Based Representation System, Intellicorp, Mountain View, California, USA.
Nau, D. (1983)
Expert computer systems, *Computer* **2**, 63–84.
Neumann, B. (1983)
Bildverstehen, *Computer Magazin*, No. 7/8, pp. 54–56.
Newell, A. & Simon, H. A. (1976)
Computer Science as Empirical Inquiry: Symbols and Search in C.A.C.M. Vol. 19, No. 3, March 1976.
Niemann, H. (1980)
Mustererkennung—Anwendungen, *Informatik Spectrum* **3** (1), pp. 1–17.
Nilsson, N. J. (1982)
Principles of Artificial Intelligence, Springer, Berlin.
Noelke, U. & Savory, S. (1984)
Prolog Systems im Vergleich, *Angewandte Informatik* **3**, 108–112.
Oakey, S. & Cawthorn, R. C. (1981)
Inductive learning of pronunciation rules by hypothesis testing and corrections, *Proc. 7th IJCAI*, Canada.
Paterson, A. M., Sachs, P. A. & Turner, M. H. M. (1985)

ESCORT—The application of causal knowledge to real time process control, in M. Merry (ed.), *Expert Systems 85*, Cambridge University Press, pp. 79–88. Supplier: PA Computers and Telecommunications, Rochester House, 33 Greycoat Street, London SW1P 2QF.
Pereira, J. & Warren, H. D. (1980)
Definite clause grammar for language analysis—a survey of the formalisms and a comparison with Augmented Transition Networks, *Artificial Intelligence* **13**.
Pohl, P. (1983)
Gateway and *Beyond the Blue Event Horizon* (SF Ńovels), Heine Verlag.
Quinlan, J. R. (1982)
Fundamentals of the knowledge engineering problem, in D. Michie (ed.), *Introductory Readings in Expert Systems*, Gordon and Breach, New York.
Rada, R., Rhine, Y. and Smallwood, J. (1984)
Rule refinement, in *Proc. Int. Symp. on Machine Learning*, The Knowledge Based Systems Centre, Polytechnic of the South bank, London.
Raulefs, P. (1983)
Software der 5ten Generation—Expertensysteme, *Computer Magazin*, No. 7/8, p. 56.
REACTOR (1982)
An expert system for diagnosis and treatment of nuclear reactor accidents, *Proc. AAAI–82*, 18–20 August, Pittsburgh, Pennsylvania, USA, pp. 296–301.
Reddy, Y. & Fox, M. (1983)
INET: a knowledge based simulation approach to distribution analysis, *Proc. IEEE Computer Society Trends and Applications*, NBS, Washington DC, USA.
Reiter, R. (1980)
A logic for default reasoning, *Artificial Intelligence* **13**.
Rendell, L. A. (1983)
Towards a unified approach for conceptual knowledge acquisition, *The Artificial Intelligence Magazine*, Winter, pp. 19–27.
Reyle, U. (1984)
Ueber die Logik der Abfrage von Datenbanken, in C.-R. Rollinger (ed.), *Probleme des (Text-) Verstehens*, Neimeyer.
Rich, E. (1983)
Artificial Intelligence, McGraw Hill, Singapore, ISBN 0–07–Y66508–7.
Rich, E. (1984)
The gradual expansion of artificial intelligence, *Computer* **5**, 4–12.
Richer, M. H. (1986)
An evaluation of expert system development tools, *Expert Systems Journal, Learned Information Systems*, (3). July.
Rissland, E. L. & Soloway, E. M. (1981)
Contrained examples generation: a testbed for studying issues in learning, *Proc. 7th Int. Conf. on Artificial Intelligence*.
Rogers, M. W. (1985)

Information technology companies' acceptance of and attitude towards Ada, in J. G. P. Barnes and G. A. Fisher Jr (eds), *Ada in Use: Proc. Ada Int. Conf., Paris,* 14–16 May.
Rogers, M. W. (1986)
ESPRIT—an IT initiative. Keynote address to the 1986 DECUS Congress, Hamburg, September 1986, published by DECUS, DEC Geneva.
Rollinger, C.-R. (1984)
Evidenzbewertung fuer Fakten un Regeln, in C.-R. Rollinger (ed.), *Probleme des (Text-) Verstehens*, Niemeyer.
Rychener, M. D. (1983)
The instructible production system: a reprospective analysis, in J. G,. Carbonell, R. S. Michalski and T. M. Mitchell (eds), *Machine Learning —An Artificial Intelligence Approach*, Tioga Publishing, Palo Alto, California, USA.
Sammut, C. (1981)
Concept learning by experiment, *Proc. 7th Int. Conf. on Artificial Intelligence*, Canada.
Sathi, A., Fox, M. & Greenberg, M. (1985)
The application of knowledge representation techniques to Project Management, *Trans. Pattern Analysis and Machine Intelligence.*
Savory, S. (1983)
A prototype Nixdorf expert system, *Angewandte Informatik* **11**, 478–482.
Savory, S. (1984)
Arbeitswerkzeuge der Kuenstlichen Intelligenz, in *COMPAS 84*, AMK Berlin pp. 1057–1065.
Savory, S. (1986)
Faultfinder and Conad: two working expert systems at Nixdorf Computer AG, *Proc. Gottlieb Duttweiler Institute Conf. on Artificial Intelligence, Rueschlikon, 1984*, North Holland.
Savory, S. (1987)
Expertensysteme: Nutzen für Ihr Unternehusen. Oldenbourg Verlag, Munich, 1987.
Schneider, H. J. (1983)
Lexikon der Informatik und Datenverarbeitung, Oldenbourg Verlag.
Schnupp, P., Schmauch, C. & Leibrandt, U. (1984)
Was ist PROLOG? *Elektronische Rechenanlagen* **4** (26).
Schwarzer, U. (1983)
Wie Rechner denken lernen, *Manager Magazin* **7**, 68–73.
Selfridge, M. (1981)
A computer model of child language acquisition, *Proc. 7th Conf. on Artificial Intelligence*, Canada.
Shortliffe, E. H. (1976)
Computer Based Medical Consultations MYCIN, North Holland.
Siekmann, J. H. (1983)
Kuenstliche Intelligenz—Bruecke in die Zukunft, *Computer Magazin*, No. 7/8, pp. 42–48.
Simon, H. (1983)

Why should machines learn? in T. Mitchell, *Machine Learning*, Tioga Press, Palo Alto, California, pp. 25–38.
Slagle, J. R. (1963)
A heuristic program that solves symbolic integration problems in freshman calculus, *J. ACM* **10**, 507–520.
Smith, R. G. (1984)
On the development of commercial expert systems, *AI Magazine*, Fall, 61–73.
Smith, R. G. & Friedland, P. (1980)
UNIT Package User's Guide, Stanford Heuristic Programming Project Memo, HPP–80–28, December.
Smith, S. F. (1984)
Adaptive search techniques for machine learning, in *Proc. Int. Symp. on Machine Learning*, The Knowledge Based Systems Centre, Polytechnic of the South Bank, London.
Stanford University (1983)
Artificial Intelligence research in the Heuristic Programming Project, *The Artificial Intelligence Magazine*, No. 3, Fall, 69–79.
Stegmueller, W. (1973–74)
Probleme und Resultate der Wissenschaftestheorie und Analytische Philosophie, Vols I to IV, Springer, Berlin.
Turing, A. M. (1936–37)
On computable numbers, with an application to the Entscheidungsproblem, *Proc. London Mathematical Society*, 2nd Series, **42**, 230–265; **43**, 544–546.
Turing, A. M. (1963)
Computing machinery and intelligence, in J. Feldman (ed.), *Computers and Thought*, McGraw-Hill, New York, pp. 11–35.
van Emden, M. H. & Kowalski, R. (1976)
The semantics of predicate logic as a programming language, *J. ACM* **23** (4), October.
Van Melle, W. (1980)
A Domain Independent System that Aids in Constructing Consultation Programs, Stanford University Report STAN–CS–80—820.
van Rijsbergen, C. J. (1985)
Turing and the origins of digital computers, *Proc. ASLIB* **37**, June/July, 281–285.
Verity, J. W. (1983)
Lisp markets grow, *Datamation*, October, p. 92.
Versonder, G. T. *et al.* (1983)
ACE: an expert system for telephone cable maintenance, *Proc. 8th IJCAI*, Karlsruhe, FRG.
Virgil
Georgies, ii, 470.
Voltaire
Candide, Chapter 30.
Waggener Group (1985)

Profile of an Expert System application for Newspaper Publishing, The Waggener Group, USA.
Wahlster, W. (1981)
Natuerlich Sprachen Argumentation im Dialog System, *Informatik Fachbericht*, Vol. 48, Springer.
Warren, D. H. (1980)
Logic programming and compiler writing, *Software Practice and Experience* **10**, 97–125.
Waterman, D. A. & Hayes-Roth, F. (eds) (1978)
Pattern Directed Inference Systems, Academic press, New York.
Wechselblatt, R. L. (1984)
N-th Generation languages, *Datamation*, 1 September, pp. 111–117.
Weizenbaum, J. (1966)
ELIZA, *CACM* **9**, 36–45.
Whiteside, D. (1984)
Artificial Intelligence—The race to make it work for managers, *International Management Europe*, September, pp. 42–48.
Wielinga, B. J. (1984)
Knowledge acquisition in practice, in *Proc. Int. Symp. on Machine Learning*, The Knowledge Based Systems Centre, Polytechnic of the South Bank, London.
Winkelbauer, L. (1984)
Learning by Examples, Technical report, Institute of Informatics, University of Vienna.
Winograd, T. (1972)
Understanding Natural Languages, Academic Press.
Winston, P. H. (1975a)
The Psychology of Computer Vision, McGraw-Hill, New York.
Winston, P. H. (1975b)
Learning Structural Descriptions from Examples, McGraw-Hill, New York.
Winston, P. H. (1979)
Artificial Intelligence, Addison Wesley, Reading, Mass.
Yasukawa, H. (1984)
LFG System in PROLOG, in *Proc. Coling 84*, Association for Computational Linguistics.
Zadeh, L. (1985)
A formalisation of commonsense reasoning based on fuzzy logic, in *Wissensbasierte Systeme, GI Kongress, Informatik Fachbericht* No. 112, October, Springer Verlag.